Reader's Guide
to
JOSEPH CONRAD

Reader's Guide to JOSEPH CONRAD

John T. Nichol

CENTRUM PRESS
NEW DELHI-110002 (INDIA)

CENTRUM PRESS
H.O.: 4360/4, Ansari Road, Daryaganj,
New Delhi-110 002 (India)
Ph.: 23278000, 23261597

B.O.: No. 1015, Ist Main Road, BSK IIIrd Stage
IIIrd Phase, IIIrd Block,
Bangalore - 560 085 (India)
Tel.: 080-41723429
Visit us at: www.centrumpress.com

Reader's Guide to Joseph Conrad

First Edition, 2009

ISBN 978-93-80106-79-3

PRINTED IN INDIA

Printed at Balaji Offset, Delhi.

Contents

	Preface	*vii*
1.	Introduction	1
2.	The Sense of Self	11
3.	"Speech Was of No Use": Conrad, a New Journalism	32
4.	'Heart of Darkness' and Late-victorian Fascination	63
5.	"Signifying Nothing": Conrad's Idiots	80
6.	Modernism and Marketplace: The Case of Conrad's Chance	93
7.	"The End of the Tether": An Old Man's	111
8.	Heart of Darkness and Apocalypse Now: A Comparative Analysis of Novella and Film	129
9.	A Personal Remembrance as Metafiction	134
10.	To Sup on Horrors: Christopher Hampton's Film	174
11.	Achievement Without Success	186
12.	Chronology	284
	Bibliography	288

Preface

Should a writer's life have interests beyond the mere writing upon which he had employed himself, this life might well be the subject of a monograph? To write: " Joseph Conrad Korzeniowski was born on such a day of such a year in the town of 'So and So' in the Government of Kieff", and so to continue would not conduce to such a rendering as this great man desired.

So, here, to the measure of the ability vouchsafed, you have a projection of Joseph Conrad as, little by little, he revealed himself to a human being during many years of close intimacy. It is so that, by degrees, Lord Jim appeared to Marlowe, or that every human soul by degrees appears to every other human soul. For, according to our view of the thing, a novel should be the biography of a man or of an affair, and a biography, whether of a man or an affair, should be a novel, both being, if they are efficiently performed, renderings of such affairs as are our human lives.

This then is a novel, not a monograph; a portrait, not a narration: for what it shall prove to be worth, a work of art, not a compilation. It is conducted exactly along the lines laid down by us, both for the novel which is biography and for the biography which is a novel. It is the rendering of an affair intended first of all to make you see the subject in his scenery.

Author

Preface

Author

Chapter 1

Introduction

Joseph Conrad (1857-1924), Polish-born English author and master mariner wrote *Heart of Darkness* (1902); "... No, it is impossible; it is impossible to convey the life-sensation of any given epoch of one's existence—that which makes its truth, its meaning—its subtle and penetrating essence. It is impossible. We live, as we dream—alone....".(ibid, Part 1)

With haunting verse Conrad has crafted a chilling tale laden with lush imagery and symbolism describing the ambiguity between good and evil. *"He was obeyed, yet he inspired neither love nor fear, nor even respect. He inspired uneasiness. That was it!"*—(ibid) With characters as anti-hero he examines man's moral complexities and capacity for corruption and evil, and the dark depths of the human psyche;

Anything approaching the change that came over his features I have never seen before, and hope never to see again. Oh, I wasn't touched. I was fascinated. It was as though a veil had been rent. I saw on that ivory face the expression of sombre pride, of ruthless power, of craven terror—of an intense and hopeless despair. Did he live his life again in every detail of desire, temptation, and surrender during that supreme moment of complete knowledge? He cried in a whisper at some image, at some vision—he cried out twice, a cry that was no more than a breath. (ibid, Part 3)

While it addresses the timeless struggle of man's self-deception and inner conflicts, influenced by Conrad's own sense of isolation from his past, the story of Marlow's journey into the Congo also exposes the clashes, exploitation and barbarity between European and African societies during 19th

Century colonial expansionism. Controversial in his time and even today, some of Conrad's works including *Heart of Darkness* have inspired filmmakers and such authors as F. Scott Fitzgerald, Gabriel García Márquez, D.H. Lawrence, Joseph Heller, Albert Camus, and Virginia Woolf.

He has also been grouped with other such esteemed authors as his friend Stephen Crane and Robert Louis Stevenson. As a young man Conrad, becoming disillusioned and having abandoned his native Poland after his parents sacrificed their lives in the fight for their country's freedom, became a world traveller on the high seas. He gained by his own sweat and blood as a seaman the life experience and sensitivity for insight into the human condition needed to produce the dozens of famous short stories and novels he wrote, many that are still in print today.

Józef Teodor Conrad Korzeniowski was born on 3 December 1857 in the Russian occupied city of Berdyczów, Ukraine. He was the only child born to Evelina Bobrowska (1832–1865) and Apollo Korzeniowski, (1820–1869) patriot, writer, and translator of such authors' works as Victor Hugo's and William Shakespeare's. Joseph would also read their works as well as those of Charles Dickens, among many others'. As members of the Polish noble gentry *szlachta* living in the Ukraine under Tsarist autocracy was a turbulent time politically and the Korzeniowski's were under constant surveillance.

In 1861 Joseph's nationalist father, who was an outspoken supporter of the serfs and critic of Poland's oppressors, was arrested along with his wife for being involved with the Polish National Committee's anti-Russian activities. They and four-year old Joseph were exiled to the province of Vologda in Northern Russia. The living conditions and harsh climate took their toll on Joseph's parents: they both contracted tuberculosis, Evelina dying of it in 1865, Apollo in 1869. He was celebrated at his death by the Poles in patriotic honour.

Polish-born English novelist and short-story writer, a dreamer, adventurer, and gentleman. In his famous preface to The Nigger of the 'Narcissus' (1897) Conrad crystallized his often quoted goal as a writer: "My task which I am trying to achieve is, by the power of the written word, to make you hear, to make you feel-it is, above all, to make you see. That-and no more, and it is everything." Among Conrad's best-known works are Lord Jim (1900) and Heart of Darkness (1902). Conrad discouraged interpretation of his sea novels through evidence from his life, but several of his stories drew the material, events, and personalities from his own experiences in different parts of the world. While making his first voyages to the West Indies, Conrad met the Corsican Dominic Cervoni, who was later model for his characters filled with a thirst for adventure.

"We live, as we dream-alone." (from *Heart of Darkness*)

Joseph Conrad was born in Berdichev, in the Ukraine, in a region that had once been a part of Poland, but was then under Russian rule. His father Apollo Korzeniowski was an aristocrat without lands, a poet and translator of Shakespeare and Dickens and French literature. The family estates had been sequestrated in 1839 following an anti-Russian rebellion. As a boy the young Joseph read Polish and French versions of English novels with his father. English was Conrad's third language; he learned to read and write in French before he knew English. Apollo Korzeniowski became embroiled in political activities. After being imprisoned for six months, he was sent to exile with his family to Volgoda, northern Russia, in 1861. Two years later the family was allowed to move to Kiev.

By 1869 Conrad's both parents had died of tuberculosis, and he was sent to Switzerland to his maternal uncle Tadeusz Bobrowski, who was to be a continuing influence on his life. On his death in 1894 Tadeusz left about £1,600 to his nephew-a sizable sum of money, well over £100,000 now. Conrad attended schools in Kraków and persuaded his uncle to let him go to the sea. In the mid-1870s he joined the French merchant marine as an apprentice, and made between 1875 and 1878 three voyages to the West Indies. During his youth Conrad also was involved in arms smuggling for the Carlist cause in Spain.

After being wounded in a duel or of a self-inflicted gunshot in the chest, Conrad continued his career at the seas in the British merchant navy for 16 years. He had been deeply in debt, but his uncle helped him out. This was a turning point in his life.

Conrad rose through the ranks from common seaman to first mate, and by 1886 he obtained his master mariner's certificate, commanding his own ship, *Otago*. In the same year he was given British citizenship and he changed officially his name to Joseph Conrad. Witnessing the forces of the sea, Conrad developed a deterministic view of the world, which he expressed in a letter in 1897: "What makes mankind tragic is not that they are the victims of nature, it is that they are conscious of it. To be part of the animal kingdom under the conditions of this earth is very well-but soon as you know of your slavery, the pain, the anger, the strife. the tragedy begins."

Conrad sailed to many parts of the world, including Australia, various ports of the Indian Ocean, Borneo, the Malay states, South America, and the South Pacific Island. In 1890 he sailed in Africa up the Congo River. The journey provided much material for his novel *Heart of Darkness*. However, the fabled East Indies particularly attracted Conrad and it became the setting of many of his stories.

By 1894 Conrad's sea life was over. During the long journeys he had started to write and Conrad decided to devote himself entirely to literature. At the age of 36 Conrad settled down in England.

Although Conrad is mostly known as a novelist, he tried his hand also as a playwright. His first one-act drama was not success-the audience rejected it. But after finishing the text he learned the existence of the Censor of the Plays, which inspired his satirical essay about an obscure civil servant. Conrad was an Anglophile, who regarded Britain as a land which respected individual liberties. As a writer he accepted the verdict of a free and independent public, but associated this official figure of censorship to the atmosphere of the Far East and the "mustiness of the Middle Ages," which shouldn't be part of the twentieth-century England.

"... one wonders that there can be found a man courageous enough to occupy the post. It is a matter of meditation. Having given it a few minutes I come to the conclusion in the serenity of my heart and the peace of my conscience that he must be either an extreme megalomaniac or an utterly unconscious being." (from 'The Censor of Plays', 1907)

Conrad married in 1896 Jessie George, an Englishwoman, by whom he had two sons. He moved to Ashford, Kent. Except trips to France, Italy, Poland, and to the United States in 1923, Conrad lived in his new home country. His first novel, Almayer's Folly (1895) was about a derelict Dutchman, who trades on the jungle rivers of Borneo. It was followed by An Outcast of the Islands (1896), less assured in its use of English. *The Nigger of the 'Narcissus'* was a complex story of a storm off the Cape of Good Hope and of an enigmatic black sailor. *Lord Jim,* narrated by Charlie Marlow, told about the fall of an young sailor and his redemption. "You have fallen terribly, my boy, fallen, perhaps, through your own self-confident dreams. Get up and try again. No skulking, no evasion! Live this thing down, humbly and hopefully, in the light of day."

Lord Jim was originally intended as a short story, but was then enlarged into a novel. It is partly based on true events: in 1880 a British captain and his crew abandoned the steamship *Jeddah,* carrying Muslim pilgrims, when the ship started to leak. *Jeddah* was brought by another steamship safely to port. Particular blame was attached to A.P. Williams, the first mate, who had organized the desertion of the vessel. The protagonist of *Lord Jim* is a British naval officer, who is haunted by guilt of cowardice, when he left his ship, *Patna,* in a storm without taking care of the passengers.

During the voyage towards Mecca, the ship had hit a submerged object, and when the small crew lowers a lifeboat, Jim impulsively jumps in it. Contrary to the crew's beliefs, the ship did not sunk and Jim is left to stand in front of the Court of Inquiry. After disgrace Jim moves through a variety of jobs ashore and finds work as an agent at the remote trading post of Patusan. The misjudged Jim gains the confidence of chief Doramin and becomes a respected figure, proving that he is "inscrutable at heart." When Gentleman Brown and his fellow European adventurers appear, Jim promises Doramin that Brown and his men will leave the island without bloodshed. He is wrong, Doramin's son is killed, and Jim is finally forced to face his past-he allows himself to be shot by the grieving Doramin. "...Jim stood stiffened and with bared head in the light of torches, looking him straight in the face, he clung heavily with his left arm round the neck of a bowed youth, and lifting deliberately his right, shot his son's friend through the chest." (Other sailor/adventurers: Ulysses, Sinbad, Hugo Pratt's comic hero Corto Maltese.)

Heart of the Darkness was partly based on Conrad's four-month command of a Congo River steamboat. The book was written in 1899 and published in 1902 in Youth: A Narrative With Two Other Stories. Conrad had learned about atrocities made by Congo "explorers", and created in the character of Kurtz the embodiment of European imperialism. Also the account of Commander R.H. Bacon, who travelled in Benin, described horrors: "... everywhere death, barbarity and blood, and smells that it hardly seems right for human beings to smell and yet live!" Moreover, Conrad was aware about Henry Morton Stanley's journey up the Congo river in the mid-1870s. Stanley's revelation of the commercial possibilities of the region had resulted in the setting up of a trading venture. However, in the novel the journey become analogous with a quest for inner truths-like in Henry Rider Haggard's novel *She* (1887). Conrad's vision has also drawn fierce criticism. In 1977 the Nigerian novelist Chinua Achebe described Conrad as "a bloody racist".

The narrator, again Marlow, who perhaps is not so reliable, depicts to his friends a trip into Africa, where he becomes curious about a man called Kurtz. Marlow works for a company that is only interested in ivory and he witnesses the suffering of the native workers. He travels up the Congo River to reach Kurtz, an agent whom Marlow expects by his reputation to be a "universal genius," an "emissary of pity, and science, and progress, and devil knows what else." As they near the inner station of the company, they are attacked, and

Marlow's helmsman is killed. At the station they meet a Russian who idolizes Kurtz, a man who has made himself the natives' god and who has decorated the posts of his hut with human skulls. Marlow tries to get the seriously ill Kurtz away down the river, but Kurtz dies, his last words being, "The horror! The Horror!" Back in Europe Marlow lies to Kurtz's fiancée, that "the last word he pronounced was-your name."

Heart of the Darkness has inspired several film version, starting from Orson Welles but his project for RKO never materialized. Kurtz fascinated Welles; a genius destroyed by inner conflicts, greatness gone wrong. During his career as a director and actor, Welles would play this kind of Faustian figure repeatedly, most notably as Citizen Kane, who also dies with a mysterious phrase on his lips. In a television performance from 1958 Boris Karloff was seen as Kurtz and Roddy McDowall as Marlow.

Francis Ford Coppola's *Apocalypse Now* (1979) was based on the novella, Michael Herr's *Dispatches*, and John Milius' 1969 script. Nicolas Roeg's adaptation from 1993 followed Conrad's work closely. "In *Apocalypse Now*, the "horror" is symbolically repressed (killed), while in *Heart of Darkness* it is brought into the light, as horrible as it might be to do so. The film, then, accepts as a premise our capacity for evil, and goes ahead to show how the colonialist psychosis of Kurtz, and by extension Western culture, translates into a social nightmare." (from *Novels into Film* by John C. Tibbets and James M. Welsh, 1999)

In *Youth* (1902) the title story recorded Conrad's experiences on the sailing-ship *Palestine*. NOSTROMO (1904) was an imaginative novel which again explored man's vulnerability and corruptibility. It includes one of Conrad's most suggestive symbols, the silver mine. In the story the Italian Nostromo ("our man") is destroyed for his heroism like Lord Jim. With his death the secret of the silver is lost forever. The English director David Lean planned to film the book, and he started to work with the screenplay with Christopher Hampton in 1986. Steven Spielberg agreed to produce the movie for Warner Bros. "I thought Conrad was a very good match for David's temperament," Hampton later said, "because he was very positive about individuals, but very pessimistic about the human race in general." Lean died in 1991 and the project was not realized.

"All ambitions are lawful except those which climb upward on the miseries or credulities of mankind." (from *A Personal Record,* 1912) - "All creative art is magic, is evocation of the unseen in forms persuasive, enlightening, familiar and surprising." (Conrad writing about Henry James)

The Secret Agent (1907) took a bleak view of prophets of destruction and utopians, but Conrad also once confessed, that "there had been moments during the writing of the book when I was an extreme revolutionist". Conrad dedicated the novel to H.G. Wells.

The period between *The Nigger of the 'Narcissus'* and Under Western Eyes (1911) is considered artistically Conrad's most productive. H.G. Wells encouraged Conrad and gave him good reviews and his work was also recognized by John Galsworthy. With Ford Madox Ford he wrote three books: The Inheritors (1901), Romance (1903), and The Nature of Crime (1924). Although Conrad was prolific, his financial situation wasn't secure until 1913 with the publication of Chance.

Last years of his life were shadowed by rheumatism. He refused an offer of knighthood in 1924 as he had earlier declined honorary degrees from five universities. Conrad died of a heart attack on August 3, 1924 and was buried in Canterbury. Conrad's influence upon 20th-century literature was wide. Ernest Hemingway expressed special admiration for the author, and his impact is seen in among others in the work of F. Scott Fitzgerald, Arthur Koestler, T.S. Eliot, Marcel Proust, André Malraux, Louis-Ferdiand Céline, Jean-Paul Sartre, and Graham Greene. Several of Conrad's stories have been filmed. The most famous adaptations include Alfred Hitchcock's *The Sabotage* (1936), based on *The Secret Agent,* Richard Brooks's *Lord Jim* (1964), and Francis Ford Coppola's *Apocalypse Now* (1979), based on *Heart of Darkness.* Conrad sold the American screen rights to his fiction in 1919. Next year he composed a screenplay entitled *The Strange Man,* based on the short story 'Gaspar Ruiz'. He did not like to work for the film business, and did not know about screenwritings. The studio rejected his script.

Major Works of Short Fiction

Critics generally divide Conrad's literary career into two periods: works written before or during 1912 and those written after 1912. Works of the first period include Conrad's widely acclaimed stories of the sea, most prominently "Youth," "Typhoon," "The End of the Tether," "The Secret Sharer," as well as the novella *Heart of Darkness*. Stories of the second period are less highly regarded and are typified by such romantic melodramas as "Because of the Dollars," "The Planter of Malata," "The Tale," and "The Warrior's Soul." Typical of the early works, *Heart of Darkness* is based in part on Conrad's personal experiences. The novella tells the story of Marlow—who also appears in *Lord Jim* (1900) and "Youth"—and his journey up the Congo River to relieve Kurtz, the most successful trader in ivory working for the Belgian government. Prior to meeting Kurtz, Marlow admires the trader and is excited at the prospect of their encounter. When Marlow finally meets him, he is repulsed by Kurtz's barbarism, subjugation of African peoples, and thirst for power. Upon Kurtz's death, Marlow realizes that the heart of darkness—the human potential for evil and savagery—lies within him as well.

Whereas in *Heart of Darkness* Conrad focused on Marlow's intensified awareness of evil in human nature through his identification with Kurtz, Conrad used the idea of a "double" in "The Secret Sharer" to portray the protagonist's growth toward self-knowledge. "The Secret Sharer" is the account of a young captain who harbors a criminal on his ship while at sea. The captain aids in the escape of Leggatt, a man wanted for murder, because he believes him to be his ideal self, his "secret sharer of life." Some critics have contended, however, that Leggatt is far from any human ideal. Instead, they argue, he displays cowardice, murderous instincts, and irrationality and represents the evil in the captain and in humankind. Conrad's ambiguous portrayal of characters has inspired extensive critical debate and stems from his goal as a writer to present the complexities of events and individuals without pretense of explanation.

While popular with readers of the time, Conrad's works written after 1912—including the novels *Chance* (1913), *Victory* (1915), and *The Shadow-Line* (1917) and the short story collections *Tales of Hearsay* (1925) and *The Sisters* (1928)—are considered inferior to his earlier writings. In such stories as "Because of the Dollars," "The Planter of Malata," and "The Warrior's Soul," Conrad abandoned complex narratives and characterizations and focused instead on romance, violence, and sentiment. "The Planter of Malata," for example, tells the story of Geoffrey Renouard, a young man in love with Felicia Moorsam, who is engaged to another man. Wanting to keep Felicia close to him, Geoffrey deceives her into sailing away to the remote island of Malata. When Felicia learns of Geoffrey's duplicity, she scorns him, and a brokenhearted Geoffrey kills himself.

Critical Reception

Most critics affirm that the superiority of Conrad's earlier stories can be attributed to their basis in his own life, particularly his experiences at sea and his private struggle with questions of morality, loyalty, and human fallibility. Some have commented that toward the end of his career, Conrad was more concerned with selling books than in creating works of literature. Moreover, critics contend that in his later works, Conrad's examination of the ambiguity of good and evil is generally considered too stylized and heavy-handed. His most highly regarded works, however, are acknowledged as masterpieces of English literature and continue to generate significant critical commentary. Critics regard him as a profound influence on several prominent twentieth-century writers, and many of his works have been adapted for the theater and film.

Chapter 2

The Sense of Self

Joseph Conrad's stories *The Secret Sharer, Heart of Darkness,* and *The Shadow Line* share a number of themes. All three stories deal with a process of maturing that involves the loss of youthful illusions, a process usually precipitated by an actual "trial" that challenges the protagonist's professional skills as well as his assumptions about his identity and sanity. In successfully dealing with the crisis, the protagonist reconstructs his identity and develops moral ideas rooted in acknowledgement of his own and others' human weaknesses and thus of men's necessary interdependence.

Each story is related from the point-of-view of one narrator: Marlow in *Heart of Darkness* and an unnamed captain in his first command in both *The Secret Sharer* and *The Shadow Line*. All exhibit a naive or idealized view of the world. Marlow chooses to go to the Congo because, since a boy, that part of Africa had always "charmed him." When the narrator of *The Shadow Line* unexpectedly wins the command of a ship as a replacement for a newly deceased captain, he looks forward to going "out to sea. The sea-which was pure, safe and friendly" (96). Likewise, the narrator of *The Secret Sharer* prematurely delights in "the great security of the sea" (23).

All three narrators are also solitary figures. The two new captains are isolated by virtue of their position; they cannot become intimate with their men without the risk of losing their respect, and Marlow is culturally isolated in the African jungle.

Each narrator encounters an actual physical trial. The new captain in *The Shadow Line* finds, when at sea and with a crew afflicted by tropical fevers, that the "mad" former captain has disposed of the store of life-saving quinine. The situation is aggravated by the fact that they are unable to find a wind to propel them, languishing for days on a stagnant sea. As Marlow makes his way up the "River," he is delayed, suffers losses, and finds the experience of the jungle more overwhelming than he anticipated. In contrast, the captain's trial in *The Secret Sharer*seems to be only that of becoming comfortable with his new command, thus an internal trial, but he then "takes on" the trial of hiding Leggatt, introducing the distressing possibility of discovery.

Yet it is the psychological crisis that each narrator goes through in response to his difficulties that Conrad is most concerned with and he uses the device of "doubling" in all three stories to bring out the psychological complexities of the narrators' struggles. *The Secret Sharer's* captain "identifies" with Leggatt, while Marlow "admires" Kurtz, and *The Shadow Line's* captain "relies on" Ransome, the able sailor with a weak heart. A second level of doubling occurs in the latter story when the pairing of the captain and Ransome are opposed to the pair of the unstable former captain and the second mate, Burns, whom the former captain has almost driven insane. Yet, both Leggatt and Kurtz are portrayed as able, even gifted men who have gone too far. Further, the double characters are associated with insanity. Kurtz has sunk into madness. Not yet mad, Leggatt, like Kurtz, cannot control his anger, and Burns and his former captain are mentally unstable.

These contrasting doubles all "pull" on the narrators; the narrators are either attracted by certain positive qualities or repelled by their double's lack of "moral restraint" or both. Yet it is through their relations with their "doubles" that the narrators learn about themselves. Stress and relating to their doubles cause all three narrators to question their own sanity and thus become familiar with their own limits. All three stories play on the imagery of darkness to represent this process; at the height of stress the darkness is most intense. The criminality of Leggatt, the brutality of Kurtz, and the self-centeredness of the former captain in *The Shadow Line* serve to underscore the dangers of giving into one's passions; their stories are a lesson in what not to do when one is under stress. At the same time, by being temporarily seduced by, then by examining and separating out the mistakes of their doubles, the narrators draw new conclusions and incorporate new knowledge not only about themselves but about the responsibilities and realities of their chosen roles. Marlow announces that he "remained loyal to Kurtz to the last" (149), and the captain of *The Shadow Line* admits survival would not have been possible without his dedicated crew who are "worthy of [his] undying regard" (120). An inkling of these signs of a maturity that acknowledges men's interdependence can also be found in the unnamed captain's last gesture toward Leggatt in his gift of the white hat. This expression of compassion for Leggatt's "mere flesh" saves the ship and indicates he has emerged from his self-absorbed isolation to begin to learn to lead his men.

In his work *Dostoevsky and the Process of Literary Creation* (1989), the French critic Jacques Catteau refers to the novel as a "barbaric art"; he claims it is an art form that can readily assimilate both "civilised and elaborate genres." The novel, he argues, is always "open to new forms, without worrying about ranks and rules" (p. 52). Dostoevsky's central importance to the development of the novel, insists Catteau, lies in his instinctive recognition of the form's malleability. In his major novels, Dostoevsky is able to unify what the critic calls a vast "pluralism of forms" (p. 53). In the typical Dostoevskyan novel, there is no "single triumphant highway"; there is, rather, a "maze of paths, a network of disparate forms" (p. 53). Dostoevsky's creative achievement, Catteau urges, lies in his ability to synthesize divergent genres such as tragedy and burlesque, political writing and comedy, within single works. One has only to consider a novel like *The Devils* (1871), which unites revolutionary anarchist politics with a comedy of provincial society manners, to recognize the pertinency of Catteau's observations.

In the same connection, it is interesting to point to Peter Kemp's broad, yet detailed synopsis of Conrad's creative method. In a 1991 *Times Literary Supplement* review, Kemp defines Conrad's achievement in terms of his ability to weld divergent literary genres into an artistic whole. Many critics, Kemp argues, have found that Conrad's fiction is riddled with heterogeneity, a strange composite of romance and scepticism, action yarn and metaphysical obstruseness.

Some of Conrad's narratives seem fashioned, as he said of 'Youth', Out of the boy's adventure story'; others derive from sailors' talk heard in Far East harbour offices or amid the click of billiard-balls in waterfront saloons thick with the smoke of cheroots. Into such robust stuff, however, he infiltrates fine-spun strands of philosophical and pyschological speculation... Conrad's fiction characteristically oscillates between contraries. (Kemp, p. 4)

In his persuasive account of Conrad's fictional world, Kemp identifies a number of literary forms — the adventure yarn, the romance story, the psychological and the metaphysical tale — all of which have been recognized as independent genres in the history and development of the novel itself. Like Catteau's appraisal of Dostoevsky, Kemp suggests that Conrad's primary achievement is his genius in unifying such diverse elements.

Though the critical establishment has long since labelled both artists as psychological, even political novelists, Conrad and Dostoevsky are also authors of what is usually called 'popular' fiction. Under this broad, notoriously problematic heading, are included such independent genres as 'adventure, thriller and detective writing'; 'romance' literature; and Gothic fiction.' Each of these literary forms, I would argue, can be claimed to exist in Conrad and Dostoevsky's complex fictional worlds. It is the world of 'Gothic' fiction that I shall focus on.

Whilst Dostoevsky's novels are recognizably Gothic in character, terming Conrad a Gothic artist might at first seem unusual, even perverse. By scrutinizing his shorter fiction, however, I hope to show that Conrad is not only an expert practioner of the Gothic form, but that much of his work refines, even extends, the original tradition. Firstly, however, it is important to identify the characteristic features of Gothic art, before establishing its significant place and function in each novelist's world. The Gothic novel had its genesis in English fiction in the later half of the 18th century.

It is generally agreed that Horace Walpole's *The Castle of Otranto* (1764) represents the first Gothic text. Walpole's novel established the general pattern the form was to take for many decades to come. The sensational popularity of *The Castle of Otranto* (1764) gave rise to its group of imitators, and a literary movement that became known as the Gothic School. Foremost among the later Gothic writers were Ann Radcliffe, whose novels *The Mysteries of Udolpho* (1794) and *The Italian* (1797) are particularly important. It should be noted that both Conrad and Dostoevsky remained great admirers of Mrs. Radcliffe throughout their literary careers. Other notable examples of the Gothic novel are Matthew Lewis' outstanding *The Monk* (1798), William Beckford's *Vathek* (1786), and Mary Shelley's somewhat later *Frankenstein* (1818).

The early Gothic novel was an extraordinarily popular form. Writing in 1797, one observer comments that the "Otranto Ghosts have propagated their species with unequalled fecundity. The spawn is in every novel shop" (Napier, p. viii). Many leading literary figures of the day adopted a deeply disdainful attitude towards the new literary sensation. In *Waverley* (1814), Sir Walter Scott makes a barbed reference to the Radcliffe school of writers, with its debased taste for "bandits, caverns, dungeons, inquisitors, trap-doors, ruins, secret passages, soothsayers, and all the usual accoutrements" (p. 33) (my emphasis). Perhaps the single most scathing indictment of Gothic art, however, must remain Jane Austen's *Northanger Abbey* (1818).

Despite this sort of hostility, it cannot be denied that the Gothic novel was the truly popular form of its day. In her illuminating work *The Failure of the Gothic* (1987), Elizabeth Napier calculates that at least one-third of the novels published in Great Britain between 1796 and 1806 were Gothic in character. By 1805, the popular magazines devoted the greater part of their space to short or serialized Gothic fiction. This initial success has not proved to be a short-lived phenomenon. The form has remained immensely popular. The works of

Stephen King amply testify to the reading public's continued, undiminished fascination with Gothic writing. Though still a distinct literary genre within twentieth century literature, the form has perhaps found a new and yet wider expression in the world of the cinema.

In attempting to define the essential nature of Gothic art, Elizabeth Napier argues that it is possible to dismantle, to deconstruct, the entire Gothic experience. "Gothicism", she writes, is "finally much less about evil... than it is a standardized, absolutely formulaic system of creating a certain kind of atmosphere in which a reader's sensibility towards fear and terror is exercised in predictable ways" (p. 29). According to Napier, a number of exact formulas, a number of characteristic elements, can be identified in all primary Gothic fiction.

The most important, single element of the Gothic novel is its overwhelming atmosphere of menace and brooding terror. This mood is usually evoked before the appearance of the central protagonists, and characteristically achieved by creating profoundly threatening landscapes. According to one critic, the early Gothic writers typically forged a landscape which became "a grotesque vision of hell" (Joslin, p. 87). Right up to Bram Stoker's *Dracula* (1897), Gothic novelists developed the initial sense of menace using an almost unvarying formula.

Writers would traditionally invoke sublime mountainous landscapes; at the top of some wild, inaccessible pass, they would place a formidable half-ruined castle or crumbling abbey. By definition, creating these menacing landscapes meant locating the action in bizarre or alien settings.

It was typical for the early Gothic novel to remove the reader from the everyday and ordinary, and place him or her in strange locations, normally the high wildernesses of Spain or Italy. In the eighteenth century, this was done to "capitalize upon the fear and superstition" usually associated with the "strangely alien... Latin and Iberian temperaments" (Joslin, p. 13). Furthermore, it was vital to isolate, to insulate, the action from any possible interference from normal society.

In this specific context, it is perhaps surprising to find

Conrad employing such traditional Gothic techniques to create an atmosphere of imminent terror. However, a short story like The Inn of the Two Witches' (1915) provides a clear revelation of Conrad's acquaintance with and understanding of Gothicism in its most basic form. In this tale, Conrad charts the story of Edgar Bryne and his search for a young seaman, Tom Corbin, who has disappeared in mysterious circumstances.

Significantly setting his action in a remote region of early nineteenth century Spain, Conrad readily adopts a number of Gothic conventions aimed at creating a mood of initial terror. A sense of brooding oppression is achieved by Conrad's references to the "wild, gloomy sky" and the "rank", "stony", and "dreary" nature of the surrounding landscape (*Within the Tides*, p. 138).

As Edgar Bryne's search intensifies, the Gothic atmosphere heightens correspondingly. Stumbling on a remote hamlet, Conrad's narrative notes that it is "hidden in a fold in the ground", in a spot which "seemed the most lonely corner of the earth and as if accursed in its uninhabited barrenness" (p. 139). In such passages Conrad's language, with its heavy adjectival stress, is ideally suited to the Gothic form, which by definition demands linguistic intensification or exaggeration.

Developing on these early narrative sequences, Conrad slowly evolves his fictional world into the realms of true Gothic nightmare. His Spanish landscape assumes an increasingly hostile, evil character. Alone in the wild, Byrne is said to toil "against wind and rain, on a barren dark upland, under a sky of ashes. Far away the harsh and desolate mountains raising their scarped and denuded ridges seemed to wait for him menacingly" (p. 145).

In characteristic Gothic fashion, Conrad's landscape has become "a grotesque vision of hell" (Joslin, p. 87). When Byrne finally reaches his destination, it is significant to note the suggestion of supernatural terror implicit in Conrad's description of the Witches' Inn. The house, we are told, seems as though it had risen from the ground or had come gliding to meet him, dumb and pallid, from some dark recess of the night. (*Within The Tides*, pp. 146-7)

Byrne's first sight of the eponymous Inn closes this clearly defined Gothic prelude. In all respects, Conrad's opening narrative sequence in The Inn of the Two Witches'(1915) follows well-established Gothic formulas designed to create a mood of initial terror. In a number of ways, I would argue, Byrne's progress towards the Inn recalls the narrator's sinister journey towards the Usher estate in Poe's 'The Fall of the House of Usher' (1839).

Though a significant example, 'The Inn of the Two Witches' (1915) is certainly not an isolated instance of Conrad's use of Gothic formulas. In many of his major texts, he exploits remote, hostile landscapes to create atmospheres of brooding terror. In fact, Conrad might be claimed to have extended the original boundaries of the form, taking the Gothic novel out of its traditional Italian or Spanish setting, and relocating it in Central Africa or the Tropics.

For Conrad's contemporary audience, these exotic regions were as unknown as Southern Europe had been for the majority of eighteenth century English readers. By turning from the traditional landscapes of earlier Gothic fiction, Conrad in effect creates a new stage for the world of menace and terror. In 'Heart of Darkness' (1899), for example, one critic refers to the "powerful impact of the setting" with its "aura of nightmarish... gloom" (Joslin, p. 148), and adds significantly that its effect is as "startling as any created in a recognized Gothic novel" (p. 163). To produce an atmosphere of growing menace prior to the appearance of Kurtz, Conrad exposes Marlow to an African jungle that seems peculiarly Gothic in its sense of brooding malice. At the Central Station, Marlow first acknowledges the power of the wilderness that surrounds him. The forest, he relates

stood up spectrally in the moonlight, and through the dim stir, through the faint sounds of the lamentable courtyard, the silence of the land went home to one's very heart — its mystery, its greatness, the amazing reality of its concealed life... The moon had spread over everything a thin layer of silver —

over the rank grass, over the mud, over the wall of matted vegetation standing higher than the wall of a temple, over the great river I could see through a sombre gap glittering, glittering, as it flowed broadly without a murmur. All this was great, expectant... I wondered whether the stillness on the face of the immensity... were meant as an appeal or a menace. (p. 81) Irrespective of the African location, Conrad's passage seems as essentially Gothic as any disquieting moonlit landscape we might encounter in Ann Radcliffe's writing.

As Marlow journeys further, Conrad develops this frightening aspect of the interior, creating a profound sense of fear and uncertainty. Fighting his way upstream, Marlow becomes aware of the "implacable", "brooding face" of the wilderness. In Conrad's narrative the jungle is realized as a living entity with an "inscrutable", malicious "intention". The forest, Marlow says, "looked at you with a vengeful aspect" (p. 93). It is significant to note how it is said to close over the shabby Eldorado Exploring Expedition' "as the sea closes over a diver", leaving no trace (p. 92). A large number of references to the "towering multitude of trees", to the rioting vegetation, all intensify the sense of suffocating oppression and gloom (p. 101). Like many Gothic protagonists before him, Marlow comes to recognize his vulnerability, his human littleness, in the face of this immense, hostile, alien landscape.

In his so-called 'Eastern' novels and tales Conrad's tropical landscapes perform a similarly Gothic function. Like the dark woods of the traditional folk or fairy tale, Conrad's tropical forests represent a world of sinister menace. Though works such as *Almayer's Folly* (1895) and *Lord Jim* (1900) have long been admired for their detailed realizations of exotic landscapes, Conrad's lavish descriptions can never be claimed to be wholly realistic. Like his Africa, Conrad's Eastern Islands are typically characterized as places of profound darkness. Even the briefest survey of his own 'Congo Diary' proves that Africa — like the Tropics — is of course a region of intense, blazing light. Conrad consistently subverts reality to achieve atmospheric, often sinister effects. In the 'Eastern' novels and stories, he typically evokes a dark underworld of tormented and twisted vegetation. In a representative early tale such as 'The Lagoon' (1898), Conrad's narrator is exposed to a hostile, even phantasmagoriac world. Mooring his boat in a narrow creek, itself described as "tortuous, fabulously deep... [and] filled with gloom" (p. 188), the narrator details a scene of impressive menace:

Immense trees soared up, invisible behind the festooned draperies of creepers. Here and there, near the glistening blackness of the water, a twisted root of some tall tree showed amongst the tracery of small ferns, black and dull, writhing and motionless, like an arrested snake. The short words of the paddlers reverberated between the thick and sombre walls of vegetation. Darkness oozed out from between the trees, through the tangled maze of the great fantastic and unstirring leaves; the darkness, mysterious and invincible; the darkness scented and poisonous of impenetrable forests. ('The Lagoon', Tales of Unrest, pp. 188-9).

Subject to this intimidating environment, Conrad's narrator can be claimed to have entered a recognizably Gothic world, a realm where nature and landscape become palpable foes. Indeed Conrad's stress on the reverberating darkness, the almost evil animation of the trees, is strikingly Gothic in its whole conception. Furthermore in this passage, it is significant to point to what Ian Watt calls Conrad's characteristic "inflation of language" (*Conrad in the Nineteenth Century*, p. 46). His lavish imagery — so typical in his descriptions of Africa and the Tropics — creates an immediate sense of apprehension, and plays a major role in evoking a mood of fear and terror. "Descriptive extravagance", as one critic puts it, is the "hallmark" of all Gothic writers (Joslin, p. 92).

In essential respects, Conrad can be seen to manipulate his exotic landscapes to promote moods of dread and oppression. Yet the innate Gothicism of Conrad's writing is not limited to these sinister evocations of the Tropics and of Africa. 'Conrad's Sea' becomes as strangely mysterious and as powerfully moving as the awesome castles and the sublime mountains of the conventional terror novel. In Conrad's novels, the sea is never depicted as merely an inanimate body of water;

from complete calm, it can rapidly assume the qualities of a raging beast, or become a brooding, malevolent foe. In *The Nigger of the 'Narcissus'* (1897) for example, Conrad's lurid description of the novel's central storm is peculiarly Gothic both in its extravagance, and its evil animation of the sea:

A fierce squall seemed to burst asunder the thick mass of sooty vapours; and above the wrack of torn clouds glimpses could be caught of the high moon rushing backwards with frightful speed over the sky, right into the wind's eye. Many [seamen] hung their heads, muttering that it 'turned their innards out' to look at it. Soon the clouds closed up and the world became a raging, blind darkness that howled, flinging at the lonely ship salt sprays and sleet. About half-past seven the pitchy obscurity round us turned a ghastly grey, and we knew that the sun had risen. This unnatural and threatening daylight, in which we could see one another's wild eyes and drawn faces, was only an added tax on our endurance. The horizon seemed to have come on all sides within arm's length of the ship. Into that narrowed circle furious seas leaped in, struck, and leaped out. A rain of salt heavy drops flew aslant like a mist. (pp. 55-6)

As in many of his novels, Conrad's tempests become hellish, even apocalyptic visions. But it is significant to note how Conrad's core imagery in this passage is almost entirely derived. The "howling" gales, the sickly "ghastly grey" sunrise, the enclosing horizon, are all well-established Gothic formulas. With only a few alterations, we might easily transplant Conrad's storm from its original context, and have it harrowing the inmates of some mouldering, medieval monastery. The extraordinary seastorms of Conrad's fiction — so central to works like *The Nigger of the 'Narcissus'* (1897) and 'Typhoon' (1903) — are, I believe, essentially Gothic in their language and their dramatic effect.

It is notable that even Conrad's tranquil seascapes can assume distinct Gothic identities. In *The Shadow Line* (1917), Conrad's young Captain comes to regard the Gulf of Siam as a wily and malevolent force. Effectively imprisoned by its placid waters, he becomes increasingly aware that an evil adversary is blocking his ship's onward progress. "Mysterious currents", he muses, drifted us here and there, with a stealthy power made manifest by the changing vistas of the islands fringing the east shore of the Gulf. And there were winds too, fitful and deceitful. They raised hopes only to dash them into the bitterest disappointment, promises of advance ending in lost ground, expiring in sighs, dying into dumb stillness in which currents had it all their own way — their own inimical way. (pp. 83-4)

The Gulf becomes an ideal Gothic location for Conrad's ship, haunted, according to the character Burns, by the dying curse of its former captain. The Gulf becomes an animate agent of evil; it is a sinister region as oppressive and frightening as any haunted graveyard.

This brief survey of Conrad's fiction tends, I feel, to overturn a number of basic critical preconceptions regarding the novelist's innovatory artistic methods. Whilst Conrad certainly remains a modernist writer, he can clearly be seen to employ a number of eighteenth century Gothic formulas in his fiction, summoning sinister land or sea scapes to create atmospheres of fear and uncertainty.

Though Gothicism plays an important role in Dostoevsky's fictional world, it is not initially evoked through narrative accounts of bizarre or exotic locations. Landscape, in the traditional sense, plays virtually no part in Dostoevsky's fiction. Descriptions of the natural world are noticeably absent in his writing. When they do occur — as in the passages describing Stephan Verkhovensky's final flight in *The Devils* (1871) — they exist solely to mirror deeper psychological states within Dostoevsky's protagonists. In essence, Dostoevsky is a writer of the city; his landscapes are predominantly urban and human. Like Dickens' London, Dostoevsky's St. Petersburg can assume a fantastic, sometimes diabolical identity. His vast tenements with their twisting, unlit stairwells, cast a profoundly disturbing shadow over characters and events in novels like *Crime and Punishment* (1866) and *The Idiot* (1869). "'There are few places'", Svidrigailov comments in the former work, "'where you'll find so many gloomy, harsh and strange influences on the soul of man as in Petersburg'" (trans. Magarshack, p. 439). In many senses, Svidrigailov's remark highlights the essentially Gothic identity of Dostoevsky's often nightmarish city. As Donald Fanger has noted, the St. Petersburg of *Crime and Punishment* (1866) is the ideal Gothic backdrop for Raskolnikov's horrific axemurders of the old pawnbroker and her sister (p. 207).

The St. Petersburg of *The Idiot* (1869) similarly highlights the Gothic aspects of Dostoevsky's art. The opening paragraph of the novel suggests that Prince Myshkin, Rogozhin and Lebedev are all entering a recognizably Gothic world:

At about nine o'clock in the morning at the end of November, during a thaw, the Warsaw train was approaching Petersburg at full speed. It was so damp and foggy that it was a long time before it grew light, and even then it was difficult to distinguish out of the carriage windows anything a few yards to the right and left of the railway track. (trans. Magarshack, p. 31)

Dostoevsky's St. Petersburg is not merely fogbound; it is blurred, unresolved. Though it is early morning, night still effectively shrouds the scene. This unnatural detail immediately defines a mood of uncertainty and oppression. Furthermore, it is significant to note that Dostoevsky employs a traditional Gothic formula towards the end of this opening sequence. "Everyone's face", the narrative notes, is "pale and yellow, the colour of the fog" (p. 31). The spectral associations conjured by this image are obvious. In choosing to open *The Idiot* (1869) in this particular way, it seems that Dostoevsky's aim is to establish St. Petersburg as a place of fear and dread. And later in the novel the city does assume a profoundly nightmarish quality. As Prince Myshkin wanders through the streets of St. Petersburg in Part Two, he is not merely followed; he is haunted by Rogozhin.

In addition to this atmosphere of terror, it is possible to distinguish a number of peculiarly Gothic landmarks within Dostoevsky's urban landscape. The interior of Rogozhin's house, for example, closely resembles the interior of the archetypal castle or monastery of Gothic fiction, despite the city location. Following established Gothic traditions, the house is a veritable maze of chambers and twisting corridors. Prince Myshkin, we are told, is led through a "number of tiny rooms, turning again and again round corners, going up two or three steps and going down as many" (p. 242). Myshkin's immediate disorientation within the confines of the house produces a mood of intense apprehension, a mood not dispelled by the discovery of Rogozhin's gloomy quarters.

Rogozhin's room, the narrative stresses, is particularly "dark and grimy", cluttered with heavy ledgers and imposing furniture. That most familiar of Gothic stageprops, the oil painting of the family elder, occupies a suitably prominent position. The canvas of Rogozhin's father, Myshkin notes, depicts an austere and menacing man, a man with a "yellow wrinkled face, and a pair of suspicious, mournful eyes" (p. 244).

In most Gothic novels, the gloomy, often dilapidated condition of the hero-villain's estate is itself an accurate reflection of the protagonist's tormented psychological state. In *The Idiot* (1869) this same Gothic association between house and character is clearly intended. Myshkin is quick to draw a parallel between the gloomy house and Rogozhin's brooding nature. "'Your house', the Prince reflects, 'has the appearance of the whole of your family and the whole of your Rogozhin way of life... Its so dark here... you dwell in darkness'. (p. 244)

And Myshkin is not the only character to draw attention to the Gothic aspect of Rogozhin's house. Writing to Aglaya, Nastasya makes a melodramatic reference to its sinister nature. It is, she comments, 'sinister and gloomy, and there is a secret in it... All the time I was in their house I could not help thinking that somewhere under the floor-boards there was a dead man hidden'. (p. 502)

With horrible irony, Ippolit also draws a similar association, terming Rogozhin's house a "'graveyard'" (p. 453). In essential respects, Dostoevsky creates an archetypal Gothic location for Nastasya's murder, right in the heart of his contemporary St. Petersburg.

It is also worth pointing to the unnamed hotel Myshkin

stays at on his return to St. Petersburg in Part Two of the novel. As the scene for Rogozhin's attempted murder of the Prince, it functions as an important dramatic backdrop within Dostoevsky's narrative. Like Rogozhin's house, the hotel is characterized as a place of darkness; it is a building that Myshkin finds entirely loathsome.

Significantly, the hotel harbours that most characteristic of Gothic locations, the winding ill-lit staircase. The staircase hiding a murderous adversary had long been recognized as an established Gothic formula, a veritable cliche of terror fiction, by the time Dostoevsky had completed his novel in 1869. Irrespective of this, the writer employs this stock item of Gothic mansionery to significant effect, substantially heightening the mood of terror. "As in all old houses", the sequence begins, "the staircase was of stone.

Dark and narrow, it twisted round a thick... column" (p. 271). As Myshkin emerges from the storm outside and proceeds up the darkened stairwell, the scene — despite its urban setting — strongly recalls a similar passage in *The Castle of Otranto* (1764). In true Gothic style, Rogozhin hides in "something like a niche" in the stairwell, a cavity "not more than a yard wide and about eighteen inches deep" (p. 271). One has only to consider the similar function darkened staircases perform in *Crime and Punishment* (1866) — they figure in all Raskolnikov's entrances and exits from the flat of the vile, old pawnbroker — to realise that Dostoevsky's inner city has a significant Gothic identity.

As well as the architecture of the Gothic novel, the Gothic storm features in Dostoevsky's urban world. The storm has long been regarded as a generic characteristic of the Gothic novel. As I have already noted, Conrad's sea storms have a descriptive extravagance that recalls Mrs. Radcliffe's pioneering method in novels like *The Mysteries of Udolpho* (1794). Although Dostoevsky does not make extensive use of the storm, his urban tempests do assume a distinct Gothic identity. The storm which forms the background to Rogozhin's attempted murder of Myshkin in *The Idiot* (1869) achieves a familiar, apocalyptic quality. "The storm-cloud", Dostoevsky's narrative recounts, "covered the whole sky and blotted out the evening light." In traditional Gothic fashion, the storm breaks the precise moment the Prince approaches, "the rain coming down in torrents" (p. 270). Rather than a realistic detail, Dostoevsky's storm functions more as a dramatic decoration to the action, significantly heightening the mood or fear and terror.

In *Crime and Punishment* (1866) Dostoevsky follows a similar Gothic strategy in detailing Svidrigailov's suicide, a St. Petersburg storm acting as the backdrop to Svidrigailov's nightmares and final hours at the end of the novel. But the influence of the Gothic school on Dostoevsky's creative method is not the only consideration here; there is also the more immediate impact of Dickens to consider. The urban storm plays an important role in many of Dickens' novels, heralding, for instance, Magwitch's dramatic return to London in *Great Expectations* (1861). Though the subject falls outside the boundaries of my current discussion, it is important to acknowledge that Dostoevsky's vision of the city owes much to Dickens' significant use of Gothic formulas.

Though I have concentrated on Dostoevsky's Gothicization of the city, I want to comment briefly on Conrad's celebrated vision of London in *The Secret Agent* (1907). In his Author's Note' to the novel, Conrad uses a number of traditional Gothic formulas to detail his fictionalized city. As with Dostoevsky, the influence of Dickens is much in evidence. In typical Gothic fashion, Conrad's landscape assumes a hostile, partly evil identity. London is seen as an "enormous... monstrous town", a "cruel devourer of the world's light." At the close of the passage, Conrad employs what is clearly a sepulchral image. His fictionalized city becomes effectively an immense urban graveyard, a place where there is "darkness enough to bury five millions of lives" (p. xii). The adjectival extravagance of Conrad's vision seems almost enough to assure it an independent Gothic identity, irrespective of content.

I hope to have shown that Conrad and Dostoevsky utilize Gothic models and archetypes to create oppressive or sinister effects in their fiction. As I have said, one can draw significant parallels between Conrad's exotic African and Eastern landscapes, and the European landscapes of the early Gothic writers. But Conrad effectively extends the geographical boundaries of the Gothic form beyond its traditional Iberian or Italian location. In the same way, his extravagant seastorms recall the narrative hyperbole of the Gothic novel's Alpine or mountain storm. In Dostoevsky's fictional world, the architectural landscapes of the genre — its gloomy buildings, its darkened staircases and tortuous passageways — are much in evidence, only relocated to a modern urban setting.

Yet despite its paramount importance, landscape and setting could be regarded as essentially a cosmetic, even decorative aspect of Gothic fiction. The most central characteristic of the genre must be the Gothic hero-villain himself. The critic Michael Joslin claims that it is possible to identify a number of characterizing features in the archetypal Gothic villain. "Power, both of purpose and mind", he writes, is the "basic trait" of all Gothic protagonists. This positive characteristic has, however, been invariably perverted to evil ends. The true Gothic villain, Joslin argues, has the capacity to benefit mankind greatly but because of his desires or because of some blighting check given to his moral development, he exerts his might only to achieve his selfish ambitions. (p. 17)

The critic cites Bram Stoker's Dracula as a classic example of one such character. The vampire hunter Van Helsing makes particular reference to the Count's illustrious past. Dracula, Van Helsing reflects, was once the cleverest as well as the bravest of men, a noble individual with a mighty brain and an iron resolution. It is this wilful perversion of extraordinary personal ability that is instrumental in creating the terror and awe associated with both the Gothic villain, and the genre itself.

By applying this critical interpretation, it is possible to draw a number of significant parallels between Joslin's archetypal Gothic villain, and leading protagonists in both Conrad and Dostoevsky's fiction. In 'Heart of Darkness' (1899),

Conrad's Kurtz might easily be defined as a major Gothic character. Like Stoker's Dracula, he possesses extraordinary personal abilities, abilities that might be directed towards entirely philanthropic ends. Conrad's narrative consistently alludes to Kurtz's genius; he is a gifted painter, an inspired musician, a formidable writer. A natural leader, Kurtz possesses enormous oratorical skills; his unusual eloquence can, and does, convert others to his ideas and beliefs. In characterisitic Gothic fashion, however, Kurtz abuses his profound natural abilities to perpetrate the most appalling crimes.

A similarly powerful, yet distorted intellect can be observed in Dostoevsky's Stavrogin. As the critic Michael Katz comments, many characters spout ideological convictions expounded by Stavrogin at some previous stage in his life. The landscape [of *The Devils* (1871)] is strewn with disciples... clinging to the vestiges of his thought. (p. Xi)

Shatov, Kirillov, and Verkhovensky all claim that Stavrogin has exerted a profound, shaping influence on their fundamental values and beliefs. Shatov's Slavophilism, Kirillov's Nietzschean individualism, Verkhovensky's pseudo-anarchist ideology, are all said to originate in heated debates with Stavrogin; he has, so each man claims, converted them to their respective causes long before the novel begins. Though Stavrogin's intellect easily embraces such diverse ethical systems, he cannot, and does not adopt them.

Like the archetypal Gothic villain, he toys with philosophies, as if they are amusing playthings, finally distorting or subverting them to evil ends. Stavrogin abuses, for example, the sacred rite of Orthodox Confession, when he uses it as a platform to celebrate his sexual depravity at his meeting with Father Tikhon. Like Kurtz, his formidable natural abilities are perverted to entirely negative and destructive purposes.

But prior to the full emergence of this evil identity, the Gothic hero-villain is usually characterized as a profoundly enigmatic figure. The Gothic novelist traditionally feeds the reader with tantalizing bits of information designed to invest his villain with a sinister, darkly charismatic identity. Van Helsing's references to Dracula's enigmatic history are, for example, particularly instumental in making Stoker's vampire a fascinating character 'per se'. This enigmatizing process, so central to the Gothic idiom, is clearly evident in Conrad and Dostoevsky's realizations of Kurtz and Stavrogin.

In Heart of Darkness' (1899), an intense aura of mystery surrounds the character and motives of Kurtz. The central station is full of strange, often disturbing rumours regarding this "remarkable person" (p. 19). As Paul O'Prey notes, a "fog of insistent vagueness" circumscribes Conrad's antagonist (p. 20). For Marlow, the name of Kurtz begins to exert a sinister fascination, a fascination that is communicated to the reader. In *The Devils* (1871), strange, often contradictory rumours reach Varvara Petrovna regarding her son's bizarre lifestyle in St. Petersburg. Just prior to his return home, Stavrogin's unusual character becomes the topic of fevered speculation in Skvoreshniki high society.

"The whole town", Dostoevsky's narrator tells us, is possessed by "the idea that his [Stavrogin's] soul might harbour a fatal secret"; some people, Govorov adds, "positively relished the notion that he was a murderer" (trans. Katz, p. 43). As with Conrad's Kurtz, Dostoevsky constructs a complex web of intrigue around his central antagonist, long before he appears in the novel. And Stavrogin's actual arrival in Skvoreshniki merely intensifies the enigma. When he drags the elderly Gaganov round the room by his nose, the petty outrage seems far more than a mere prank; Stavrogin's inexplicable behaviour carries its own sinister resonance. With this action, Dostoevsky's narrator warns, "the wild beast" had "suddenly unsheathed its claws" (p. 45). In many ways, Dostoevsky's realization of Stavrogin follows a well-established Gothic pattern. Like Conrad's Kurtz, Dostoevsky's character progresses from fascinating enigma to evil genius.

In his survey of the Gothic genre, Michael Joslin identifies a further important characteristic of the form. The achetypal Gothic protagonist, Joslin claims, typically has his familiar', a grotesque, often comic foil who idolizes the hero-villain (p.

139). In Stoker's *Dracula* (1897), the Count has his slavish adherent in the lunatic Renfield. Stoker's madman insists that he is Dracula's servant. This devil-disciple' relationship', so characteristic of the Gothic idiom, can also be identified in Conrad and Dostoevsky's writing.

Stavrogin and Kurtz both have their respective familiars. In an important passage in *The Devils* (1871) Peter Verkhovensky insists that Stavrogin is his "idol". "You're my leader, you're my sun, and I'm your worm'", he informs Dostoevsky's antagonist in Part Two of the novel (trans. Magarshack, p. 420). Though Verkhovensky is undoubtedly an accomplished manipulator, it does seem possible to interpret many of his actions as attempts to impress or gratify Stavrogin. Verkhovensky is like an eager dog keen to please his master.

Though Rogozhin cannot be regarded as a genuine Gothic hero-villain, it is worth noting that Dostoevsky's brutal, sensual protagonist has his clownish familiar. Particularly in Part One of *The Idiot* (1869), the civil servent Lebedev proves slavishly faithful, offering to "'walk upside down'" for Rogozhin (p. 36). "'Thrash me and you shall have me'", he tells Semyon Parfyonovich. "'By thrashing me, you shall put your seal on me... " (p. 41). Rogozhin readily accepts the attention of this avaricious buffoon, and contemptuously terms Lebedev his "'leech'" (p. 38).

In 'Heart of Darkness' (1899), it is the aptly named Harlequin who acts as Kurtz's familiar. Like the archetypal Gothic villain, Conrad's antagonist treats his disciple with complete contempt, threatening to shoot him should he so desire. As Marlow notes, the Harlequin idolizes Kurtz. In Marlow's opinion, "the man [Kurtz] filled his life, occupied his thoughts, swayed his emotions" (Penguin ed. p. 95). Conrad's comic figure is as devoted to Kurtz as the lakeside savages who regard him as their deity.

In this essay, I have endeavoured to show how one distinct, perhaps surprising, literary genre proves to be a common and significant factor in both Conrad and Dostoevsky's fiction. Though I have concentrated on the specific issue of Gothicism, many recent critics have shown that other literary forms are common to both writers' worlds.

The genres of 'adventure', 'thriller', 'romance', and 'detective' fiction are prominent and readily evident features in each author's novels. This innovative ability to successfully weld such disparate forms into their writing is, I believe, an indication of the significant bond existing between Conrad and Dostoevsky's fundamental creative processes.

Chapter 3

"Speech Was of No Use": Conrad, a New Journalism

It is a familiar and still-venerated truth that the novels of Joseph Conrad despair at the insurmountability of subjectivity, and consequently effect a retreat "inward," away from the real; but without much notice, this truth is usually said to be a necessary consequence of these works' narrative structure alone, regardless of whether it is also expressed in their thematics or explicit discourse. Ursula Lord's recent formulation is paradigmatic:

Heart of Darkness and Lord Jim disclose in narrative structure the relativism of modern epistemology.... Conrad's creation of Marlow and his embedding of Marlow's narrative within another acknowledge that we always perceive the world many times removed, filtered through our own consciousness and that of others, as through a glass darkly. (63-64)

The notion that the mere existence of an "internal" narrator necessarily puts the reader at a remove from a reality and a truth that would have revealed itself in the absence of his mediation might seem to have been exhumed from a theoretical debate that died out years ago. We might not find it surprising that there has never actually been a thorough poststructuralist analysis of the narratological foundation of this idea, since it seems just another iteration of a well-traversed "metaphysics of presence."

The still-tenacious presumption that an "embedded" narrator necessarily occludes a transparency that would otherwise be available is not, however, simply the effect of a depth model exerting its centuries-old influence from within Western intellectual discourse. What I would like to demonstrate with a review of the twentieth century's criticism of Conrad's narrated narrators is that its general suspicion of a reporter like Marlow-as a "filterer" of truth and an obstacle to the real-is an expression of an historically traceable cultural politics of attestation. From this vantage it will become clear that Conrad's famous break from prevailing narratological norms is inextricable, for instance, from his constantly reiterated loathing of the daily press.

Both the politics and the metaphysics of what might be called anonymous versus testimonial authority have been disseminated most effectively, since the latter half of the nineteenth century, by a ubiquitous and solidly institutionalized public journalism. Conrad's novelistic theater, in which the social or even juridical forums of all narration are insistently located, and where no interrogator escapes visibility or responsibility, is deliberately opposed to an increasingly influential power of anonymous authority at the fin de siecle, one that has been sustained most effectively by what the author calls "the perspectiveless manner of the daily papers" (Notes 141). Not simply a recoil from the "devouring publicity" of newsprint that haunted a figure like Henry James, Conrad's opposition is more precisely to the "new journalism" emerging concurrently with his writing career.

The former "age of verbatim report," in Harold Herd's words, was now in decline; the series of testimonials that had formerly constituted the newspaper were now being sifted, readily paraphrased, and framed with commentary to "help [the reader] in absorbing the news." "The journal" was thus being elevated more distinctly above its constituent elements, and had attained an extradiegetic purchase from which it could claim "comprehensive coverage of... modern life" in general (Herd 223). As I hope to show, the promise of comprehension that had come to be demanded of the newspaper, the most popular and pervasive disseminator of narrative norms the modern world had known, would also henceforth be demanded of the novel. In an 1889 edition of London's The New Review, Tighe Hopkins initiated a colloquium on anonymity in the newspaper. Unsigned articles had long been the norm in the English press, and another discussion of their efficacy in combating the suppression of reformist voices would have been unremarkable. But here at the twilight of the century, Hopkins and several journalistic and literary allies argue at length against anonymity.

The progressive voices that had once feared the blunt power of crown and title now see a new enemy: anonymous authority itself, a power said to be conjured by the very organs of mass communication that had been weapons against the old order. "The power of the press," writes L.F. Austin, who will ultimately oppose Hopkins in the debate, "is a purely impersonal force.... The Times is the power, not the men who write in it" (I: 517).1 William Archer also calls it an "impersonal force," one that exerts itself from behind a mask of superhuman, ineffable wisdom which imposes so ludicrously on the multitude.... Men tell each other with bated breath, "The Tribune says this, the Oracle says that; the Reverberator is of such an opinion," forgetting that Tribune, Oracle, and Reverberator are only Hobson, Dobson and Jobson speaking grandiloquently through a resonant mouthpiece. (1: 530)

The New Review debate is not about whether the use of an anonymous voice really does effect a distinct and instrumental authority: all of its participants, including Bernard Shaw, agree that anonymity creates an identifiable, autonomous authority with an operative power. At issue, rather, is whether the press ought to wield the "mysterious power," as James Runciman puts it, "which the anonymous article gives" (1: 528).

Whereas Hopkins and his allies lament a reading public "willing to impose on itself... a belief that the use of the 'We' in place of the T endows [a] writer with a semi-miraculous wisdom" (I: 524), L.F. Austin and others warn that "the power of the press in England" would be devastated without its anonymous voice (I: 517). Austin contrasts English practice with that of Paris, where "the authority of this or that journal is of no account" precisely because articles are attributed to particular writers. The Parisian news reader "enjoys the performances of his favourite literary swordsmen, the clash of whose weapons amuses the Boulevards and sometimes startles the birds in early morning in the Bois de Boulogne" (I: 517).

For Austin, open acknowledgment that articles are ultimately constituted by the personal testimony of particular writers and witnesses turns the serious business of journalism into a contemptible game. French journalism is said to deserve demotion into the "literary" not because it is tainted by fictitiousness, but because it does not affirm a transcendental relation to the personal testimony of which it is composed. A report bound to a signature or name will for that reason alone contribute more to the memoir than to the history, more to the literary than to the real.

Few of the New Review contributors fail to compare, favorably or not, the English habit of anonymity with France's systematic attribution. The portrait of a French public discourse rendered impotent by its rejection of anonymous authority is made intelligible by a cultural logic well known to Austin's readers: the greater insistence across the Channel on the testimonial nature of journalism is readily understood as an expression of the debilitating relativism and subjectivism for which Paris is the Western world's bastion. The New Review debate, to which we will return at the end of this study, reveals the extent to which an industry whose product is public discourse had come to depend on cultural codes and philosophical imperatives that establish the moral value-and even necessity-of anonymous authority in itself.

To the cultural and institutional forces with a stake in such authority, there would always be available a long-standing philosophical rhetoric that conceptually degrades, or "marks" in deconstructive parlance, the category of testimony itself. In his 1988 Le Differend, Jean-Francois Lyotard draws attention to the logic by which this marking occurs: even when it is taken for granted that there is no historiography that is not ultimately dependent on individual testimonies, it is always possible that any one such statement is, if not a lie, corrupt because it is biased, or "interested," or sees only "one side" of the event in question. If the witness to an event "claims to see everything," Lyotard writes, "he or she is not credible.

If he or she is credible, it is insofar as he or she has not seen everything, but has only seen a certain aspect" (45). The contemporary inquiry Lyotard takes as his case study reveals the potential height of the stakes involved: the never-adequate testifier is the witness to mass executions in Nazi concentration camps who has now been called back to the witness stand by scholars contesting the historicity of the holocaust.3 It is an inquiry made possible by a movement of "zooming out," to borrow the photographer's term; a re-examination of the statement from a widened scope that brings into view the scene of deposition as such.

What had been the sole, "outer" frame of the scene created by the statement-a boundary identical with that of the testimony itself-now recedes within a new, larger frame; it recedes into full view as a foregrounded object. Before the zoom out, the object of inquiry had been the "content" of the statement; now it is the statement as such, its content bracketed. Before, there was no other authority, no authoritativeness outside the testimony; but now the testifier is inescapably suspect, and final authority can reside only in what we will see is an imaginary comprehension effected by the new scene of deposition.

Lyotard's work has also come under the consideration of Shoshana Felman, who argues convincingly that the Holocaust brought about a "historical crisis of witnessing," and inaugurated what she calls our "contemporary Age of Testimony." Faced with the Holocaust as "an event eliminating its own witness," Felman claims that "the cryptic forms of modern narrative... [bear] testimony, through their very cryptic form, to the radical historical crisis in witnessing the Holocaust has opened up" (200-01, emphasis in original). It is precisely this picture, however, of modern narrative embracing the condition of the witness because of its absolute inadequacy that I would like to revise.

Felman's portrayal of modernist narrative as a "cryptogram," which presupposes a hidden but determined comprehension that such narration deliberately withholds or evades, occludes at the outset the tendency of this writing to question the very possibility of comprehension beyond testimony. As the survey below will remind us, the critical tradition that has rendered the modernist novel with a metaphorics of cryptography usually begins by looking at pre-war writers like Conrad.

If there is an "age of testimony" contemporaneous with literary modernism, it is one that rather grows out of a mounting tension-as exhibited by the literary and journalistic participants of the New Review roundtable-between testimony and an anonymous authority to which the masters of "public discourse" increasingly appeal. For a writer like Conrad, the "problem" of the witness is not that she cannot survive to tell the tale, but that her report, as Lyotard suggests, is said to fall short of an imaginary narrative that would depict the event in its comprehensive entire, beyond her mere "perspective."

That the operation of attestation, deposition, and confession is a primary subject of Conrad's scrutiny has been both a truism and an impossibility for literary criticism. Although we no longer follow Henry James in pulling Conrad's scenes of narration out of the realm of a novel's proper "content" and into an externality of "treatment," the still-active rhetoric of epistemological "filtering" owes a great deal to this long-standing banishment.

James had gotten the ball rolling in his 1914 summation of Conrad in "The Younger Generation," which focuses exclusively on the author's staged narration, and is, rather remarkably, the only formal study of Conrad he would ever articulate. Purely "the exhibition of method," according to James, and therefore external to content, Conrad's investigation of Marlow's investigations cannot possibly be conceived as a subject under treatment. "What shall we most call Mr. Conrad's method," James writes, "but his attempt to clarify [his subject] quand meme... steeping his matter in perfect eventual obscuration" (157).

James arrives at this essay, we might recall, with a theory of narration that had already been infused with the logic to which Lyotard draws our attention: Attestation, once it is framed or made visible as such, is necessarily untrustworthy. In a 1911 letter to H.G. Wells, James had written:

I make my remonstrance-for I do remonstrate-bear upon the bad service you have done your cause by riding so hard again that accurst autobiographic form.... Save in the fantastic and the romantic... it has no authority, no persuasive or convincing force-its grasp of reality and truth isn't strong and disinterested.... There is, to my vision, no authentic... report of things on the novelist's... part unless a particular detachment has operated, unless the great stewpot or crucible of the imagination, of the observant and recording and interpreting mind in short, has intervened and played its part.... (Henry James 500)

The authority of a novelistic statement hinges at the outset on a disavowal of its status as testimony, even as that authority retains its own "interpreting mind" that would "intervene" in our quest for the "reality and truth" it grasps. Hence the axiom in "The Younger Generation" that the lack of true authority in Conrad's Marlow is entirely due to his status as "a reciter, a definite responsible intervening first person singular." Authority can reside only in a non-responsible narrator, a "single... impersonal and inscrutable... omniscience, remaining indeed nameless" ("Younger" 157).

As it pretends to cite bvit actually inscribes into orthodoxy "the general law of fiction" that Conrad disobeys, James's essay begins by explaining that the scene of deposition Conrad habitually keeps in view should rather be suppressed; the reader should remain unconscious of the interrogative or confessional arrangements that are the precondition of testimony.

It has been the course... of [Conrad's] so multiplying his creators or, as we are now fond of saying, producers, as to make them almost more numerous and quite emphatically more material than the creatures and the production itself in whom and which we by the general law of fiction expect such agents to lose themselves. We take for granted by the general law of fiction a primary author... [who] works upon us most in fact by making us forget him. Mr. Conrad's first care, adversely to this, is expressly to posit or set up a reciter, a definite responsible intervening first person singular. (157)

The language of law serves to preempt inevitable questions about why we should "take it for granted" that the "primary author" of, say, The Ambassadors remains "nameless" and non-locatable. For in fact this refusal in Conrad to let his "projected" storyteller disappear as a responsible intervener confronts James with something that inevitably precludes his law: the inescapable possibility that what a reader takes for granted is precisely a historical determination of this author-e.g., a determination of a Mr. Henry James, of various facts and lore constituting his public persona. To ensure that we "forget" this author, and to establish that its "observant and recording and interpreting mind" is categorically distinct from Marlow's-that "beautiful and generous" interpreter of events (157)-what is available to James is no law, but only his own decree. As we will see, however, it is a decree that will become the very foundation of a later "narratology," the only means of establishing both the discretion and totalization of a given "structural" schematic for a novel, as well as that structure's independence from "content."

As are later narratologies, James is careful not to play the trump card of "omniscience" to establish the difference in authority that would exist between Marlow and the proper Jamesian narrator to which he is necessarily opposed; rather, he gives the term to Marlow himself: "Marlow's omniscience... is a prolonged hovering flight of the subjective over the outstretched ground of the case exposed. We make out this ground, only through the shadow cast by the flight,... to the no small eclipse of intrinsic colour and form and whatever, upon the passive expanse" (157). James does not allow his all-important "methodological" distinction to be based on a godly power that, if achieved merely by avoiding the "first person singular," an author could so easily and arbitrarily give himself, and which Conrad would thus have austerely renounced.

Instead, the essay achieves its abjection of the Conradian testimonial by strategically grafting onto its narrative agents designations of subject and object. Marlow is said to be effectively omniscient; but he also allows himself to be "seen" as an object of study, which places him merely "within" the comprehension that ought always to "enclose and confine" determined objects (158). In contrast, the Jamesian narrator is perforce freed from all qualities and effects attributed to an object, such as the inevitability of casting a "shadow," the shadow of his own "subjectivity."

To pick just one point of its entry into the subsequent history of critical thought, the imaginary comprehension that would "enclose" all objectified narratives reappears in narratology's conception of "external focalization." As Gérard Genette writes in Narrative Discourse, this externality becomes evident when a literary hero "performs in front of us without our ever being allowed to know his thoughts or feelings." Ernest Hemingway's "Hills Like White Elephants" is said to be an exemplary case, "which carries circumspection so far as to become a riddle." Genette continues:

> But we should not limit this narrative type to a role only in works at the highest literary level. Michel Raimond remarks rightly that in the novel of intrigue or adventure, "where interest arises from the fact that there is a mystery," the author "does not tell us immediately all that he knows." (190)4

There is an epistemological contract peculiar to the whodunit, which first promises then unveils a predetermined answer to a mystery. Genette identifies the mystery of this determined truth with the mysteries supposed to belong to Hemingway's fiction: the truth of a fictional hero's consciousness and the "riddle" of the story as a whole, the encoded truth it ultimately speaks. Despite Genette's ostensibly gratuitous movement toward the sub-genre of the mystery as if toward another illustrative case, the activity peculiar to such books-of manufacturing a screen behind which secrets are said to lie, thereby assuring the advent of truth in the mere drawing of the curtain-has been presumed all along to belong to fiction in general.

There would then always have been an answer to the riddle of fiction, and the truth that literature speaks will be identical to the establishment and completion of such circuits of veiling and unveiling. In order to establish what, exactly, would constitute full disclosure in a story like "Hills Like White Elephants," the critic must draw up a contract to designate the question(s) whose answer shall be the ultimate revelation.6 In the pact Genette would impose on Hemingway's story, the designated question is of the "thoughts and feelings" of the hero. If an answer to this question had been answered in the fiction, the author would reportedly have given us "all that he knows"-despite the fact that there remain countless other possible questions, pooled from the psychological knowledge-systems Genette faintly evokes, that could just as easily have been the designated one: questions about the hero's childhood, sexual habits, relationship with his mother, and so on.

Long after Narrative Discourse, narratologists continue to be alarmed at the modernist novel's failure to oblige a contract of comprehension. With an eye on "internal focalization" and a rigorous policing of "modal locutions," David Herman, for instance, alerts us to the epistemological danger of Franz Kafka's The Trial. Joseph K. is said to lack a reliable "grammatical (and conceptual)" measure by which he can evaluate his own shirting conceptions of the world; from among the "possible worlds" K. imagines he inhabits, he needs to choose that which will serve as the best "model world" (137). "In relating only the sort and the amount of information immediately available from within K.'s own perspective," The Trial bars us from the correct presentation, the determined comprehension that ought to be our goal (100).

Herman's Universal Grammar and Narrative Form offers itself as a cure for the disease of Kafka's narrative form: "What we require are grammatical (and conceptual) resources for ranking possible worlds as better and worse candidates for model worlds in a given case. Such resources might help us to avoid the radical disactualizations in which Kafka's narrative form continually involves us" (137).

In a similar narratological diagnosis of Heart of Darkness, Diana Knight applies the term "paralepsis"-"the inclusion of more information than is strictly accessible to the perceiver's visual or aural viewpoint" (23)-to Marlow's statement that, upon meeting Kurtz's intended, he "perceived she was one of those creatures that are not the playthings of Time" (Darkness 76; qtd. in Knight 23). Knight writes: "This may be presented as an act of straight perception, yet the capitalization of 'Time' indicates the infiltration of an abstract noun which... strictly belongs to a different level of perception" (24).

Measured against a "level of perception" that could finally discern the truth of Time and all other such capital concepts, Marlow, and thus any witness, will always be inadequate. Even when such witnesses could be portrayed as acknowledging this inadequacy with what narratology calls "modal locutions"-such as "I seemed to hear" or "I perceived"-these, according to Knight, must be read as "unavowed paralepses" (23). Sealed inside his subjectivity, Knight suggests, the witness would do well not to pretend to achieve the "level of perception" apparently attainable by another, unnamed perceiver.

The almost automatic identification of what Frederick Karl calls "surrogate narrators" with a programme of subjectification has penetrated even into projects that would locate Conrad within a purely philosophical field. At work in Mark Wollaeger's Conrad and the Fictions of Skepticism, for instance, is a great shibboleth in modernist studies-originating with Ford Madox Ford, and persisting into Fredric Jameson's depiction of Conrad's "aestheticizing strategy"-of attributing to Conrad's prose a fundamental "impressionism."

Wollaeger posits the "subjectification of Marlow's narrative" in Heart of Darkness at the outset of his study, attributing it to the novella's "emphasis on sensation" (8-9). What is not made clear in such criticism is the measure by which the novel's depiction of sensation is said to be "emphasized" over its much more prevalent discourse of ideas-the like of which is in fact the primary object of Wollaeger's study-or even over its narrative incident, or its explicit historical depiction of colonial operations in Africa. By what rule or what logic can we say that the impressionistic passages in the story come to govern the entirety of Marlow's discourse, establishing the essentiality and continuity of its "subjectification"?

For a rigorous engagement with such questions we can appeal to Fredric Jameson's The Political Unconscious, which gives a name to this continuity. Lord Jim is said to create a "sensorium" that makes its depiction of "working life at sea... available for consumption on some purely aesthetic level" (213-14). The sensorium is said to be effected primarily by the text's sensory signals toward point of view. As if alerted to the inadequacy of founding the sensorium entirely on a mode of presentation-a foundation solidly in place when the narrator reports Jim "seeing" or "hearing" an event, but which would disappear in the absence of such terms-Jameson posits additionally an active motion of narrative "displacement."

The novel's "intermittent vision of the sea's economic function," which exhibits both the "reality of production" and "Conrad's unquestionable and acute sense of the nature and dynamics of imperialist penetration," is an authentic "content" occluded by the aestheticized content in the interstices of this intermittence (215). The trope of displacement seems to locate the otherwise elusive activity of aestheticization-the exhibition, then derealization of "content"-in the temporal progression of narrative; that is, over the course of "the nonstop textual production" of this, "the first half of Lord Jim" (214, 219). Jameson thus protects the working reality of aestheticization by affixing it to the reality of textual production; he rescues its operation from the very "abstract structure of temporality" he claims to be endemic to modernism itself (261). The authentic content of Jim's relation to the production of imperial capitalism, the like of which appears in the early rendition of the firemen aboard the Patna, is said to be displaced by the subsequently rendered "vision of the ship" (214).

Jameson carries us to the question: If authentic content in

a narrative is placed, then displaced, can it be re-placed upon further textual production? In its wideranging appeal to other works "in Conrad" wherein displacement takes place, The Political Unconscious answers affirmatively: displaced in one text in the Conradian arena, authentic content can be re-placed in a subsequent work.

If we were to allow this re-placement across works, but disallow it "within," we would have a critical project governed by precisely the strategy of "aesthetic containment" Jameson would expose in Conrad. The questions that inevitably ensue, about the attribution of comprehensive governance to one but not another "place" in this chain of textual displacement-i.e., to the aestheticization that appears in one passage, but not to the "authentic content" that will inevitably arise in a subsequent one, whether within this or the "next" authorial production-are too many for us to host here; they must be submitted ultimately to the crucial and ongoing debates within Marxist thought about the univocality of ideology, about its place or khora.

For Jameson's reading of Lord Jim and Conrad in general, these questions are posed rather insistently by the very existence of a further Conradian production I will examine at the end of this discussion. Two 1912 essays on the Titanic disaster, which angrily name specific corporate and industrial interests that the author sees poised against sea laborers, force us to ask: Given the chain of content-displacement that had begun (again) in a novel of 1900, what could halt that chain-and suspend it finally in the purgatory of "aestheticization"-before it reaches the depiction of labour and capital in these English Review essays?

With The Political Unconscious, Jameson verifies that the projection into Conrad of an epistemological hermeneutic, which finally exists only in the operation of the critic, does not require allegiance to a formal narratology:

Conrad's elaborate narrative hermeneutic [in Lord Jim]-what really did happen? who knows it all? what impressions do people have who possess only this piece of the puzzle, or that one?-tends to reinforce and supply powerful narrative demonstrations of... [an] ideology of the relativity of individual monads. (222)

The precedent for this formulation is so extensive and familiar we might pass right over it without verifying whether the questions it ventriloquizes could possibly be evoked by this novel. Yet from the perspective of the "individual monads" to which Jameson alludes-Marlow, Stein, the French lieutenant, and so on-we have to ask: Is there any fact about Jim's "story" or his desertion of the Patna that Conrad leaves in question? In the "elaborate" narrative environments of Lord Jim, Chance, Nostromo, or Under Western Eyes, does there ever remain for the reader any mystery about "what really did happen"? Do not these fictions rather stage as their primary conflict the pathetic attempt of an embattled conscience to breach the inviolability and irreducibility of an established fact?

As Marlow reminds us repeatedly about Jim's story, "[t]here was no incertitude as to facts" (56). What we see in Jameson here, as well as in countless critical approaches that claim an allegiance with Conrad, is another case of forging the signature of modernism on the epistemological contract of the whodunit. The trope of the scattered puzzle is vital to this purpose. The succession of narrative "impressions" that could adequately be depicted, and with the greatest simplicity, as superadditions-a purely productive vision of Conradian narrative which Jameson himself had conjured three pages earlier7-are designated as "pieces" or fragments.

With respect to the "history" that is Lord Jim, each character's narrative is thus marked with an historiographie inadequacy imposed arbitrarily as a structural principle, and which is patently false in terms of the diegetic facts of the novel.

In Lord Jim, Marlow recites and comments on narratives he obtained from Jim. As there is no controversy or incertitude "as to facts" between these figures, the differences that might exist between their narratives could only be those of interpretation, of their judgments about those facts. all of the novel's questions, whether they be called existential, ethical or political, would have remained questions without Marlow's participation, even if we had obtained these stories from Jim himself, and even if the entirety of the novel had been voiced in third-person omniscience.

The persistence into contemporary criticism of the opposing notion, that a staged narrator necessarily keeps us from certain "answers" to which we would otherwise have had access, can be attributed partially to the narratological metaphor of "embedded" narration. Onto the narrative series that constitutes a Conradian novel, this image superimposes an activity of receding "inward" with each new embedding.

So, although Marlow's discourse is actually no further from the facts than Jim's or a third-person's hypothetical narration, this imaginary movement of ever-greater "enclosure" posits for the critic an immediacy that has been left behind. This is not to say that such an image cannot play an illuminating role in interpretation. In the case of a novel whose various narratives are arranged with the rigorous symmetry and regularity of nesting dolls, that arrangement becomes a gesture, a theme, and just as much an object of attention as anything in the fabula.

For this reason, critics have been eager in Conrad's case to reinforce the trope of subjective enclosure they have imported into his work by demonstrating therein an operation of narrative nesting. For his instructive narratological analysis of Heart of Darkness, for instance, Peter Brooks depends heavily on a diagram of symmetrical brackets; yet he acknowledges that upon close examination "we realise that the diagram is false: the inner frame of Kurtz's narrative has no such shapely coherence, and-perhaps as a consequence-neither Marlow's narrative nor the first narrator's appears to 'close' in satisfactory fashion" (351n8).

Lacking brackets, these narratives are said to be ruled nevertheless by a bracketing structure-more precisely, by the failure of Kurtz's narrative to achieve such structure. This absence is something that might even have "consequential" power over the other narratives. The pervasive depiction of Conrad's narrative landscape in primarily negative and reactive terms, as a rebellious destroyer of structural coherence, helps to confirm that this writing does in fact orient itself according to the rules of a structuralism, but that its project just happens to be a perverse thwarting of those rules.

After a half-century of criticism has thoroughly anatomized Conrad's failure to construct "the neat pattern of nested boxes... we should have" (256), we can now begin to investigate how and why the injunction behind this "should" has never belonged solely to an extra-critical "tradition" of narrative nesting imposed by the nineteenth-century novel.

For the task of historically situating Conradian narrative, literary criticism has not been eager to trace it through eighteenth-century epistolary fiction, whose strategies of testimonial narration were so crucial to the novel's development. Tony Jackson's astute The Subject of Modernism represents an exceptional case, but he makes the connection, ultimately, only to implicate both Conrad and the epistolary form in a general ploy to manufacture authority through the posture of the witness. The authority established by the "face-to-face" relationship of "oral narrative" is said to be the hidden desire of any and all first-person novels:

[The early novel] stands apart from the time-proven classical literary genres, and so is missing the ready grounding of an already authorized and authorizing readership. Consequently, we find, especially in earlier novels, writers feeling the need to establish the truth and value of their work from within that work.... One of the most common means of self-authorization is the attempt to imitate the immediate personal presence of the oral storyteller.... The first novelists who consciously strive for some form of realistic representation seem acutely aware of what they might lose in not having the face-to-face, teller-listener relationship of oral narrative, and they take pains to establish their authority in story teller fashion.

Thus, we find the first-person narration of Defoe and the very personal voice of the epistolary novel. (35-36) As it posits in the epistolary novel a gambit for "face-to-face" authority, and as it denies third-person narration and its readers the effects and consequences of a "teller-listener" relationship,

Jackson's literary-historical map begins to lose conceptual coherence.

Yet what remains intact is the more important and fundamental assumption, not at all peculiar to Jackson, that the predominating first-person mode of the new prose form had always constituted a circumvention, a turning away from a narrative ordinance to which the novel would have held itself if not for its historically contingent need for an aura of authority. The evaded ordinance, of course, could only be some form of third-person presentation; and with this conception we find ourselves having posited a norm for the novel that has nothing to do with its actual, historical instantiation.8

Despite its presumption that first-person presentation throughout the novel's history has always already been a deviation from another, more primary practice, literary criticism has not detected in early epistolary and travel fiction the thicket of philosophical problems it sees in the testimonial narration of modernism. It is not until we turn our eyes to the twentieth century that we discover the dangerousness of the first-person novel, its purported capacity, as Samuel Hynes writes, to raise "uncertainty about the nature of truth and reality to the level of a structural principle" (55). This historically selective emphasis of epistemological problems that would have to inhere in any and all testimonial structures is the trace of a philosophical and cultural programme, one that seeks to define the modernist novel in terms of an unprecedented psychic withdrawal and retreat from the real.

Yet for some critical discourses, the perfection of this move inward is also the means by which an aging modernism finally fulfills a contract of comprehension. Although it has failed to construct a circuit by which "the nature of truth and reality" would be unveiled, modernism finally answers the question to which Hemingway had been contracted-about the "thoughts and feelings" of a fictional persona-with its perfected forms of interior monologue. In the "immediate speech" of a Molly Bloom, for instance, narratology sees, in Genette's words, an unprecedented "emancipation," a means of "obliterating the last traces of the narrating instance" that would normally come between a character's consciousness and ourselves (ND 173-74).

Even as it places a premium on character-bound narration, however, the narratology that declares this victory for modernism remains fully dependent on the abjection of personal testimony. Modernist innovations in "psycho-narration" are said to show that a character's consciousness can be borne faithfully-more faithfully, at least, than ever before-by iteration. Yet the rule that denies the power of comprehension to a framed narration requires it to be impossible that the character herself could ever accomplish that iteration.

Thus, of the relation between an external narrator and a character who might testify about her own psyche, Seymore Chatman can assert categorically that "[o]nly a narrator can provide language" to convey "the deepest of all [her] internal experiences" (125).9 The self-expression of a Pamela could never under any circumstance achieve the immediacy in relation to her own consciousness that "Penelope" achieves in relation to Molly Bloom's; and if the latter had been introduced in Ulysses as a radically de-formalized entry in Molly's diary, we would no longer be allowed to call it an unadulterated glimpse into her mind, even if its text were identical to the final chapter of the novel as it exists now.

It would take only the minute addition of a single set of quotation marks at the beginning and end of the chapter to mark the discourse as testimony, and thus transform it from something immediate and emancipated into a fallen "narrating instance."

As the herald of a narrating instance, quotation marks are functionally indistinguishable from a novel's title page, or from its position as a bound volume in the fiction section of a bookstore-from all the features that variously objectify the literary text, and without which a narratological mapping of Ulysses, or any novel, could not begin. What is the criteria by which narratology selects some but not other of these features to be operative signals of a narrating instance? For narratology, legitimate signals must have been authorized as such, demonstrably asserted by the text either in explicit statement or through conventional signs like quotation marks.

We might want to ask what it would mean that the objective, structural features of the novel are said to be constituted not by any and all operative framing effects, but by a selection thereof established by decree, by a mere assertion of the novel? Yet even this question will always have been precluded by another: Did not the same kind of authorizing intentionality also inscribe the novel's title, and often a signature beneath, thereby intending and announcing that what follows is an instance of narration?

Jacques Derrida has already demonstrated why the frame that would be established by a fiction's title must, for any structuralism, remain invisible as such, or just outside critical consciousness.10 For narratology, as for Henry James, the power to frame can belong only to a designated "outer" narration that must never itself be subject to even the possibility of framing. The frame of the outermost narration takes on a unique spectrality: for if it were fully visible as such, it would be an object, and we would have to acknowledge the new framing standpoint, even further "out," that we now occupy.

The hermeneutic would dissolve, and it would be impossible for there ever to have existed an autonomous structure that could disable the framing effect of a title, banishing it to an "outside" of the novel; and neither could there have been a "law of fiction" to determine the illegitimacy of this frame. Just as James had been compelled to draft such legislation as modernism began its emphasis on testimony, Genette's seminal work updates the ordinance to better police its post-Edwardian development. In Narrative Discourse, he writes,

Nothing claims that Meursault or The Unnamable wrote the texts we read as their interior monologues, and it goes without saying that the text of the Lauriers sont coupes cannot be anything but a "stream of consciousness"-not written, or even spoken-mysteriously caught and transcribed by Dujardin. It is the nature of immediate speech to preclude any formal determination of the narrating instance which it constitutes. (230)

Here is a logocentrism that does not privilege speech: for even if the monologue had been "spoken," it would not have escaped its iterability, its participation in "writing in general." This speech would have been implicated with writing in its distance from present consciousness, from an "immediate speech" prior to speech. Speech and writing, once determined as such, could only be a report: mere testimony about presence. In order to ascend the testimony that is writing in general, the writing that is said to articulate consciousness cannot be writing.

Since Genette, of course, narratology has significantly evolved, and subsequent theorists have done much to stabilize the spectrality of this writing that, nevertheless, narratology would still like to remove from the scene of writing. Mieke Bal's 1997 Narratology, for instance, takes pains to strip from the "external focalizer" any claim to a non-localized vocality. "From a grammatical point of view," she argues, all narration stems from "a 'first person.' In fact, the term 'third-person narrator' is absurd: a narrator is not a 'he' or a 'she'" (22). Hence, "where the focalization level is concerned, there is no fundamental difference between a 'first-person narrative' and a 'third-person narrative'" (157).

Yet it remains in Bal's narratology a structural certainty that a "character-bound focalizer... brings about bias and limitation" (146). As exemplary proof of this categorical statement, Bal points to the in-the-dark detective of a mystery story, albeit a "literary" one: in Henry James's What Maisie Knew, the child hero is besieged by signals difficult for her, but easy for us, to decode. The epistemological contract here is distinct from the whodunit only in the reader's position in the circuit of veiling and unveiling. We the readers are in the know, backstage during the magician's performance, and we watch Maisie all alone in the auditorium struggling for comprehension. The essential, relevant truth of the fiction, identified by Bal as "what is actually going on," is then easily determined: it is comprised of whatever facts of the fabula that have become clear to us but which Maisie evidently does not know (147).

Reminding us that "the narrator and focalizer" are not to be conflated in this or any novel, Bal confirms a more general narratological principle: "When an external focalizer [EF] seems to 'yield' focalization to a character-bound focalizer [CF], what is really happening is that the CF is being given within the all-encompassing vision of the EF" (157-58). For each bit of knowledge that had been produced for the reader by a stretch of Maisie-bound focalization, Bal's narrato-theology requires the positing of a further "external focalizer" that had been extant, somewhere, during each such passage, existing independently of the "focalized" text.

Thus, even if each and every prepared and encoded signal of what Maisie does not know had been generated through a focalization "bound" to the girl, the total knowledge thus produced for the reader is necessarily exceeded and "encompassed" by the other, external focalization, since otherwise the two would be identical. Loosed from the finite sum of the encoded signals that mostly fly over Maisie's head, this "all-encompassing" vision is bound to no particular finitude whatsoever. It has remained a defining feature of narratology's metaphysics that any imaginable nook or cranny of the fictional world, left unarticulated in the text, will have always already been determined in the heaven of external focalization. The external focalizer will always be identical to this general comprehension.

Taking it as given that writing in general is an obstacle to comprehension, Jameson explicitly subsumes "the alienation of the printed book" into the historical emergence of Conrad's narrated narrators. In its strongest Lukacsian register, The Political Unconscious hearkens back to "that older concrete social situation" of bards and storytellers, wherein the spoken signifier was never subject to the possibility of diversion, misreading, or ungoverned reiteration. In the "communicational situation" of pre-capitalist narrative practice, the signifier is said to have always arrived at its proper destination. In his account of Marlow as a literary phenomenon, Jameson thus appeals to Plato's Phaedrus: It is clear that to return from the primacy of the Jamesian narrative category of point of view to the older fiction of the storyteller and the storytelling situation is to express impatience with the objective yet ever intensifying alienation of the printed book, those bound and portable novels which "when they have been once written down... are tumbled about anywhere among those who may or may not understand them, and know not to whom they should reply, to whom not: and, if they are maltreated or abused, they have no parent to protect them; and they cannot protect or defend themselves." (219-20)

The role assigned here to Conrad in a literary-historical dialectic is all the more startling considering the near impossibility of finding any body of work that demonstrates with as much force and repetition that no "storyteller situation" could ever secure the testifier's ability to protect, defend, or otherwise govern the career of his testimony. Jim is given the floor at his public inquiry, but no matter: in that forum, "speech was of no use to him any longer" (33). And even the monologist aboard the Nellie in Heart of Darkness must ask his "concrete" listeners, half-asleep and occluded in shadows, "Do you see the story? Do you see anything? It seems to me I am trying to tell you a dream" (172).

Having confidently left behind years ago almost all debate about the effect of such critical logocentrism on our conception of the modernist novel, we might reasonably expect our fresh post-postmodern eyes to have perceived anew, and finally in positive terms, the significance of Marlow's emergence in the English novel. Yet if we take Michael North's recent re-evaluation as an exemplary instance, the idea that Conrad's narrated narrator puts us at a remove from a reality and a truth that would have revealed itself in the absence of his "mediation" appears to be as indispensable as ever.

As evinced by a singularly compact and efficient paragraph in the opening pages of The Dialect of Modernism, it appears that literary criticism has in fact only streamlined the procedure by which the whodunit's contract of comprehension enables a metaphysics of presence to produce the structural truth, reportedly "confessed" by Conrad himself, of the degenerate nature of testimony:

... Conrad's works often confront us with the laboriously physical process by which dry print becomes a visual and auditory experience. If this task to which Conrad dedicates himself can be understood as something actually seen, then it is a task to which he frequently confessed himself unequal. Lord Jim, to take just one example, degenerates from an omniscient and all-seeing account into Marlow's version, told "audibly," and then into the packet of written documents left for the "privileged man" in chapter 36, declining from the seen to the heard to the written as the story compounds its mysteries. The aesthetic attempt to conjure out of some sensually unrewarding marks on paper a full sensory experience is constantly qualified in this way by Conrad's sense of its structural impossibility. (38)

As with Jameson's depiction of the novel as a factual "puzzle," this portrayal of Lord Jim's abrupt shift-from omniscient reporting to Marlow's narration-as a "degeneration," a fall from certainty to perplexity, transparency to occlusion, has remained indelible." If we listen carefully, on the other hand, to the transition from omniscience to testimony as the novel actually presents it, we can hear its very different evaluation of "Marlow's version," especially in its relation to the posture of epistemological comprehension struck by the "omniscient and all-seeing" voice of the opening chapters. What Conrad stages is in fact a narratological coup over the anonymous authority he has set up precisely for this purpose.

The author even implicates this anonymous omniscience with institutional powers depicted in the fiction: specifically, with the forces mobilizing the public inquiry that triggers the narrative transition in the first place. The shift takes place between two chapters, but right in the middle of Jim's deposition at the tribunal investigating his abandonment of the crippled, pilgrim-laden steamship, the Patna. It is a remarkable moment in the history of novelistic courtroom drama for the precision with which it ties the usual promise of a scene of deposition-the promise of comprehensive disclosure-to that of the anonymous third-person narrator.

Following the climax of the episode at the close of the fourth chapter, both the theater of deposition and the anonymous narrator heretofore governing the novel are simultaneously ousted by Marlow's voice. Aside from a few momentary resurfacings, the omniscient narrator will never regain the reins of the novel, not even to provide the symmetry of a narrative "end bracket."

Far from a degeneration, it is a succession that takes its mandate even from the fiction itself: Marlow takes over at precisely the moment when Jim's testimony is revealed to be irrelevant within the frame of a spectral, corporate authority. The statement Jim hopes to make, with its "shades of expression" and "complicated aspect," has been precluded by a well-circulated story already established before he took the stand, a "tale that was public property," but which the novel keeps from us (31, 41).

The authorless tale of the Patna's latest voyage and its scandal, pointedly suppressed in these opening chapters, and which a normal omniscient narrator would have articulated by now, has indeed been spelled out already to the tribunal and its audience by the likes of the Home News edition a stranger later hands Marlow in a cafe. What we are shown instead is the posture of diegetic removal these authorities assume, and which creates the imaginary comprehension that will render the statement of the witness always already inadequate, because perspectival, and possibly corrupt, because biased. As a stranger murmurs in Marlow's ear during the inquiry, speaking of the defendants: "Of course they would lie" (135).

The novel has a long history of using the trial scene to duplicate within itself the diegetic divide between its characters and the anonymous judging reader.12 In Lord Jim, however, the reader is not allowed to judge at the scene of trial. We don't know the facts of the case until the effectively diegetic divide between Jim and the anonymous inquiry has been erased by the subsequent chapters; these rewrite the scene of deposition in a blend of confession and interrogation between Jim and Marlow.

The disclosure we expect at the inquiry-a scene of the confessor rendering himself intelligible to an official prozess-comes later, but it does so through an interlocution between subjects commonly disciplined and responsible to one another. Until then, the mariner's formerly spontaneous, self-generated and gratuitous rime has become, under Conrad's pen, coerced testimony in a tribunal.13 As elsewhere in modernist literature, the courtroom proves to be the crucial trope in a depiction of the degraded status of the testifier in a culture of anonymous authority.

The official unidirectional gaze encompassing Jim's testimony belongs to the same entity Conrad will later rail against in two essays on the official inquiries into the Titanic disaster: The British Board of Trade. "Some Reflexions, Seamanlike and Otherwise, on the Loss of the Titanic," published soon after the event in The English Review, is certainly the most passionate public statement the author ever penned, and its sequel, "Certain Aspects of the Admirable Inquiry Into the Loss of the Titanic," is only slightly more restrained. "It is with a certain bitterness," the first essay begins, "that one must admit to oneself that the late S.S. Titanic had a 'good press'" (304).14 Despite having "no great practice of daily newspapers" and "scant respect for the Organs of public opinion,' as they fondly believe themselves to be," the former seaman has much to say about the collusion of their "irresponsible paragraphs" with the more official public inquiries into the disaster that were underway in England and the US. (SR 304, CA 581, SR 305).

The purpose of all these inquiries, in Conrad's eyes, is to deflect responsibility from the profit-motivated decisions of technocrats and "commercial men" to the ship's crew and captain (SR 305). All the "established authorities" at work in this deflection-the Board of Trade, the "passage-selling Combines," the "high priests" of technology (who would "fain forbid the profane from inquiring into its mysteries") and even a US Senate board of inquiry-are implicated together in the "calumnious, baseless... lie charging poor Captain Smith with desertion of his post by means of suicide" (SR 306; CA 590, 582; SR 315). That charge, Conrad writes in conclusion to the "Reflexions," is "the vilest and most ugly thing of all in this outburst of journalistic enterprise" (315).

This crescendo infuses into "journalistic enterprise" all the "commercial and industrial interests" under scrutiny throughout the essay (309). Exerting themselves through both the tribunal and the newspaper, all these authorities, Conrad suggests, contribute to the single "admirable inquiry" of the later essay's title.

The corporate power Conrad strains to keep in view is not that which derives from the juridical and political influence of raw industrial might. He rather traces the inexorability of this power precisely and almost exclusively to its dislocation and anonymity. As we might then expect, the pivotal and ubiquitous term in his analysis is the same that had governed Tighe Hopkins's New Review debate on anonymity in the press: "responsibility."

When a participant like G.B. Shaw had insisted that he writes "more carefully, and with a keener sense of direct personal responsibility for the soundness of my utterances, when what I write appears over my signature" (II: 271), the warning he received in return was that such a position endangers "the journal" as a corporate entity. "The editorial 'We'," writes Lynn Linton, "is the sign of a unified multitude, and its force is both great and legitimate.... By the adoption of the signature the journal repudiates responsibility" (I: 516). The invective of the "Reflexions," against a general inquest conducted through multiple public forums, carries forward the terms of this reporters' debate. In his quarrel with the Board of Trade, Conrad cites "some exasperated wit" who described such entities as having

> no souls to be saved and no bodies to be kicked, and thus [are] free in this world and the next from all effective sanctions of conscientious conduct.... The Board of Trade is composed of bloodless departments. It has no limbs and no physiognomy, or else at the forthcoming inquiry it might have paid to the

victims of the Titanic disaster the small tribute of a blush. (307). The Board is composed of "irresponsible gentlemen... with no care in the world; for there can be no care without personal responsibility-such, for instance, as the seamen have...." Among the principal initiators of the Titanic public inquiry Conrad can find no responsibility, no named accuser to which the crew can respond: "A Board of Trade-what is it?... A ghost.... Less than nothing; a mere void without as much as a shadow of responsibility" (306).

More Articles of Interest

"Signifying nothing": Conrad's idiots and the anxiety of modernism - Joseph...

Joseph Conrad

'Heart of Darkness' and late-Victorian fascination with the primitive and the...

Seeing the Animal: Colonial Space and Movement in Joseph Conrad's Lord Jim

Colonizers, Cannibals, and the Horror of Good Intentions in Joseph Conrad's...

Conrad's own testimony in this public proceeding is made possible by the authority he claims as a former marine officer. To further their argument, however, the Titanic essays are surprisingly hesitant to appeal to personal experience; that is, to adopt a testimonial mode. The shift in the "Reflexions" away from its caustic editorial stance is distinct and clearly announced; but it also comes reluctantly, even apologetically. It is 2,500 words into the essay before the author offers for instruction an "incident I witnessed" during his tenure at sea, one that had not been "boastfully paragraphed all round the Press, because that was not the fashion of the time."

He tells his story "not for the vain pleasure of talking about my own poor experiences, but only to illustrate my point," assuring his Review audience that "what I am going to relate" is a "fact." He interrupts his account with a repeated assurance that "I am sticking all the time to my subject to illustrate my point" (310-13). The defensiveness of the storyteller finding himself amidst this journalistic proceeding, now just one of many voices in a public debate-this, combined with the diction and especially the circumstance of the remarks, calls to mind Jim's fictional attempt to give his own testimony on the witness stand about the Patna.

In the novel, the inquiry is no more closed an affair than that of the Titanic: the entire Malay Archipelago, the whole of the seafaring world attends. The magistrates "wanted facts. Facts! They demanded facts from him" (29). The young seaman has hope, at first, in "a meticulous precision of statement" on his part; but in his delivery of this testimony he was "becoming irrelevant; a question to the point cut short his speech.... He was coming to that, he was coming to that-and now, checked brutally, he had to answer by yes or no" (31). The voice that demands Jim more than once to answer "to the point" is the same inquisitor Conrad seems to feel over his own shoulder-twelve years after the novel, still firmly within a tacit role as seamen's advocate-writing his own testimony in a public controversy about, among other things, a marine officer fleeing his duty in the face of catastrophe.

It is as if the author is compelled to exorcise from his report the specter raised in the New Review debate of the great danger to a journal's authority: a Frenchified mode of memoir-writing. Whatever authority he might otherwise wield, the realm of the literary that Conrad dangerously skirts by recounting yet another story of the sea would disqualify him from the authority governing this inquiry. His foray into public debate struggles to escape the status of a merely "amusing" performance, to recall L.F. Austin, of a "literary swordsman."

Hopkins's two essays will be abbreviated as I and II

Hopkins's colloquium has also drawn the attention of Marc DaRosa, who argues that its participants conceive the newspaper as "a text that invalidates the notion of an originating consciousness" (829). The New Review observers thus display a prescient anxiety, DaRosa concludes, about the pure domination of text upon the death of the author. It is a tempting argument, but one that ultimately requires a blindness to the authority these writers consistently re-condense into the journal itself, an entity discrete but unlocalized. For Hopkins and his colleagues, neither anonymity nor any appeal to an authority that would transcend personal testimony precludes univocality. As Edward Russell writes, a newspaper had "an individuality[,]... a continuity, a policy and even a manner independent of its personnel" (I: 517).

The New Review writers consistently and automatically project behind the article an originating consciousness; they reify an author effect even in the absence of a determined author, even where there is no possibility of signature. The general conceptual effect of corporate or anonymous histories-of-the-now, written in a voice that would be extradiegetic in relation to the world it reports, has not been the dissolution of the author; the massive proliferation of this writing since the "new journalism" has rather normalized, as Russell might have predicted, a projection of comprehensive consciousness behind the extradiegetic pose.

Lyotard singles out Robert Faurisson, who synopsized his argument for Le Monde on Jan. 16, 1979.

Genette quotes from Raimond's La Crise du roman, des lendemains du naturalisme aux annees 20 (Paris, 1966), 300.

I am echoing here Jacques Derrida's reading of Lacan's "Seminar on The Purloined Letter"; see "La Facteur de la Verite" in The Post Card.

The thesis that this imposed contract is instead something that always already structures narrative itself is more explicitly articulated in Roland Barthes's S/Z.

Jameson writes, "Certainly the first half of Lord Jim is one of the most breathtaking exercises in nonstop textual production that our literature has to show, a self-genera ting sequence of sentences for which narrative and narrator are mere pretexts, the realization of a mechanism of well-nigh random narrative free association, in which the aleatory and seemingly uncontrollable, unverifiable generation of new detail and new anecdotal material out of the old... obeys a logic of its own" (219).

Aside from the confusion of a productivity that would obey "a logic of its own" and yet remain "random," Jameson borrows the theoretical vocabulary of Gilles Deleuze in his discussion of Proust: "[T]he modern work of art is a machine and functions as such.... To the logos, organ and organon whose meaning must be discovered in the whole to which it belongs, is opposed the antilogos, machine and machinery whose meaning... depends solely on its functioning, which, in turn, depends on its separate parts" (128-29). Narrative(s) may "remain partitioned, fragmented, without anything lacking: eternally partial parts, open boxes and sealed vessels, swept on by time without forming a whole or presupposing one" (142-43, emphasis in original).

For relevant histories, see Davis and Showalter, "Prehistory." The former verifies that even the printed ballads of the sixteenth and seventeenth centuries habitually took the form of a first-person testimonial, and that an important part of their drama would often involve the spying activities that had been required of the narrating witness to get the story. Showalter's survey of the "prehistory of omniscience" suggests that the seventeenth century's omniscient narrator in Europe was usually born in a given conte as an actor within the fiction itself; his penetration into a private space and his attainment of omniscience, whether by covert or supernatural means, was often a major element of the plot.

Chatman here follows Cohn, who writes that an external narrator can "effectively articulate a psychic life that remains unverbalized, penumbral, or obscure," and can do so-always, in every possible case-"better than the character himself" (46).

The metaphysics of testimonial "degeneration" in North's reading of Lord Jim does not, however, derail his important larger project of writing race into the critical consciousness of modernism.

In The Novel and the Police, Miller draws our attention to the first page of Wilkie Collins's The Woman in White, in which the narrator writes of the "case" about to unfold: "As the Judge might once have heard it, so the Reader shall hear it now" (Collins 33).

The best full-length study of dialogue and interrogation in Conrad is certainly Fogel's Coercion to Speak, although I disagree with what Foucault would call the repressive hypothesis of the book. For Fogel, the ubiquitous scenes of "forced speech" in Conrad are not matters of productive incitement, as I think is usually the case, but rather coerced disclosures.

The rich Kafkan comedy of Razumov's "interrogation" in Under Western Eyes is an illustrative case: the phlegmatic Russian official asks nothing at all of Razumov, whose lengthy jabbering comes from a compulsion to construct for the eyes of the state a coherent subjectivity, personal and political, that simply does not exist.

The articles will be abbreviated hereafter SR and CA. They were slightly revised for their inclusion in the 1921 Notes on Life and Letters. See Stape for an excellent reading of these essays.

In a letter to Edward Garnett five years earlier, Conrad anticipated the effect of their public participation in a coordinated "literary" protest, in the form of a letter to The Times, against the office of the Censor of Plays. As readers peruse the names of the forty belletristic signatories, Conrad imagines they will "perceive dimly that we are not stockbrokers, not clerks, not manufacturers or bankers, or lawyers.... We will in short appear to be unauthorized persons" (Collected Letters III, 489).

Chapter 4

'Heart of Darkness' and Late-victorian Fascination

A fascination with primordial darkness, the oxymoronic "fascination of the abomination" that Marlow in Heart of Darkness offers to his listeners (6), was prevalent in the late nineteenth century, reflecting a belief in man's animal origins. A perusal of the main periodicals of the period such as Nineteenth Century, Fortnightly Review, Cornhill Magazine, and Macmillan's Monthly Magazine reveals that they aimed to tell the unvarnished truth about the ugly and frightening realities of man's nature hidden behind an attractive facade.

The articles published include those by R. A. Proctor, Henry Rowley, G. J. Romanes, Grant Allen, W. J. Corbett, James Sully, H. G. Wells, and Lionel Johnson."(1) Essentially, the discourse of primitivism and degeneracy reverses the idea of evolution; it deconstructs the ethos of the improving spirit of the times.

A marked premise of nineteenth-century ideology, generating more colonial rhetoric, is the superiority of the white races in the evolutionary scheme to the "primitive" or "savage."(2) Rowley's essay might well have been written as a critique of this racist vision. It states that all creatures are united in the primitive natural state, and the highest/lowest hierarchy is blurred:

Nothing more astonishes an inexperienced traveller than the discovery that in all men, differ how much so ever they may in outward circumstances or acquired habits, our race still preserves its social character; that there are the same instincts, the same natural feelings... with the most degraded equally with the highest. (684)

Substantially, this suggests Marlow's observation about the connection between himself and the "savages":

No, they were not inhuman. Well, you know, that was the worst of it—this suspicion of their not being inhuman. It would come slowly to one. They howled and leaped, and spun, and made horrid faces; but what thrilled you was just the thought of their humanity—like yours—the thought of your remote kinship with this wild and passionate uproar. (36-37)

Overall, Heart of Darkness offers a paradoxical reading of black and white:

It was very curious to see the contrast of expressions of the white men and of the black fellows of our crew, who were as much strangers to that part of the river as we, though their homes were only eight hundred miles away. The whites, of course greatly discomposed, had besides a curious look of being painfully shocked by such an outrageous row. The others had an alert, naturally interested expression; but their faces were essentially quiet. (41)

In this perspective, Edward Tylor argued for the unsettling of rigid hierarchical separation between races, which he ranged on a spectrum of cultural evolution. He observed that

The character and habit of mankind at once display...

Similarity and consistency of phenomena, which led the Italian proverb-maker to declare that 'all the world is one country.'... It appears both possible and desirable to eliminate considerations of hereditary varieties or races of man, and to treat mankind as homogeneous in nature, though placed in different grades of civilization.... In comparing mental and artistic culture among several peoples, the balance of good and ill is not quite easy to strike.... Savagery and Civilization are connected as lower and higher stages of one formation. (I: 6, 7, 28, 37)

The title of his book itself signifies that primitive people, in their communal capacities, are makers of culture—which discounts claims to cultural bias.

Many readers of the 1890s would surely agree with what Sully stated in "The Dream as a Revolution":

Psychology has of late occupied itself much with the curious phenomenon of double or alternating personality. By this is meant the recurrent interruption of the normal state by the intrusion of a secondary state, in which the thought, feelings, and the whole personality become other than they were. This occasional substitution of a new for the old self is sometimes spontaneous, the result of brain trouble. (361)

Similarly Oscar Wilde, in The Picture of Dorian Gray, sees a possibility that "we can multiply our personalities," and hence a human being can appropriate "myriad lives and myriad sensations," and Dorian tells Basil Hallward, "Each of us has Heaven and Hell in him" (142, 157). This sense of the alliance of good and evil in the psyche is evident in Bram Stoker's Dracula, when Professor Van Helsing remarks, "This evil thing is rooted deep in all good" (231), and also in Marlow's observation about Kurtz: "The pulsating stream of light, or the deceitful flow from the heart of an impenetrable darkness" (48). Madame Blavatsky is in agreement on this co-existence of contradictory selves working within the same person, as she remarks that "as flitting personalities, to-day one person, to-morrow another—we are" (85).

It is a safe assumption that the outline of this thought lies behind the efflorescence of what may be termed as neo-primitivist novels and short stories, within a few years of each other at the end of the century, by writers as varied as Robert Lewis Stevenson, Rudyard Kipling, Bram Stoker, H. G. Wells, Grant Allen, Oscar Wilde, and Henry James. Darkness is the controlling metaphor for these narratives which, in their different ways, have as their theme the phenomenon of two consciousnesses—the human "primitive" duality (the idea of the secret sharer is of vital concern for Conrad) and the interconnectedness of genius and insanity.

Titles such as The Strange Case of Dr. Jekyll and Mr. Hyde, "The Mark of the Beast," Dracula, The Invisible Man, The British Barbarians, "The Beast in the Jungle" would not be in the least out of place in any one of the above-mentioned journals. My approach to Heart of Darkness is by way of such texts, as it displays sufficient affinities to them. The "dark" Kurtz, although drawn in much darker colors, is not an uneasy ally of the predatory Moreau, Dracula, and Hyde—all are mad and savage geniuses. Yet it must be said that while Heart of Darkness works with well-nigh common materials, it manages to be highly esteemed for its far more rich and complex rendering of the darkness theme, and remains a brilliant work anticipating modernist techniques which appeal to the modern sensibility.

Kurtz is seen in a double focus; genius and nobility of personality and purpose find themselves in easy partnership with insanity and monstrosity: "His intelligence was perfectly clear—concentrated, it is true, upon himself with horrible intensity, yet clear.... But his soul was mad" (67-68). Initially he is one in whom "sweetness and light" prevail. We are provided with examples of the breadth of his considerable talents. He is accorded adulation as "a universal genius" (28). The brickmaker pays tribute with hyperbole to the mind that has equipped itself with human empathy, science, and civilized order: "an emissary of pity, and science, and progress, and devil knows what else" (25).

He is verbally gifted too: he has a reputation for an "unbounded power of eloquence" (51). "The point was in his being a gifted creature, and that of all his gifts the one that stood up pre-eminently, that carried with it a sense of real presence, was his ability to talk, his words—the gift of expression" (48). To Marlow, prior to meeting him, "The man presented himself as a voice" (48).

Kurtz's cousin comments, "But Heavens! how that man could talk! He electrified large meetings.... He would have been a splendid leader of an extreme party" (74). And his financee remarks of his rhetorical skill, "Who was not his friend who had heard him speak once?" (77). That he is "a remarkable man" is kept alive in the reader's mind through reiteration (62, 72, 76).(3) He gives the Russian, his devoted and largely uncritical follower, a sense of linguistic inadequacy whenever he speaks: "You don't talk with that man—you listen to him"

(54). Appropriately, Kurtz's listeners become corpselike, they cannot muster words for debate with him.

As befits an artistic genius, Kurtz has a considerable poetic talent (65). His essential creativity and imaginative energy extend to the field of music ("Kurtz had been essentially a great musician" I73~), painting (25), and journalism (73, 74). Kurtz's oil sketch—a true engagement in the creative, artistic experience—shows that he finds inspiration easy. The Russian says, "Oh, he enlarged my mind!" (65), and "He made me see things" (56). His greatness of mind is also established by his unselfish commitment to the good of the savage people.

Genius tends to promote evil;(4) the uncommonly gifted individual surrenders to madness. Kurtz is repeatedly described as "mad" (57, 68 I twice~). In a letter to his publisher Conrad perceives the story on one plane as "an anecdote of a man who went mad in the Centre of Africa" (Collected 417). Kurtz's descent into madness begins in the sepulchral city: "'Ever any madness in your family?' I the trading company's doctor~ asked, in a matter of fact tone" (11). To be clever and insane is an essential part of the pathology of H. G. Wells's Moreau: "His curiosity, his mad, aimless investigations, drove him on" (139). Prendick, the narrator, whose knowledge at the end of the novel is far from rudimentary, points to his own real satanic nature: "I, too, was not a reasonable creature, but only an animal tormented with some strange disorder in its brain, that sent it to wander alone, like a sheep stricken with the gid" (191). This is not alien to the interpretation of warped genius given by Sully in The Human Mind—genius is co-extensive with insanity:

The man of great intellect or genius has so frequently been characterized by marked moral failings, weakness of will in control of the passions and so forth that this fact... has led certain writers to regard the organic basis of all genius as a neurosis or abnormal deviation from the healthy type of nervous organization. (309)

Further, the psychology of insane genius is developed in "Genius and Insanity"—Sully sees mental imbalance connotated with genius:

The idea that there is an affinity between genius and mental disease seems at first foreign to our modern habits of thought. In the one, we have human intellect rejoicing in titanic strength; in the other, the same intellect disordered and pitiably enfeebled. Yet, as has been hinted, the belief in the connection of the two is an old and persistent one.... Among our own writers we have so healthy and serene a spirit as Shakespeare asserting a degree of affinity between poetic creation and madness:

The lunatick, the lover, and the poet Are of imagination all compact...

A more serious affirmation of a propinquity is to be found in the well-known lines of Dryden:—

Great wits are sure to madness near allied.

Dracula can be regarded as akin to Jekyll in the confluence of genius and dark qualities. In one passage Stoker depicts him as a distinctly imposing figure, a most wonderful man. Soldier, statesman, and alchemist—which later was the highest development of the science-knowledge of his time. He had a mighty brain, a learning beyond compare, and a heart that knew no fear and no remorse. He dared even to attend the Scholomance and there was no branch of knowledge of his time that he did not essay. Well, in him the brain powers survived the physical death. (290-91)

Dracula has assembled in his library "a vast number of English books, whole shelves full of them, and bound volumes of magazines and newspapers.... The books were of the most varied kind—history, geography, politics, political economy, botany, geology, law," which, in his own words, "have been good friends to me" (19). In Professor Van Helsing's view, "He is clever, oh, so clever!" (303), has a "more subtle brain... than any man," (308) and is further "spoken of as the cleverest and the most cunning, as well as the bravest of the sons of the 'land beyond the forest'" (231). The connection between crime and cleverness has not gone unnoticed by the Professor: "The philosophy of crime... is a study of insanity.... The criminal... is clever and resourceful" (328). Dr. Moreau is a mad and tyrannical man of science-as-evolution. His outrageous expressions of pragmatic intelligence are centered on an expert knowledge of "grafting" (102) in pursuit of his doctrine of beasts as humans-in-becoming, with no thought for scientific ethics. He is plunged into a darkness similar to Kurtz's. The narrator dwells upon the result of the amoral experimenter's dominant passion for research:

He was so irresponsible, so utterly careless. His curiosity, his mad, aimless investigations, drove him on, and the things |animals~ were thrown out to live a year or so, to struggle, and blunder, and suffer; at last to die painfully. They were wretched in themselves, the old animal hate moved them to trouble one another, the Law held them back from a brief hot struggle and a decisive end to their natural animosities. (139)

Prendick's statement, "I lost faith in the sanity of the world when I saw it suffering the painful disorder of this island" (139), is premised on his belief in Moreau's terrorist impulses.

In his review of The Picture of Dorian Gray Walter Pater argued that

To lose the moral sense therefore, for instance, the sense of sin and righteousness, as Mr. Wilde's heroes are bent on doing as speedily, as completely as they can, is to lose, or lower, organization, to become less complex, to pass from a higher to a lower degree of development. (264)

The same judgment might well apply to Heart of Darkness. Kurtz embodies all forms of an urge to be more or less than human. He employs his faculties for aims in the opposite direction from the idealism announced in his self-deconstructing report as a civilizer. His writings designate in Marlow's view an "exotic Immensity ruled by an august Benevolence" and they appeal to "every altruistic sentiment." His predisposition for benevolent sympathy is clear in the statement "We whites... must necessarily appear to them |savages~ in the nature of supernatural beings.

By the simple exercise of our will we can exert a power for good practically unbounded" (51). The Central Station manager quotes Kurtz, the exemplar: "Each station should be like a beacon on the road towards better things, a centre for trade of course, but also for humanizing, improving, instructing" (33). Kurtz's inexperienced, scientific self in the fiery report is alive with the possibility of the cultivation and conversion of the "savages." He would have subscribed to Moreau's proposition that "a pig may be educated" (104).

But theory is one thing, practice is another. Idealism, which has a Utopian quality, is inappropriate in a world where corrupt interests abound and where there are many who go on all fours. The last sentence in the report, an added footnote—"Exterminate all the brutes"—refers us to the dark other side of his identity, "the soul satiated with primitive emotions" (69); it shows a descent from high to low, and that his civilizer's concern for the distressed savages has turned to hatred—a Jekyll-to-Hyde turn.

Of particular relevance in this respect is the significance of the portrait he has painted, the blindfolded torchbearer against the black background (25), which could be said to suggest, among other things, the simplicity of the ideal and the complexity of reality, the illusion of light and the truth of darkness. The monstrous prevails, and the human and artistic potential miscarries. There is a downward tug in Kurtz's involvement with the wilderness and he descends into a brute existence. He is reduced to madness, and his aggressive impulses take control of him:

> The wilderness had patted him on the head, and, behold, it was like a ball—an ivory ball; it had caressed him, and—lo!—he had withered; it had taken him, loved him, embraced him, got into his veins, consumed his flesh, and sealed his soul to its own by the inconceivable ceremonies of some devilish initiation. He was its spoiled and pampered favourite.... How many powers of darkness claimed him for their own.... The wilderness... had whispered to him things about himself which he did not know... the whisper had proved irresistibly fascinating. It echoed loudly within him because he was hollow at the core.... The heavy, mute spell of the wilderness... seemed to draw him to its pitiless breast by the awakening of forgotten and brutal instincts, by the memory of gratified and monstrous passions. (49, 59, 67)

One thinks of Jekyll's statement, "My devil had been long

caged, he came out roaring.... As the first edge of my penitence wore off, the lower side of me... began to growl for license" (90-92). Lucy Westenra, an infectious prey to Dracula's bite, is a close manifestation of the possibility of conversion from goodness and purity to a female vampire:

The sweetness was turned to adamantine, heartless cruelty, and the purity to voluptuous wantonness.... The lips were crimson with fresh blood.... The stream had trickled over her chin and stained the purity of her lawn death-robe.... She flung to the ground, callous as a devil, the child that up to now she had clutched strenuously to her breast, growling over it as a dog growls over a bone. (203)

Kurtz possesses an immense charisma; he displays a mysterious hold on the natives. In the Russian's words, "They adored him.... He came to them with thunder and lightning." Although Kurtz harbors murderous thoughts about the Russian, the latter responds with further devotion: "He wanted to shoot me one day.... But I didn't clear out. No, no. I couldn't leave him" (57). Appropriately, "He had taken a high seat among the devils of the land" (50). The men-animals treat the dictatorial Moreau on terms not much different; he is deified and his power means mortal terror to others:

'His is the House of Pain.' 'His is the Hand that makes.' 'His is the Hand that wounds.' 'His is the Hand that heals.' (85)

Kurtz's humanity is visible only in expressions of self-disgust. When close to death he reflects, with a sense of loss, on his brutality. His words, "The horror! The horror!" show the Promethean shame that follows pride, and further constitute "a judgment upon the adventures of his soul on this earth" (71). It is both ironic and revealing that Kurtz dies at the moment of self-knowledge.

In the novels under discussion, persons have their echoes—a function of doubling, replication. Dracula is the signifier of insanity, which seems to have infected all male characters—a collective hysteria. It recurs in different degrees in the lunatic Redfield, who is confined to a mental asylum (111, 269), Jonathan Harker (96, 178), Arthur Godalming (199,

221), Dr. Seward (185), and even the learned Professor Van Helsing (187, 327). The helmsman's madness may be juxtaposed to Kurtz's—"He had no restraint, no restraint—just like Kurtz" (52)—and their deaths are somehow linked in our minds (47).

Clues make it clear that early experiences that befall Fresleven, Marlow's predecessor, killed because of his insanity and destructiveness, parodically foretell Kurtz's own death. Moreau, like Fresleven, is killed in an agitated flurry of fury. Both are cruel, at a terrible cost to themselves. Montgomery is Moreau's metonymical associate. He is another case of atavistic regression. Prendick is not particularly distinct from these two; he has some of their savage nature. Remarkably enough, he undergoes a change on the island:

> I too must have undergone strange changes. My clothes hung about me as yellow rags, through whose rents glowed the tanned skin. My hair grew long, and became matted together. I am told that even now my eyes have a strange brightness, a swift alertness of movement. (181)

It is not surprising to find him admitting, "I, too, was not a reasonable creature, but only an animal tormented with some strange disorder in its brain" (191). Montgomery acts as an instrument of Moreau's will; his adventures are more or less the duplicate of those of his master. He is a creature of irrational impulse: in a bout of insanity he burns up the boats "to prevent our return to mankind," the narrator points out (161).

Marlow's role may be said to correspond with that of Montgomery. Apart from his role in the mediation for the auditors of the truths of Kurtz, he is aligned with Kurtz in the reader's mind from the very beginning. From Kurtz's first mention, he is homesick for him. Marlow is like a mesmerized person; Kurtz has gained ascendancy over him. Dracula's assault on Mina has left her subordinated to his will, "And you... are now to me, flesh of my flesh; blood of my blood; kin of my kin" (276).

The confrontation of Marlow's identity with Kurtz is a figuration of the inner conflict between the two selves of

Marlow, the self's downward journey into its own unconsciousness: "We penetrated deeper and deeper into the heart of darkness" (35). The journey of Dracula's pursuers upriver in the direction of the Castle is a similar figurative descent into the unconscious mind: "We seem to be drifting into unknown places and unknown ways; into a whole world of dark and dreadful things," remarks Jonathan Harker (344).

The conversation that takes place between Marlow and Kurtz seems like a monologic discourse of self-articulation: "I tried to break the spell.... If anybody had ever struggled with a soul, I am the man" (67). There are implications that Marlow is placed in the same existential arena as Kurtz: when he pursues the missing Kurtz, he remarks that "I was anxious to deal with this shadow by myself alone—and to this day I don't know why I was so jealous of sharing with any one the peculiar blackness of that experience" (66), and later on he observes, "It is his extremity that I seem to have lived through" (72).

Marlow strikes his aunt as "an emissary of light, something like a lower sort of apostle" (12); so too Kurtz is characterized by the brickmaker as an "emissary of pity, and science, and progress" (25). Marlow taking pleasure in telling a bizarre story is perhaps a mark of insanity; passion can seize him: "I had some difficulty in restraining myself from laughing in their faces" (72-73). Watching the natives dance, he responds with the thought of a "remote kinship with this wild and passionate uproar" (37).

Caught in recognition of imminent death, Marlow stresses his primitive, bestial predisposition, and describes how he is spared destruction. "I was within a hair's breadth of the last opportunity for pronouncement.... He had stepped over the edge, while I had been permitted to draw back my hesitating foot" (72). Kurtz's death implies the death of Marlow: Kurtz "was as good as buried. And for a moment it seemed to me as if I also were buried.... That next day the pilgrims buried something in a muddy hole. And they very nearly buried me" (63, 71). Kurtz "was very little more than a voice" (48, 49) and so is his double—the frame narrator takes Marlow to be "no more... than a voice" (28). We may note, incidentally, that Jekyll recognizes in Hyde his "other self," and also maintains that "he thought of Hyde, for all his energy of life, as of something not only hellish but inorganic. This was the shocking thing; that the slime of the pit seemed to utter cries and voices" (95), which in a sense suggests an atmosphere of supernatural dread and the elemental.

Van Helsing and Dracula may also be considered a double, even if not so explicitly confirmed as Jekyll and Hyde. It matters that Van Helsing has an "iron jaw," "bushy eyebrows meeting" (126, 236), and a propensity for madness which recall Dracula's. Both men are old, alien, and threatening; they are related to vampirism—one by pursuing the mastery of vampire lore and influencing the endangered away from evil, and the other by deed—and Van Helsing, in a manner reminiscent of Dracula, tells Lucy, "No trifling with me! I never jest! There is grim purpose in all I do" (126).

It is possible to regard Jonathan Harker as a shadow Dracula. Harker looks into the depths of his shaving glass at Castle Dracula expecting to glimpse the count's face reflected in it, "but, there was no sign of a man in it, except myself" (24). The woman whose child was stolen has, in her tragic position, a tacit assumption that Harker is the culprit, never suspecting the count, who is disguised in Jonathan's garb: "Monster, give me my child" (44).

In Quincey Morris, too, we find a displaced Dracula. The reader's attention is drawn to him in the scene in which he occupies Dracula's physical position outside the window, and with his gun at hand strikes terror in Van Helsing and all the men, who "jumped to their feet" (232). Marlow remarks that duality has its collective—not merely personal—aspect: "The mind of man is capable of anything—because everything is in it, all the past as well as all the future" (37)—which fits a Jungian perspective. This meaning is recognizable in Van Helsing's words, "All men are mad in some way or the other" (115). Prendick, speaking of the "metamorphosed brutes" (120) on Dr. Moreau's island, notes:

I would see one of the clumsy bovine creatures who worked the launch treading heavily through the undergrowth, and find myself asking, trying hard to recall, how he differed from some really human yokel trudging home from his mechanical labours; or I would meet the Fox-Bear Woman's vulpine, shifty face, strangely human in its speculative cunning, and even imagine I had met it before in some city by-way. (121)

When he returns to London he remarks of Londoners, "I feel as though the animal was surging up through them.... I shrink from them... they seemed no more my fellow-creatures than dead bodies would be" (190-91). Jekyll learns "to recognise the thorough and primitive duality of man" (82); and suggests that "the terms of this debate |the Jekyll-Hyde duality~ are as old and commonplace as man" (89). Such statements perhaps recall, if only distantly, Walter Pater's remark that "the mind of the race, the character of the age, sway him |man~ this way or that," and Coleridge's "the infinite I AM" (Appreciations 67, Biographia 1: 202).

The discourse of primitivism is at the core of Dr. Jekyll and Mr. Hyde. Jekyll admits that the pleasures he "made haste to seek were... undignified.... But in the hands of Edward Hyde they soon began to turn towards the monstrous" (86). Jekyll attributes the brutality of Hyde to a vehement attachment of self: "His every act and thought centered on self; drinking pleasure with bestial avidity from any degree of torture to another; relentless like a man of stone" (86). Kurtz's "soul |is~ satiated with primitive emotions" (69), his primitive dehumanizing egotism—reversing his altruism—fills the self and causes otherness to be obliterated.

He relates everything to his inflated self: "'My intended, my ivory, my station, my river, my—' everything belonged to him" (49). "My intended, my station, my career, my ideas—these were the subjects for the occasional utterances of elevated sentiments" (69). Kurtz's is a discourse of unrestrained will; we are told that "He had kicked himself loose of the earth" (67), and the Russian tells Marlow of his rapacious greed: "Evidently the appetite for more ivory had got the better of the—what shall I say?—less material aspirations" (57-58). Typical of a thunderers's is Kurtz's belligerent demand for ivory (56), and he succumbs to homicidal mania: "those heads drying on the stakes" which were "only a savage sight" (59) and "showed that Mr. Kurtz lacked restraint in the gratification of his various lusts" (58).

These decapitated heads recall the terrorist Nero's human torches (victims covered with wax and set on fire) that lit his gardens—as Tacitus informs us.(5) Moreau's demonic manipulation of others manifests itself with some force in his account of the physical metamorphosis of his subjects: "I made my first man. All the week, night and day, I moulded him" (109). The self-assertive effect of the words is apparent. Jekyll acknowledges, not surprisingly, the absence of restraint to curb brute instinct: "I had voluntarily stripped myself of all those balancing instincts" (90).

A link between criminality and selfish impulses characterizes Dracula: "As he is criminal he is selfish... his action is based on selfishness, he confines himself to one purpose" (329-30). Like Kurtz, he relates all to himself, grounding vision of others within his own power. He tells Van Helsing and his group, "Your girls that you all love are mine already; and through them you and others shall yet be mine—my creatures, to do my bidding and to be my jackals when I want to feed" (295). One thinks of Sully, who in his article "Self-Esteem and Self-Estimation" saw an affinity between the feeling of self-esteem and primitive consciousness. He argued that "Far down, so to speak, below the surface of distinct consciousness... the connections between the idea of self and this emotion of esteem have been slowly woven through long ages of animal development" (164).

The novels have in common the use of animal imagery to signify the "primitive." A simple image brings out Kurtz's status: when left to himself, he becomes a quadruped "crawling on all-fours" back to his station, back to a prehuman state (66). He must have had immense stamina ("ruthless power" 71) required for the performance of his cannibalizing task. There are instances of the man-demon equation: "He looked at least seven feet long" (60), his eyes are described as "fiery" (68), his love as "diabolic," and his hate as "unearthly" (69). He is represented emblematically by his gaping mouth: initially Kurtz appears to Marlow with his mouth open wide—"it gave him a weirdly voracious aspect, as though he had wanted to swallow all the air, all the earth, all the men before him" (61). Moreover, Marlow has "a vision of him on the stretcher, opening his mouth voraciously, as if to devour all the earth with all its mankind" (74). This reference implies a literal element of devouring which brands him as a predator. The anatomical description further suggests animality:

I saw the thin arm extended commandingly, the lower jaw moving, the eyes of that apparition shining darkly far in its bony head that nodded with grotesque jerks.... I could see the cage of his ribs all astir, the bones of his arm waving. (60)

Hyde surely would feel at home among animals: he is explicitly described as "the brute" (94) and "ape-like" (47, 96, 97), with his "savage laugh" (40), and his "quick light way" "like a monkey" (67-68). His wildness is also signified metonymically by his hand, described as "lean, corded, knuckly, of a dusky pallor, and thickly shaded with a swart growth of hair" (88). Enfield testifies to his degeneracy:

There is something wrong with his appearance; something displeasing, something downright detestable. I never saw a man I so disliked, and yet I scarce know why. He must be deformed somewhere; he gives a strong feeling of deformity. (34)

Dr. Lanyon describes Hyde's regressive appearance: "small... with the shocking expression of his face, with his remarkable combination of great muscular activity and great apparent debility of constitution" (77). "Particularly small and particularly wicked-looking, is what the maid calls him" (48). To Utterson "Mr. Hyde was pale and dwarfish... hardly human! Something troglodytic" (40). He assaults Carew "with ape-like fury" (47). Poole describes him as "cry l ing~ out like a rat" (66). Hyde speaks of "the animal within me licking the chops of memory" (92).

The animal image is equally appropriate in Dracula's case. This is largely suggested by his landing in England in canine form, through his nocturnal incarnation as a wolf, and crawling "face down" like a bat, and his direct description as "a tiger," a "man-eater," and "panther-like in the movement" (33, 188, 228, 230, 308, 294). His "aquiline nose" with "great nostrils" (271), "very massive eyebrows almost meeting over the nose," "bushy hair that seemed to curl in its own profusion," hairy palm, and "pointed" ears (17) suggest the animalistic quality of his features.

His "peculiarly sharp white teeth" (17) "like those of a wild beast" (271), "eye-teeth long and pointed" (294), "broad" hand "with squat fingers," "long" nails (17), and "terrible grip" (271) bespeak his vampirism. His "hair growing scantily round the temples but profusely elsewhere" (17) brings him close to Dr. Moreau's "animal-men," who are described as having "scant bristly hair upon their heads" (60).

The animal context is present throughout The Island of Dr. Moreau; it controls our reading of the novel. Although the bulk of the "beastly" characters (153) reveal new properties and new capacities, essentially they have "the unmistakable mark of the beast" (61). The awesome figure of Moreau shares to some degree the features of animals. Wells depicts him as "a powerfully built man" with "rather heavy features" "and the fall of his heavy mouth at the corners gave him an expression of pugnacious resolution" (38). His rage, as described by Prendick, is close to that of an animal:

In a moment he had gripped me by the shoulder with a hand that was smeared red, had twisted me off my feet, and flung me headlong back into my own room. He lifted me as though I was a little child. I fell at full length upon the floor, and the door slammed and shut out the passionate intensity of his face. (73)

Even his "directness in discussion" is described as "brutal" (48). At the end of his beastly career, after the beast-men have turned against him, he turns into a beaten animal: "He lay face downward in a trampled space in a cane brake" (151). There is also Montgomery, who "was in truth half akin to these Beast Folk, unfitted for human kindred" (157).

In conclusion, Kurtz, no less than other neo-primitives, is an evolutionary throwback, the "man-that-was" (Dracula 231).

He is an exemplification of the duality of human nature, of how darkness is a component of light, and when it prevails, brings anarchy and corruption of others as well as self. Appropriately, he ends up ignominiously: "Suddenly the manager's boy |probably burlesquing the manager~ put his insolent black head in the doorway, and said in a tone of scathing contempt: 'Mistah Kurtz—he dead'" (71).

Jung's definition of the "experience that furnishes the material for artistic expression" could well apply to Heart of Darkness and to each of the other novels: "It is something strange that derives its existence from the hinterland of man's mind, as if it had emerged from the abyss of prehuman ages, or from a superhuman world of contrasting light and darkness. It is a primordial experience which surpasses man's understanding and to which in his weakness he may easily succumb" (90).

Chapter 5

"Signifying Nothing": Conrad's Idiots

On or about 25 July 1894, Conrad wrote to Marguerite Poradowska:

Man must drag the ball and chain of his individuality to the very end. It is the [price] one pays for the infernal and divine privilege of thought; consequently, it is only the elect who are convicts in this life—the glorious company of those who understand and who lament, but who tread the earth amid a multitude of ghosts with maniacal gestures, with idiotic grimaces. Which do you prefer—idiot or convict? (Collected Letters 1: 163)

Metaphorically extended, this impossible choice between two modes of being—idiot or convict—is both a theme and a structuring principle that runs across the best of Conrad's mature modernist work, written during the first decade of the century. But it is not really a matter of choice.

The author who cannot will himself into idiocy is willy-nilly a convict, imprisoned with in his own skepticism, sentenced to a lifetime of hard labour, anxiously trying to quarry meaning out of the brute matter of existence.(1) In what follows, I would suggest, on the same forensic note, that one may detect the "voice prints" of that Modernist anxiety in one of Conrad's earliest and most problematic short stories, a text that is both a symptom and a diagnosis of the same cultural crisis. The symptomaticity of the story is evident in its ultimate failure; the diagnostic power that turns it into a text of some cultural significance lies in its apparent awareness of that failure. "The Idiots," written in May 1896, during Conrad's honeymoon in Brittany, has been almost unanimously treated by critics as an embarrassing bit of juvenilia. In his Author's Note, written in the summer of 1919, Conrad himself had, according to Najder, dissociated himself from the story "unobtrusively but quite clearly," dismissing it as "such an obviously derivative piece of work that it is impossible for me to say anything about it here" (Najder 441). The story was subsequently described in Guerard's influential study as "an amateur's desperate search for a `subject' after a dismal experience of `writer's block,'" a verdict that seems to have foreclosed any further critical discussion (95).(2)

The story did, however, draw some attention as a suggestive source of speculation for psycho-biographical or pathographical studies. Hardly a honeymoon piece, it is, no doubt, highly interesting if one takes the liberty of studying the author's psychosexual life. Bernard C. Meyer, for instance, has focused on the figure of the wife, the half-demented murderous woman who was to feature more fully in Conrad's later work as Winnie Verloc (the surrogate mother of another congenital idiot, who, like her early prototype, stabs the father-figure in a fit of fury).

It is probably Meyer's rather ruthlessly clinical discussion that Najder has in mind when he observes, a touch acerbically perhaps, that the story "was to provide great fun for all Conrad's future psychoanalytical critics" (195).

I would argue that "The Idiots" is indeed interesting mainly for its symptomatic significance, but the anxiety it articulates, in the most inarticulate manner, is not merely the private mental torments of a troubled individual trying to adjust to the marital state, but a much wider-reaching cultural malaise.

I believe that the biographer's justified refusal of facile, sometimes vulgar psychoanalytic or pathobiographical speculation does not necessarily rule our the perception of symptomaticity where psychic, textual, and cultural vectors are significantly related. The following discussion would question the still prevalent distinction between the psychic (private, subjective, internal) and the cultural parameters of human reality, and suggest that any such watertight compartmentalization is ultimately less productive than the rather messier practice of watching these enclosures intersect and blend into each other.

"The Idiots" is one of Conrad's most pointless stories. It is the story of a peasant couple whose children are all born mentally deficient, a story of remorseless, fortuitous disintegration. By the end of the story Jean-Pierre Bacadou and his wife, Susan, are both dead. No ending, it seems, can be more final and absolute. And yet, the story seems to remain unfinished. The absolute and final end does not yield the "sense of an ending" that would endow the plot with significance, that retrospective illumination on which narratives—both traditional and modernist—depend for their ultimate justification. Stripped of all narrative scaffolding that would turn it into a neatly packaged unit of meaning, the story collapses into a meaningless tale of woe. It is a narrative without a proper ending, without a moral.

"Man is that which is in relation to his end in the fundamentally equivocal sense of this word" (Derrida 123). The structural dependence of narratives on some retrospective sense of significance and the Modernist "crisis of closure" have been articulated in depth in the notable studies of Kermode, Brooks and Ricoeur. A beautifully poetic rendering of the same crisis is Walter Benjamin's epigrammatic postulate: "Death is the sanction of everything that the storyteller can tell. He has borrowed his authority from death" (94). The meaning of a life, according to Benjamin, can only be finally consolidated and transmitted as a memory of that life, in a narrative that frames it. The traditional "wisdom" imparted by the storyteller can only be gathered from the full trajectory, which includes the end.

The reader of novels... [looks] for human beings from whom he derives the "meaning of life." Therefore he must, no matter what, know in advance that he will share their experience of death: if need be their figurative death—the end of the novel—but preferably their actual one.... The novel is significant, therefore, not because it presents someone else's fate to us, perhaps didactically, but because this stranger's fate by virtue of the flame which consumes it yields us the warmth which we never draw from our own fate. What draws the reader to the novel is the hope of warming his shivering life with a death he reads about. (101)

The same etiological relationship between authoring and authority is perceived as the very condition of the aesthetic relationship in Bakhtin's early work. The creative position of the author (defined as "a principle of seeing"), a position of outsideness or transgradience that enables him to enframe his characters "can be founded only upon a deep trust in the highest level of authority that blesses a culture—upon trust, that is, in the fact that there is another—the highest other—who answers for my own special answerability, and trust in the fact that I do not act in an axiological void" (206; emphasis added). The position of ultimate transgradience is that of God, and "the divinity of the artist consists in his partaking of the supreme outsideness" (191). The sense of an ending, that meaningful death which should warm our shivering life is attainable, according to the early Bakhtin, only when the omniscient human author derives his authority from the transcendental Auctor Mundi.(3)

It is, of course, not a coincidence that the omniscient, enframing narrative mode that characterized the novel throughout the eighteenth and nineteenth centuries came to be perceived as obsolete when the death of God was publicly diagnosed by Nietzsche. The "wisdom" of the storyteller, the authority that he derives out of his knowledge of the end, the retrospective illumination that is brought about by the closure of the narrative frame are only viable within a metaphysical frame of reference. That omniscient authorial consciousness which transcends the sphere of action and consciousness within which the characters act, and views the narrative as a temporal and axiological whole, is analogous to and dependent on the conception of metaphysical grounding.

Conrad, too, is well aware of the desire for "the sense of an ending." In his essay on James he wistfully comments on the "usual methods of solution by rewards and punishments, by crowned love, by fortune, by a broken leg or a sudden death," which, he says, are legitimate inasmuch as they satisfy the desire for finality, for which our hearts yearn, with a longing greater than the longing for the loaves and the fishes of this earth. Perhaps the only true desire of mankind, coming thus to fight in its hours of leisure, is to be set at rest. (18-19)

The desire for the end is not only the motor of narration. It is the incurable need for a final significance, appropriately related to the loaves and the fishes, and—just like them—no longer available in a secular world.

But narrative is not only a structure of aesthetic production. Narrativity is, as most postmodernist thinkers have come to realise—paradoxically at the moment when all master-narratives have been invalidated—a cognitive structuring category of a Kantian magnitude. The very idea of selfhood, of a coherent sense of identity, is related to the possibility of narrativization:

We are forever telling stories about ourselves. In telling these self-stories to others we may, for most purposes, be said to be performing straightforward narrative actions. In saying that we also tell them to ourselves, however, we are enclosing one story within another. This is the story that there is a self to tell something to, a someone else serving as audience who is oneself or one's self. When the stories we tell others about ourselves concern these other selves of ours, when we say, for example, "I am not master of myself." We are again enclosing one story within another, On this view, the self is a telling. (Shafer 345; emphasis added)

A fuller treatment of the interdependence of human subjectivity and narrative constructions is beyond the scope of the present inquiry, but it is arguable that the distinctive Modernist enterprise is precisely that search for a "narrative order," to use Musil's phrase, a construction that would endow the subject with a sense of coherence. As we shall see, the protagonist of "The Idiots," like its author, is a citizen of a world that has been stripped of its narrative framework.

If textual closure is the ultimate goal of the text, its

"desire," to use Brooks's psychotextual terminology, the road leading to it often goes through the detour of "repetitions serving to bind the energy of the text so as to make its final discharge more effective" (108). Folk stories, fairy tales, mythological narratives and other formulaic literary genres are typically structured on serial principles that generate a sense of significance through sameness and variation. The protagonist of "The Idiots," desperately trying to place his fife within some significant framework, is temporarily deluded by the apparent pattern that seems to emerge out of the recurrent disasters that hit him. It is precisely this need to find some narrative order in life that moves Jean-Pierre Bacadou to the point of religious conversion. A man of strong anti-clerical convictions, he breaks down at the suggestion that there may, indeed, be some mechanism of reward and punishment that has determined his fate:

> Jean-Pierre felt the [Republican, anti-clerical] convictions imbibed in the regiment torn out of his breast-not by arguments, but by facts. Striding over his fields he thought it over. There were three of them. Three! All alike! Why? Such things did not happen to everybody—to nobody he ever heard of. One yet—it might pass. But three! All three... Forever useless, to be fed while he lived and... What would become of the land when he died? This must be seen to. He would sacrifice his convictions.
>
> One day he told his wife—
>
> "See what your God will do for us. Pay for some masses." (66-67)

Jean-Pierre Bacadou capitulates to the illusory significance of his tragedy, the narrative force generated by mere repetition, by the magic number of three. It is the repetition of the event that turns the calamity into a story that might yet end—as stories do—on a note of recognition and a reversal of fortune.

Bacadou's "new credulity" is soon belied. Three black-soutaned priests come to the christening of the new baby, and Mme Lavaille, with her unique combination of piety and avarice, serves as her godmother. But the fourth child, too, turns out to be an idiot. It is at this point that Bacadou, cheated out of his precarious narrative, is moved to a gesture of hollow defiance. Rattling the iron bars of the church gates, he calls out: "Hey there! Come out!" He, too, is a convict, realizing that the transcendental Being that is supposed to "be there" is, like himself, a nobodaddy.

But the question of origins and ends—the question of metaphysics—is not merely a conspiracy of the clergy, a "swindle of the crows," as Jean-Pierre naively believes, along with a number of quite sophisticated intellectuals much closer home. In the narrative of human continuity the question of origin and destination is transformed into a question of paternity. It is this inescapable fact of life that smuggles the Trojan Horse of metaphysics into the very heart of a thoroughly disenchanted, secularized civilization.

Robert Con Davis, who proposes a Lacanian "psychoanalytic anthropomorphism of the text," focuses on the structural role of the father, or rather the absence of the father, in narrative. Davis argues that "a Freudian theory of certain laws of transformation suggests a paradigm for textuality—for the structural relations within a text.

Since the operations of the psychoanalytic subject and the text are synonymous—rather, since textuality is an inscription of the subject—many of the same laws govern both" (3). Davis discusses the paradigmatic status of The Odyssey in terms of this Lacanian psychopoesis: the father's absence, the son's quest, the recognition scene and the re-assertion of the law of the father are "laws of transformation" that operate within the subject and the text alike.

Just as in Lacanian theory where the initial absence of the father inaugurates a desire for the father's function, and the child thereby becomes the embodiment of knowledge about the father (and the absence associated with him), the Odyssean son begins the epic as he gazes toward a fatherless horizon and answers Athena's question about what it is to know a father. The paternal absence at the beginning of The Odyssey, then, has a necessary structural function in the evocation of a lack, but this lack is not irrevocably bound to father figures. Absence can also be indicated in complex and indirect ways....

The development of narrative... is fully dependent on the structural absence that initiates it.... This lack... is an originary feature of every narrative. (7-8)

I would suggest that the Negative Theology of the Lacanian formula is merely the obverse of the same metaphysical paradigm. If the absence of the father—a metaphoric extension of the primordial manque—a-etre—is the lack that produces discourse, that triggers all narratives into motion, it is the assumption of an eventual homecoming that is ultimately the enabling condition of narrative closure.

Predicated on a secure relationship of origins to ends, the analogy between the textual dynamics of narrative and the psychic dynamics of paternity ultimately depends on a metaphysical frame of reference. In the absence of that framework, the analogy collapses.

However, the need to insert oneself and one's private narrative into some "transindividual order," a metanarrative that would contain and unify the incoherent private one, is not obviated in the absence of religion. That need for grounding—the primary metaphysical need—becomes painfully real with the fact of parenthood.

The individual, we might say, makes raids on a putative master plot in order to remedy the insufficiencies of his own unsatisfactory plot—unsatisfactory because unclosed and thus not fully coherent, unilluminated. It is as if the individual, in order to be able to narrate his life story to himself in such a way as to make it coherent and significant, had to reach back toward the idea of a providential plot which, for better or for worse, would subsume his experience to that of mankind, to show the individual as a significant repetition of a story already endowed with meaning. (Brooks 280)

The sense of a totality larger than the self, a family, a community, or a nation, is the obvious alternative to religious faith. But Jean-Pierre Bacadou is not offered the comforts of any such alternative master-narrative, communal or familial. One by one, all the conventional idealizations of peasant life—Nature, Community, Tradition—are demolished in the telling. There is no sense of significance to be found in the bleak landscape, the cynicism, the greed and the indifferent callousness of the characters. The "pathos of authenticity," to use Vattimo's phrase, fails to work.(4) Even "the land," that altar at which Bacadou religiously serves, which seems to be invariably capitalized in his thoughts, can offer him nothing but its heavy, indifferent silence, It is the state of "the land" that motivates him to get married soon after his return to the village:

"It is not for me that I am speaking," insisted Jean-Pierre. "It is for the land. It's a pity to see it badly used. I am not impatient for myself." The old fellow nodded over his stick.... The mother was pleased with her daughter-in-law. (59)

There is no transition from the discussion of the badly-used land to the wedding, not a word about the courtship or the bride, not a word about love. The marriage is an offering to the Land that is the ultimate, terminal value against which the lives of individuals are measured. It is also in terms of the service of the land that Jean-Pierre thinks of his retarded children a few years later:

All three... Forever useless, to be fed while he lived and... What would become of the land when he died? (66) He looked at the black earth, at the earth mute and promising, at the mysterious earth doing its work of life in death-like stillness under the veiled sorrow of the sky. And it seemed to him that to a man worse than childless there was no promise in the fertility of the fields, that from him the earth escaped, defied him, frowned at him like the clouds, sombre and hurried above his head. Having to face alone his own fields, he felt the inferiority of man who passes away before the clod that remains. (71)

Faced with the unresponsive earth, trapped into the "antipathetic fallacy" that Watts has diagnosed as one of Conrad's "absurdist techniques," Jean-Pierre Bacadou is stripped of the last metaphysical consolation. There is no master-plot that can subsume and justify this pointless tale of sorrows. It is, one might say, an "idiot reality," a reality that resists narrativization with the indifferent force of brute matter.

When the psychic and the cultural parameters of human

reality intersect, it is hard to draw the fine that marks the diagnosis from the symptom. The failure of paternity is not contained within the text; it spills over onto its borderlines and turns into a failure of narrative. If the reader, unlike the protagonist, may sometimes find a sense of communality in the very act of narration—implying a bond between an implicit authorial figure or an embodied narrator and his listeners—that meager consolation is also denied us. The story begins as a personal reminiscence: "We were driving along the road..." (56). But the first-person narrator disappears with the beginning of the tale, and the omniscient narrative mode that seems to follow does not entail any comforts of providence and wisdom. The failure of the narrative is echoed in the failure of narration. The failure of paternity is ultimately the failure of authorship.

"The Idiots" is a dead end at the very beginning of what was to develop into a singular literary journey. Its symptomaticity points to a junction at which various authorial anxieties, both psychic and cultural, intersect and merge into a highly explosive mixture. It is the spring of 1896, when fatherhood becomes a real possibility, when the decision to become a professional, fully committed writer is about to be made. Having broken away from his own heritage, the familial and the communal narratives were no longer readily available to Conrad as a transindividual narrative of continuity: he was about to become a father outside the familial narrative, a storyteller without the wisdom and the sanction of a meaningful literary death.

Shortly before he wrote the story, Conrad fell ill.

It remains unclear whether the difficulties with writing or other distressing factors were the cause (which seems likely) or the effect; at all events, Conrad fell ill suddenly... "he became more and more incoherent and rambling in his speech.... He raved in grim earnest, speaking only in his native tongue.... All that night Joseph Conrad continued to rave in Polish, a habit he kept up every time any illness had him in its grip." (Najder 198) Fourteen years later, upon the completion of Under Western Eyes (another work that revolves around similar issues), Conrad was afflicted by a similar reaction. But the collapse of the narrative is over-determined: its underlying anxiety is not only that of a particular uprooted individual.

It is related to a much deeper sense of cultural and epistemic crisis. When the metaphysical outlook is no longer viable, the possibility of narrative framing becomes a mere aesthetic fiction, and the concept of paternity is thoroughly shaken. It is here that the cultural and the private realms blend into what I have called "the anxiety of Modernism," which Conrad was to grapple with in the best of his work.

Nineteenth-century narrative was, typically, "the narrative of an attempted homecoming: of the effort to reach an assertion of origin through ending, to find the same in the different, the time before in the time after" (Brooks 110). The twentieth century, heralded by Nietzsche and Vaihinger, is the age of homesickness. "It's a wise child that knows its own father," says Telemachus to Athena. It is, to extrapolate, an idiot child who does not. The modernist narrative is plagued by the suspicion that we are all idiots in that sense.

When narrative ends can no longer signify and be true at the same time, the author can either opt for the silence of the idiot or for the forced conviction of the convict, the willed and desperate construction of meaning, "as if," to use Vaihinger's paradigm, there were really a home to come back to. The central question of modernism turns on the very possibility of any homecoming. The centrality of exile, the persistence of nostalgia, are all the symptoms of this modernist ache, the suspicion that narratives—"real" narratives with beginnings and ends—are mere fictions. The narrative of the self, that construction which enables us to sustain a sense of coherent identity, is no exception to this.

In one of his most memorable letters to Cunninghame Graham, written on 14-15 January 1898, just a few hours before the birth of his eldest son, Conrad seems to be at his bleakest best:

Life knows us not and we do not know life—we do not know even our own thoughts. Half the words we use have no meaning whatever and of the other half each man understands each word after the fashion of his own folly and conceit. Faith is a myth and beliefs shift like mists on the shore; thoughts vanish; words, once pronounced, die; and the memory of yesterday is as shadowy as the hope of to-morrow—only the string of my platitudes seems to have no end. As our peasants say; "Pray, brother, forgive me for the love of God." And we don't know what forgiveness is, nor what is love, nor where God is. Assez. (Letters to Graham 65)

Nothing, it seems, is left to the author of this bleak, hopeless message. Nothing but silence. But the dark conclusion of the letter is reversed by a curious postscript:

PS. This letter missed this morning's post because an infant of male persuasion arrived and made such a row that I could not hear the Postman's whistle. It's a fine commentary upon this letter! But salvation lies in being illogical. Still I feel remorse. (Letters to Graham 65)

The truth of this odd postscript outweighs, if only by the smallest of margins, the apocalyptic tone of the letter. Conrad, we know, had chosen to turn away from the dead end of his own lethal skepticism, to attend to the tiny voice of the infant and all it stood for rather than listen for the postman's whistle. A convict of his own making, he had apparently chosen—as if it were a matter of choice—to join the company of "the elect," those cursed with the "infernal and divine privilege of thought," "who understand and who lament." Salvation, it seems, does lie in being illogical. (1) See Erdinast-Vulcan, Joseph Conrad... 1-24, 139-56.

(2) One exception to this unanimous critical silence is a comment made by Daniel Schwarz who, in trying to redeem the story from critical oblivion, describes it as "a penetrating study of emotional and moral idiocy," where "the blighted offspring are stark symbols of a community where family, clerical, and political structures are undermined by the hypocrisy, selfishness, and vanity of those in positions to provide moral leadership," and argues, with very little support from the text, that the narrator's "values" are "a humanistic alternative" to those of the Ploumar parish that fails "to provide responsible care for the helpless children" (Schwarz

23-24). Schwarz's commentary itself is a case in point, for in providing the story with a didactic message, a moral that is obviously not to be found in the text, it exposes a sense of acute readerly discomfort that does not derive from an aesthetic weakness in the text but from what is clearly an ethical issue.

(3) On the ambivalence of Bakhtin's early work see Erdinast-Vulcan, "Narrative..." and "Bakhtin's Homesickness...." (4) Vattimo uses the phrase in his "apology for Nihilism," with reference to the "resistance to the accomplishment of nihilism," which he defines as the "reduction of Being to exchange value" in the absence of the "terminal, interrupting instance of highest value (God)" (21). My own use of the phrase, in a somewhat extended sense, denotes the substitution of religious with other forms of metaphysical ballast.

Chapter 6

Modernism and Marketplace: The Case of Conrad's Chance

Many early twentieth-century authors now associated with protomodernist or modernist experimentation appeared initially in weekly or monthly journals before proceeding to book form, partly as a matter of economic necessity, partly to ensure a broad dissemination of their work. Experimental writers relied on journal publication in the British Isles and the United States to make a living, while their innovations in narrative method often failed to fit the contexts of their initial appearance. Thus, three of Joyce's Dubliners stories, "The Sisters," "Eveline," and "After the Race" were first published in 1904 in a popular Dublin agricultural journal, The Irish Homestead, a journal Joyce later referred to in Ulysses as "the pigs' paper" (Joyce 1992, 27).

Moreover, a distinctive eclecticism characterised many journals in the period, where writers such as Thomas Hardy or Joseph Conrad appeared in Harper's (then a far more broadly-based journal than the current publication) or The Pictorial Review alongside the romances of Baroness Orzcy, Marjorie Bowen or Marie Corelli. Instalments of fiction were often framed by features on beauty and fashion, advertisements for household goods, articles on topical issues, and photographs of distinguished personalities. In the July issue of The London Magazine for 1912 an advertisement directs its female readers to "Obliterate Fatness and Restore Beauty," while the October number offers a fictional romance by Arnold Bennett, whose content questions the very conventions of representation that implicitly shape female identity in this context.

Recent critical debates have revealed the complexity of the relationship between modernism and popular forms. Tim Armstrong, for example, asks whether modernism might not be understood as "a phenomenon of the market" (2005, 48). He cites competing accounts presented by Lawrence Rainey (1998) and Mark Morrisson (2001), who both establish, in different ways, modernism's response to market forces and the emergence of popular journal publication.

Both critics try to avoid the polarisation implied by Andrea Huyssens's notion of "the great divide," in which modernist authors' relationship to mass culture is seen as "an anxiety of contamination" (1986, vii). Even so, Rainey's account of the development of Little Magazines sometimes reflects the enduring Greenbergian distinction between "lowbrow" and "highbrow." As Armstrong observes, Rainey argues for modernism's elitist tendency "to create a new niche market for an 'advanced literature' structured by scarcity rather than abundance" (2005, 48).

It is true that with the development of the Little Magazines and literary journals, experimental fiction moved out of the broad-ranging popular contexts like Pall Mall, London Magazine, and Metropolitan Magazine and found a more exclusive niche. Pound and Eliot's The Egoist, which ran 1914-1919 as a mouthpiece for Imagism, serialised Portrait of the Artist as a Young Man; John Middleton Murry's The Adelphi published Dorothy Richardson in London, Margaret Anderson's Chicago The Little Review published work by Wyndham Lewis, T. S. Eliot, Ford Madox Ford and chapters of Ulysses.

However, Rainey's account of modernism's emergence through systems of patronage rather than through direct commercial relations changes the emphasis from a polarisation of "high" and "low" to a more nuanced identification of authors' individual relations with figures associated with the mass market, such as the newspaper magnate, Alfred Harmsworth (Lord Northcliffe) or C. Arthur Pearson in

England, Randolph Hearst or S.S. McClure in the United States. On the other hand, Morrisson suggests a more fluid interaction between modernism and the popular market, outlining the ways in which modernism exploits techniques of advertising and popular publishing, "even where it seems to create a 'counter-public' sphere" (Armstrong 2005, 48-49).

Morrisson argues for the adaptation of mass publication techniques by contemporary political groups such as suffragists, socialists, and anarchists and the argument for a strong relationship between experimental work and the popular press can be illustrated by the fact that the popular context for "highbrow" fiction does not disappear in the twentieth century. After all, Sylvia Plath published short stories such as "Sunday at the Mintons" in Mademoiselle in August 1952, and "Initiation" in January 1953 in Seventeen.

Studies such as those of Rainey or Morrisson give rise to general theories of modernism's relationship to the marketplace, yet they have not always explored fully the close textual problems arising from this context, in particular the implications of a transformation from serial to book text of much modernist writing.

Critics such as Alfred Habegger (1989) or R.B. Kerschner (1996) have led the way by exploring the periodical publication of the works of protomodernist and high modernist figures ranging from Henry James to James Joyce. Likewise, Linda Hughes and Michael Lund have observed an important relationship between the serial context and the protomodernist novel, noting that "serialization was the dominant form for the first appearance of major works by Stevenson, Hardy, Wells, Kipling, James, Conrad, and others" (Hughes and Lund 1991, 230).

Yet for those writers who sought a wide readership as well as integrity for the novel as art form, a tension often arose in the period between aesthetic aims and marketing incentives, where the themes and content of fiction did not always meet the generic expectations of a mass audience. The censored serial text of Hardy's Jude the Obscure, for example, appeared in Harper's in 1895 under the editor's somewhat misleading title of Hearts Insurgent. As Hughes and Lund observe, this title suggests the "romantic fulfilment, ascension through the social ranks and expansion of real influence" that conformed more readily to serial readers' expectations than to the harsh scepticism of Hardy's book text (1991, 232). Moreover, Hardy's manuscript was bowdlerized in the serial, the editor having cut such events as the pig-killing or Arabella's seduction of Jude (230).

In fact, the serial text of late nineteenth- early twentieth-century protomodernist fiction has often been dismissed out of hand by contemporary critics and editors. It sometimes occupies a similar place to that of the "The Bad Quarto" of Hamlet—where the text has in the past been almost too easily dismissed as inferior, unreliable copy without reference to its more elusive potential. The serial version of novels of this period, cranked out to deadline, unchecked at proof stage, brutally censored and edited, nevertheless retains, in its context, an "improvisational" quality, not least in its often disjunctive combination of text and illustration.

Of course it could be argued that the apparently naive mismatch between fictional texts and the surrounding visual material used for illustrations of fiction, advertisements and feature articles incorporates the discourses of freedom and individual worth. But you could polemicize this phenomenon in a different way. Images for advertisements and illustrations for fiction usually conform to a limited taxonomy, promoting received conventions of genre and of gender identity according to standards of contemporary taste or fashion and often eliding generic ambiguities in the texts themselves. Instead they emphasise the conservative tendencies that shaped the desires of readers of popular romance.

In this respect, textual studies have provided useful models for rethinking critical assumptions associated with modernist writers. Theorists of the history of the book, ranging from Pierre Macherey and Pierre Bourdieu to Jerome McGann have increasingly encouraged us to engage with the context in which the text is produced (see Macherey 1966, Bourdieu 1993, McGann 1983). D. F. McKenzie's theory of the "Sociology of the Text" has similarly led to a radical revision of critical attitudes in the examination of all pre-publication and published states of the text, identifying a more fluid, open and inclusive framework (McKenzie 1986).

Man can embody truth but he cannot know it." Nowhere is William Butler Yeats's adage more clearly illustrated than in the narrative of Charlie Marlow in Heart of Darkness. Throughout the text, Marlow insists upon the distinction between truth and lies; between men and women; between civilization and savagery; and, most of all, between Self and Other. Of these, the most important distinction is between Self and Other, for it is this opposition that sustains the colonial enterprise.

The lure and the fear of the Other initiate the pursuit and "discovery" of colonialism; the conviction of the inferiority of the Other justifies the undertaking. Yet despite Marlow's insistence, all binary oppositions collapse in the course of his narrative: colonists prove to be conquerors, the gang of virtue is indistinguishable from the gang of greed, the illusions of women merely echo the illusions of men, and there is no clear distinction between lies and truth. Most importantly, the fundamental difference between Self and Other disappears and, with it, the unbridgeable gulf between men and women and between savage and civilized that sustains the power structure of western civilization. But this awareness offered by the text eludes Marlow for, enmeshed in his own culture, he would find this awareness "too dark—too dark altogether."

More Articles of Interest

'Heart of Darkness' and late-Victorian fascination with the primitive and the... Moral Conditions for Genocide in Joseph Conrad's Heart of Darkness1, The Joseph Conrad

"Signifying nothing": Conrad's idiots and the anxiety of modernism - Joseph...

"Speech Was of No Use": Conrad, a New Journalism, and the Critical...

In psychological terms, the Other is but the undiscovered territory in the self. In the colonial enterprise, this territory of the unconscious is displaced onto another people who both allure and terrify. The colonizer, fearing to succumb to the Other, attempts to contain it—through subordination, suppression, or conversion. These strategies of containment are designed to preserve the opposition and inequality between Self and Other that justifies the imperialist enterprise. The central trope of imperialism is what Abdul R. JanMohamed terms "the manichean allegory" that converts racial difference "into moral and even metaphysical difference" (80).

This allegory characterizes the relationship between dominant and subordinate culture as one of ineradicable opposition (82). Although the opposing terms of the allegory change—good and evil, civilization and savagery, intelligence and emotion, rationality and sensuality—they are always predicated upon the assumption of the superiority of the outside evaluator and the inferiority of the native being observed.

Colonialist literature, as byproduct of the imperialist enterprise, necessarily reinscribes the manichean allegory either to confirm or to interrogate it in an effort to move beyond its limits. As a result, colonialist texts take two forms, which reflect, respectively, these two different responses: the "imaginary" and the "symbolic" (JanMohamed 84). These designations derive from Jacques Lacan's descriptions of sequential stages of human development.

The "imaginary," according to Lacan, dates from the mirror stage of infant life, in which the child of six to eighteen months jubilantly identifies itself with its mirror image, the wholeness and integrity of which belie the internal flux and fragmentation the child experiences (Lacan 4). Because of the unbridgeable distance of the specular image with which the child identifies, the child situates within it rivalry, opposition, and aggressivity (Gallop 59). The relation between the self and its image, which Lacan terms "the imaginary," is one in which mirroring forestalls intersubjectivity or the interaction between two separate selves, each with its own distinct perspective.

In the "imaginary" colonialist text, JanMohamed observes, "the native functions as an image of the imperialist self in such a manner that it reveals the latter's self-alienation" (84). This self-alienation consists in the failure to recognize as inherent within the self despised attributes the imperialist projects onto the Other. Thus, the "imaginary" colonialist text adheres to a fixed opposition between the self and the native, insisting upon the homogeneous identity of the indigenous population and taking refuge in the "superior," more "enlightened," and more "civilized" perspective of the dominant culture. Interpreted through the narrative perspective of Marlow, Heart of Darkness exemplifies the "imaginary" colonialist text.

The second type of colonialist fiction, the "symbolic," parallels the stage at which the young child, once having become convinced of its wholeness and integrity, is able to recognize and identify with an imago or subject-image as a counterpart; and is then able to enter into a dialectic that links the self or I "with socially elaborated situations" (Lacan 5). At this stage, the child is able to enter into social exchange, dialogue, and relationship (Gallop 59-61).

An equivalent stage in culture would make possible a dialectic encounter between Self and Other in which the dominant culture is able to bracket its own values and thus radically to question its basis for cultural inference and interpretation. Such a dialectic or exchange would aim at resolving cultural oppositions through syncretic solutions (JanMohamed 85). Such, I would argue, is the larger narrative perspective of Heart of Darkness, which exposes the limitations and self-contradiction of Marlow's views to open up a complex dialogue on issues of history, culture, race, and gender. Thus the entirety of Heart of Darkness attempts to deal with the Other in symbolic terms, although Marlow is able to deal with the other only in the realm of the Imaginary.

Heart of Darkness points to awarenesses beyond Marlow both by revealing his limitations and by systematically undercutting the polarities and distinctions that Marlow takes pains to establish. From the first, Marlow's narrative invites the reader to reach an understanding beyond him when he states that his experience was "not very clear. And yet it seemed to throw a kind of light" (70). Among his many limitations in dealing with cultural differences, Marlow displays his xenophobia when he reluctantly accepts his relatives' choice of living on the Continent, explaining, "It's cheap and not so nasty as it looks, they say" (71). Further, he exhibits contradictory ideas about entering another culture, revealing his determination to get to Africa "by hook or by crook" but, once there, feeling like "an imposter" (77) when he observes that the natives (unlike him) "wanted no excuse for being there" (78).

He insists that he detests and avoids lies, yet acknowledges three separate lies in the course of the narrative—to the station manager, to Kurtz, and to the Intended. He maintains that the conquest of the earth is redeemed by "an unselfish belief in the idea—something you can set up, and bow down before, and offer a sacrifice to" (69-70). Not only is this assertion undercut by the language of idolatry, but it prefigures evidence, as the narrative unfolds, that Kurtz' belief in the idea of "humanizing, improving, instructing" (101) leads to the most ruthless exploitation and most appalling idolatry of all, as Kurtz turns himself, the emissary of the idea, into an object of worship.

Further, Marlow dismisses as foolish his aunt's notion of "weaning those ignorant millions from their horrid ways" (76), but describes as "a beautiful piece of writing" Kurtz' kindred assertion, "By the simple exercise of our will we can exert a power for good [among the natives] practically unbounded" (123). Throughout the text, Marlow works hard to separate savage customs from civilized behaviour, yet an observer might be pressed to distinguish Marlow's noisy jig with the boiler-maker (when he finally gets rivets to repair his boat) (98) from the "whirl of black limbs" (105) on shore that he condescends to regard as "not inhuman" (105).

Similarly, Marlow's distinction between the comprehensible language of civilized discourse and the incomprehensible noise of savages—"the roll of drums" (105), "abrupt burst of yells" (141), "savage clamour" (113), "savage discords" (110), "tumultuous and mournful uproar" (110)—breaks down. All voices, European and native, degenerate in

Marlow's memory into "one immense jabber, silly, atrocious, sordid, savage, or simply mean, without any kind of sense" (120-21).

Because most of Marlow's attempts at separations prove unstable and many of his distinctions blur, they serve to reveal his intense need to sustain the manichean allegory so necessary to his sense of Self in contradistinction to the Other. Underlying Marlow's efforts to maintain binary oppositions is the colonizer's intense anxiety about being taken over by the Other. Marlow's strategy of containment emerges most forcefully throughout the text in his parallel descriptions of women and of natives.(1)

Throughout his account, Marlow both denigrates and overestimates the power of women. Through synecdoche, Marlow reduces the women he sees in the waiting room of the Belgian shipping company to "one fat and the other slim" (73), one young and one old, "knitting black wool as for a warm pall" (74). At the same time, they are oddly "uncanny and fateful" (74); and Marlow after his encounter with Kurtz observes, "the knitting old woman with the cat obtruded herself upon my memory as a most improper person to be sitting at the other end of such an affair" (142). Analogously, the secretary, who seems to know all about Marlow's fate, he reduces to "a white-haired secretarial head, but wearing a compassionate expression" (74).

Similarly, Marlow downplays his aunt's power, while inadvertently revealing his reliance upon her. After disavowing his dependency on women—"Then—would you believe it?... I, Charlie Marlow, set the women to work—to get a job. Heavens!"—he acknowledges that he relied upon his aunt to get him the job as captain of the Congo steamer. His aunt, who clearly wields more social power than Marlow, he describes patronizingly as "a dear enthusiastic soul" (76), although her influential recommendations of him haunt him along his Congo journey and serve to ally him with the similarly "gifted" Kurtz.

As he describes her, he confines his aunt to a drawing room "that most soothingly looked just as you would expect a lady's drawing room to look" (76), a description that contrasts markedly with his later description of the disquieting drawing room in which he encounters Kurtz' Intended.

Marlow's adverb "soothingly" suggests his discomfort at the idea of encountering a woman who is not contained in a drawing room, a discomfort he will experience at its most extreme in his meeting with the "savage" woman in the jungle. Once he returns from the Congo, no lady's drawing room will again be a "soothing" place because he will have found out—although he never consciously admits it—that neither women nor domestic space offer sanctuary from the knowledge of the pervasiveness of evil.

Marlow's self-deluding ability to polarize his experiences—in particular, to separate the "soothing" female world of illusions from the larger male world of shocking realities—collapses in his interview with the Intended. Despite Marlow's efforts to keep these worlds separate, after his jungle encounter with Kurtz, they fuse in the nightmare atmosphere of the Intended's drawing room, inhabited by Kurtz' ghost, whose words echo and eerily combine with hers to form the ghastly chorus Marlow hears.

This chorus suggests a terrifying intertwining of purpose between Kurtz and his Intended—a collusion between the "soul as translucently pure as a cliff of crystal" (149) and the "soul that knew no restraint, no faith, and no fear" (144). For this reason, when Marlow asserts, "I saw them together—I heard them together" (154) in the drawing room, he experiences "a sensation of panic in my heart as though I had blundered into a place of cruel and absurd mysteries not fit for a human being to behold" (154). (The phrase "cruel and absurd mysteries" eerily echoes the "unspeakable rites" attributed to Kurtz in Africa). In this scene, Marlow's language and observations suggest, although his panic and confusion indicate he does not consciously understand, that domestic bliss and female innocence in Belgium are predicated upon the exploitation of natives and the pilfering of ivory in the Congo; that marriages between ambitious young men of insufficient means with young women of substance are facilitated by the colonial enterprise, in which enterprising young men make good in the name of doing good. ("I had heard that her engagement with Kurtz had been disapproved by her people. He wasn't rich enough or something... He had given me some reason to infer that it was his impatience of comparative poverty that drove him out there" [155]).

Many apparently innocent features of the drawing room recall sinister aspects of the colonial enterprise presented earlier in the story. Thus, the grand piano "like a sombre and polished sarcophagus" (153) recalls the image of Brussels, the city outside her door, site of the colonial Company's offices, as "a whited sepulchre" (73); the piano, symbol of feminine refinement, has keys of ivory, the ivory Kurtz pilfered from Africa; the apparently noble image of the Intended's white forehead "illumined by the unextinguishable light of belief and love" (154) against the dark background of the room recalls Kurtz's ominous painting of her "draped and blindfolded, carrying a torch" in which "the effect of the torch-light on the face was sinister" (92).

In the drawing room scene, she is in effect blindfolded by her enduring and willful illusions about Kurtz and she carries the torch of his ideas, which cast a sinister light back upon her. Fittingly, the image of her hair as an "ashy halo" associates her apparently angelic goodness with death. Consequently Marlow, in acknowledging that the Intended's claim, "I knew him best" (107), may be accurate, aptly notes that "with every word spoken the room was growing darker" (107)—that is, more unfathomable, more remote from truth, more connected with evil, more suggestive of death. In this scene all details combine to point out that domestic innocence colludes with global evil in death-dealing conspiracy. Yet, in the Intended's drawing room, as in other stations along his pilgrimage, Marlow shrinks from the enormity of the knowledge he is offered.

Similarly, in his descriptions of the African natives, as in his glib generalizations about women, Marlow likewise attempts to deny the power of the Other he fears by resorting to stereotypes. Just as his descriptions of women are reductive, so too are his accounts of the natives, whom he acknowledges only in generic descriptions.

"Dark human shapes could be made out in the distance.... two bronze figures, leaning on tall spears, stood in the sunlight under fantastic head-dresses of spotted skins, warlike and still in statuesque repose" (136). Even when described individually, they are stereotyped: "The man seemed young—almost a boy—but you know with them it's hard to tell" (82).Marlow's stereotypical descriptions of both women and natives serve a strategy of containment that enables him to deny both their importance for him and his affinity with them.

Nowhere, however, is Marlow's containment of the Other through discourse so sustained as in his treatment of the "savage" woman, the figure in which race and gender emblematically intersect. This is not to say that racial and sexual difference are to be equated. Since the value attributed to each is culturally determined, interpretations of racial and sexual superiority vary from one culture to another; and within any particular culture these constructions may conflict rather than intersect. Yet when Heart of Darkness presents an African tribal culture that reverses both the racial and sexual hierarchy of the West, these reversals constitute a powerful double threat to Western social constructions that Marlow views as natural and inevitable.(2)

Marlow's compelling but ambivalent description of the "savage" woman enables the reader to see the contrast between her authority and unique attributes and Marlow's repeated attempts, throughout the text, to deny the power and individuality of African natives. Marlow responds to her dangerous allure—dangerous because he sees her as partly responsible for Kurtz's "going native"—by insisting on her ineradicable twofold otherness, the savage and female as distinguished from the civilized and male. By designating her the living embodiment of these dualities, Marlow shores up the binary oppositions upon which his understanding of Western civilization rests.

The "savage" woman, as Marlow describes her, is a distillation of alluring but frightening otherness. His view of her highlights her beauty, leadership, and ferocity. She is "wild," "gorgeous" (136), and proud. Wearing a helmet, armor, and magic charms, she is fearless in the face of the pilgrims' bullets, and is obeyed by her tribesmen. She is "like the wilderness itself, with an air of brooding over an inscrutable purpose" (137), a description sufficiently ominous but all the more so for echoing the previous description of the wilderness as "an implacable force brooding over an inscrutable intention" (103).

Although she is without words, the "savage" woman is not without purpose—and this, her "struggling, half-shaped resolve" (137), is all the more menacing for being unknowable. Her threatening otherness is most fully articulated by Marlow's parodic double, the Russian "man of patches" (88) who finds her so frightening that he proclaims: "If she had offered to come aboard [the steamer] I really think I would have tried to shoot her" (88). The contrast between the harlequin's nervousness and the "savage" woman's composure, between his ragged attire and her "gorgeous" adornment highlights her formidable power.

In her overt sexuality and aggressive claims upon Kurtz's person, Marlow finds her both enticing and menacing. Voracious and diabolical, she appears to belong to a matriarchal and polyandrous female warrior culture. Equated with the wilderness—she is its "tenebrous and passionate soul" (137)—she is a kind of succubus that has made Kurtz her concubine and thereby drained him of his vitality:

> The wilderness had patted him on the head.... it had caressed him, and—lo!—he had withered; it had taken him, loved him, embraced him, got into his veins, consumed his flesh, and sealed his soul to its own by the inconceivable ceremonies of some devilish initiation. He was its spoiled and pampered favourite (121).

The "savage" woman is one with the wilderness that has claimed Kurtz for its harem. This image of Kurtz as the "spoiled and pampered favourite" in a male harem directly threatens the patriarchal and ostensibly monogamous structure of the society from which he has emigrated.

So threatening is the "savage" woman in her sexual otherness that Marlow adopts a strategy of subduing her power through grief: "she stopped as if her heart had failed her" (137). Finally the text supplants her with—in effect, turns her into—the Intended, in perpetual mourning and domestic confinement, whose outstretched arms mirror the "savage" woman's gesture but lack her power to command a tribe or to enshroud a pilgrim ship in shadow: "Suddenly she [the "savage" woman] opened her bared arms and threw them up rigid above her head.... and at the same time the swift shadows darted out on the earth, swept around on the river, gathering the steamer into a shadowy embrace" (88). Thus Marlow's narration quells the anxiety the "savage" woman evokes: It demonstrates that her "barbarous" charms are in fact "powerless" (156). Her inconsolable grief, in paralyzing her, restores the male—in the person of her paramour, Kurtz—to primacy.

The colonialist anxiety of being taken over by the Other surfaces even more frighteningly in the cannibalism that Marlow imputes to the native workers aboard his boat who, at any moment, may devour Marlow and the pilgrims. In Heart of Darkness, cannibalism serves as the metaphor for the absolute violation of boundaries between one human being and another, the physical equivalent of the cultural absorption or ingestion by the Other that the colonizer fears.

On another level, the cannibalism Marlow imputes to the natives may be merely a guilty projection of the rapacity of the white colonizers who, as Jonathan Swift noted about earlier British colonial exploiters in "A Modest Proposal," have already devoured the native population in less literal ways. Since the European intruders have invaded territorial boundaries, have violated property rights, and have in fact confiscated the natives' most personal property—their bodies—for their own uses, the Europeans are but one step from literally devouring the inhabitants.

In fact, Marlow describes the insatiable Kurtz as threatening to do so: "I saw him open his mouth wide—it gave him a weirdly voracious aspect, as though he had wanted to swallow all the air, all the earth, all the men before him" (135). Even Marlow's approval of the apparent restraint of the natives aboard ship, whom he takes to be hungry cannibals, may simply suggest the guilt he feels at the Europeans' lack of restraint toward the indigenous population.

Marlow's attribution of cannibalism to the natives—an accusation never borne out by their behaviour—is a violence Marlow inflicts on the culture. This violence is characteristic of all linguistic descriptions of the members of one culture by members of another culture who exercise power over them and exploit them. Throughout, Heart of Darkness suggests that physical violence originates in the violence of language—the language that is used to justify intrusion, usurpation, and conversion.

As Jacques Derrida observes, human violence originates in the violence of the letter, which takes many forms:(3) in Heart of Darkness, the map of Africa, divided and colored according to the greedy claims of European nations; the inscription upon the land of roads and railroads; the delivery of mail from home to European intruders; the keeping of accounts to tally the loot; the written recommendations of outsiders to legitimize the coercion of natives; the Bible that justifies the pilgrims in converting and (if resisted) in killing the natives; and the law that labels some natives "enemies" and others "criminals" and thereby legitimizes clapping them in irons and forcing them into chain gangs.

Thus Marlow correctly describes Kurtz primarily as a "voice" whose "unextinguishable gift of noble and lofty expression" (146) authorizes and smoothes the way for indulging his consummate greed.(4) The text suggests the inevitable course of Kurtz's report to the International Society for the Suppression of Savage Customs that begins by arguing that the godlike status of white men in the Congo enables them to "exert a power for good practically unbounded" and ends by urging "Exterminate all the brutes!" (123). As Marlow ironically yet revealingly suggests, this last admonition "may be regarded as the exposition of a method."

The text's recognition of the violence inherent in language

also helps to explain the narrative event most puzzling to critics, Marlow's apparent lie to Kurtz's Intended. In reply to her request for "His last word—to live with," Marlow responds, "The last word he pronounced was—your name."

By this assertion, Marlow inadvertently tells her the truth. For Kurtz, the Intended is not a distinct person. Just as she has no name of her own, she has no intrinsic reality for Kurtz. She is the expression of his intentions, of the life he intends for her, one that reflects his culture-based ideas about marriage, sexuality, and the subordination of women. She is, in effect, colonized by Kurtz's intentions, which confine her in the drawing room and limit her discourse to an echo of his.

Similarly, the African natives exist in the text as expressions of Kurtz's—and Marlow's—intentions. They exist for Kurtz's uses and are confined to Marlow's conceptions of them. To have intentions toward a people is to appropriate for oneself the right to subdue, to convert, and to use—all in the name of benevolence. Thus "the horror" is indeed the name of the Intended: it designates the violence that results from the intentions of the powerful who impose their will upon the powerless.(5)

Further, the designation "the Intended" signals an awareness that permeates the text of the unreliability and slipperiness of language. "The Intended" is the shifting signifier, sign of the unbridgeable gulf between aim and achievement, the gap in meaning that cannot be sutured. Without heeding the text's warning about the unreliable and equivocal nature of language, the reader may trust too much to Marlow's words, just as Kurtz' adherents have trusted too much to his eloquence; and potential colonist-conquerors may fool themselves as well as others into believing in their noble intentions.

Repeatedly, in recording the booming voice but essential hollowness of Kurtz, the text underlines the tricky nature of language itself that conceals as it apparently reveals, that denotes presence while signifying absence, that signals meaning while lacking it.

By the time Marlow tells the truth he considers a lie when

he suggests that "the horror" is the name of Kurtz' Intended (that is to say, the name for what he had intended), the text has effectually blurred the distinction between truth and lies, much as it has blurred the distinctions between colonists and conquerors, between savagery and civilization, between men's realities and women's illusions.

If, as has often been claimed, Marlow represents a white, patriarchal, Eurocentric view of late nineteenth-century history,(6) the text suggests, although it does not develop, a perspective on contemporary global politics that is more complex and more problematic than Marlow's. Unlike Marlow's conflation of all historic periods into one universal time and his insistence that Africa mirrors the beginnings of Western civilization, the text marks a specific moment in the European imperialist enterprise, the moment in which late nineteenth-century England, disconcertingly akin to the more overtly ruthless Belgium, was frantically grabbing territory in outlying regions of the world.

Unlike Marlow's erasure of class differences through his creation of an artificially egalitarian community aboard a yacht (in which a plain seaman rubs elbows with a lawyer and a director of companies), the text recognizes that even in the jungle class barriers exist between colonial officials and working men, such as mechanics and boiler-makers.

Further, although Marlow posits an essential and innate ideological difference between men and women, the text recognizes that late-Victorian society assigns very limited roles to women so that, if their social views are unrealistic, it is because they lack education and therefore merely echo male platitudes. In addition, the text briefly notices—in the dress and status of the "savage" woman and in the dialect of her tribe—the particularities of a specific African tribal culture and recognizes that this culture has language and meaning, while observing that these are unreadable to outsiders. Thus Marlow's dying helmsman appears to want to speak but cannot do so to those who do not and will not understand him (119).

Finally, the narrative stipulates that what it arbitrarily

equates with darkness is in fact universal—an ineradicable core of evil in all human beings, whatever their culture of origin. When Marlow observes about modern England, "And this also... has been one of the dark places of the earth" (67), his use of the perfect tense brings his observation into the present.

By the time Marlow ceases to speak to his audience on the "cruising yawl," symbolically the privileged site of the dominant culture, all persons on board must acknowledge that the apparently "tranquil waterway" of modern European history leads "into the heart of an immense darkness" (158), located not only in the outposts of empire but always already within the human breast.

Chapter 7

"The End of the Tether": An Old Man's

Holger Nüstedt (Göttingen)

While it may be a not so very surprising attempt to demonstrate that Joseph Conrad, in order to throw into relief the development of the mostly youthful protagonists of his sea stories, leans rather heavily on the idea of initiation, it must at first sight appear paradox to claim something similar for a man as old as Captain Whalley in "The End of the Tether". For initiation, in simplified terms, is understood to be a phenomenon that exclusively marks the transition of young people from childhood to adulthood in so-called 'primitive' societies and may therefore seem a plausible enough mataphor for a number of changes experienced by young persons in literature, but would appear out of place in connection with a hero in his late sixties.

Yet that is really only correct if the combination of 'initiation' with the development of a literary character is automatically understood to be a thematic one, as has been the case with most critics in the past. If initiation, on the other hand, is taken to be the entire complex of meaningful dramatizations, symbols, and myths it really is – if, in other words, it is taken to be the anthropological concept as a whole rather than the superficial phenomenology of events so termed, then it may offer itself as a ready enough critical tool for the analysis of something more than just a thematic strain, which would result in the detection of yet another story of initiation at best. In the same manner, it can be a versatile artistic device in the hands of an author familiar with its details.

In this latter case, the concept provides, above all, a set of structural and mythico-symbolical parallels with which to create a more poignant picture of various forms of human transitions amounting to a similarly far-reaching and radical existential alteration as does a young person's actual initiation without, however, necessarily being the same.

As this article proposes to show, "The End of the Tether" is a case in point. In this story, Conrad portrays an old man's existential crisis and transformation and to do so, as in all of his sea stories, he makes use of the anthropological concept of initiation as outlined above. For the purpose of this demonstration, a quick glance at the concept itself is unavoidable, though it can only be very briefly sketched out here.

In his seminal book *Les Rites de passage*, Arnold van Gennep2 has demonstrated that the phenomenon of initiation belongs to the larger group of rites of passage, by means of which various occasions in the course of human existence are marked in scriptless societies – such as birth, initiation, engagement, marriage, pregnancy, and death, to mention only the most important ones. All these ritual scenarios have a tripartite basic structure, its elements being *séparation* (separation), *marge* (transition), and *agrégation* (incorporation), and all of them invariably entail an alteration of the social status of the individuals concerned by them, but it is initiation alone that brings about a concomitant existential transmutation of considerable proportions. The function of the above elements or phases may be described as follows:

*The so-called rites of passage [...] are distinguished by formal, and usually very severe, exercises of severance, whereby the mind is radically cut away from the attitudes, attachments, and life patterns of the stage being left behind. Then follows an interval of more or less extended retirement, during which are enacted rituals designed to introduce the life adventurer to the forms and proper feelings of his new estate, so that when, at last, the time has ripened for the return to the normal world, the initiate will be as good as reborn.*3

What is termed "exercises of severance" here, in connection with initiation is more commonly known as the so-called *ordeals,* which comprise various forms of bodily mutilation destined, among other things, to leave the candidate with some unalterable marks indicative of his (or her) new status and often supported in this function by the adoption of a new name, a ritual change of clothes, and the use of a new language in the third phase. The purpose of all this is a full assertion of the initiate as a distinct adult *individual* as opposed to the rather nondescript child he or she has been before.

During the more or less extended middle phase the candidate is isolated away from the rest of the tribe, only accompanied by an initiation helper or mentor, who right from the start guides the novice through all of the rituals and determines their exact time and course as a sort of master of ceremonies, who supplies the novice with food during isolation and whose specific task in this phase is the impartation of "the mores of adult life",4 the "transmission of the tribal lore with its instructions about proper behaviour, both through formalized teaching and through various ritual activities"5 as well as an introduction to the tribe's religious traditions, a revelation of the beliefs, myths, and taboos of the adults. 6 Because of the candidate's ostensible disappearance, this phase usually symbolizes death preceding his rebirth as a different being, which is thought to take place in the third phase.

Like the manifold rites, which show a surprising correspondence throughout the world in totally unrelated societies, the myths accompanying them "make use of a symbolic inventory of initiation which can be found in the mythology of almost every known culture".7 This inventory consists mainly of four universal motifs: (1) *regressus ad uterum,* (2) *descensus ad inferos,* (3) the being swallowed by a monster and the night-sea journey, and (4) the paradoxical passage. While the *regressus ad uterum* illustrates the initiation process as a return to the womb of the great chthonic mother and a subsequent new birth, the *descensus ad inferos* represents it as a descent into the underworld and a victorious and purged return from there. Victorious, because various agencies of the underworld will attempt to hinder the hero from his return just as much as they try to deny him access at the beginning; and while access may be gained by successfully passing a 'threshold adventure', the return is often supported by magic help from other, friendly instances.

As the underworld is both hell and the realm of the dead, the descent into it means the initiate's taking upon himself the trials meant for the dead; as it likewise is the stronghold of knowledge and wisdom, the descent, especially in classical hero myths, is often undertaken to win "the ultimate boon", "the elixir"8 that restores the world. Both previous motifs may also be rediscovered in the third, in which the hero is either swallowed by a monster – often a giant fish or whale – or deliberately throws himself into its throat.

The corresponding myths combine the idea of the hero's sojourn in the belly of the monster, from where he must re-emerge by himself, with that of the monster's west - east movement following the nightly course of the sun, thus making his progress a night-sea journey. Finally, the paradoxical passage, most conspicuously symbolized in the clashing rocks of Jason's voyage in the Argo, represents the idea of overcoming a seemingly insurmountable obstacle. In that way, the notion is illustrated that whoever is to gain passage into another form of being has to achieve what is normally impossible in daily life.

In sum, initiation may be said to be a process of human transformation and development taking place in three steps or stages and effective on three levels: on a psychological level it is a process of individuation, on an interpersonal level a process of socialization, and on a religious level a process of revelation. 9 Its result is an existential alteration so fundamental and radical as to suggest a symbolic visualization in terms of the death of the former, and the rebirth of a renewed human being.

On first encountering Captain Henry Whalley, the central character of "The End of the Tether", the reader finds him in an unmistakable situation of isolation. Whalley, the once successful and daring sailing ship's captain ("Dare-devil Harry Whalley", 167),[10] who has discovered a new passage and given his name to a previously unknown island, seems alone to have been left over from a time in which spirit of enterprise and personal initiative were the most important guarantors of professional success at sea.

At age 67, he has survived most of his contemporaries and, above all, "the conditions that had gone to the making of his name" (176). And he might turn his back on the affairs of an era that knows nothing of his former merits and the respect for his person resulting from them, if he had not lost almost his entire fortune in a bank crash. As things are, however, he is forced to continue his activities and appears like a relic[11] whose friends and benefactors, just like his wife, have long been dead, whose programmatically-named daughter Ivy[12] lives far away in Australia and now, forced by an unhappy stroke of fate, clings to him primarily by means of letters asking for his help. Thus the old sailing ship's captain is as much separated from the people with any meaning to him as from the changed environment of merchant shipping, which is more and more dominated by steamers with a "time-table of appointed routes like a confounded service of tramways" (176).

At the same time, the opening scene of the story opens the reader's eyes to the symbolic frame of the three-phase underground journey in which Conrad allusively envelops his direct events. This frame compresses Whalley's longer development in the *Sofala's* last voyage – a development which is also subdivided into three distinct phases, extends over fairly exactly three years, and is presented in its entirety only by means of a number of selective flashbacks. Elements of this frame are the way up the river darkened by the overgrowing jungle, the arrival late in the evening and the stopover at the leg's end as well as the opposite passage back to the open sea – and also the *serang's* decisive support for Whalley in the initial crossing of the mud bar outside the mouth of the river, which may be understood as assistance in the passing of an almost literal threshold adventure and which, therefore, also provides an early hint at the activity of helper figures in this narrative. Other characters with a similar role as that of the *serang* are the harbor-master Eliott, who unknowingly saves Whalley by telling him about the shipowner-engineer Massy and his difficulties in finding a captain for his steamer; Mr. Van Wyk, who will still have to be considered more closely; and finally Massy himself.

In his case this function appears to be most perplexing, for at a glance he is mainly a failure and a gambler at that, albeit one favored by fortune more than once. Nevertheless his significance for Whalley is tantamount to that of a mentor in real rites – not as an instructor and an immediate helper, but the more effectively as a kind of master of ceremonies who exerts a decisive influence on the course of events and finally also as the one who, again unintentionally, helps Whalley to have a guiding insight.

At the end of his steamer's leg into the jungle of Borneo Whalley meets another *isolato* in the person of Mr. Van Wyk. This young Dutchman, who has retired from his former surroundings because of a disappointment in love and has acquired wealth and the respect of the natives as a tobacco planter in the loneliness of the jungle, thus forms a parallel to Whalley's situation, though one which is not fully elaborated but only indicated. 13 Above all, however, two analogies appear on an anthropological and a mythological plane, which assign a helper status to him, too.

On the one hand he invites Whalley to dinner in his house on the latter's arrival, thus giving him food in the middle phase of his journey just like the mentors in real scenarios; 14 on the other hand he averts the greatest danger which might hinder Whalley from returning from his underground journey by vaguely promising the first officer Sterne to make him captain of the *Sofala* on her next round trip if he will keep silent until then. For the mate has discovered Whalley's secret – he is gradually losing his eyesight – and in his eager ambition is only waiting for an opportunity to push Whalley out of his office, if possible even before leaving Van Wyk's jetty.

Furthermore, Van Wyk's role is confirmed by the fact that Captain Whalley himself chooses him as a kind of confessor to whom he entrusts his hidden misfortune. It is true, though, that the relative positions of both men and their relationship with each other forbid an immediately advising and helping activity of the planter to result from this fact; rather, the latter has to limit himself to paving Whalley's way behind his back by preventing Sterne's intrigue, of which the old captain has no suspicion as yet.

Together with this inventory for an initiation-like change as becoming visible in the story, a status resembling that of a novice can be discerned in the old captain though it must seem paradox at first sight. Yet Whalley has made a completely new beginning in an age not his own and now commands a steamer for the first time in his life. Furthermore he is never described as an actually old man but rather as someone firmly planted in the midst of life ("He was at home in life", 171) or, allusively, even at its beginning – he himself playfully calls his fifty years at sea "a pretty thorough *apprenticeship*" (167, italics added).

And also physically Whalley does not appear really old: "No single betraying fold or line of care disfigured the reposeful modelling of his face" (187), his glance is even "like a boy's" (187), and his frame conveys an impression of strength and vitality. 15 All in all, he thus seems to be exempt from the natural chronology of life: "Time – after, indeed, marking him for its own – had given him up to his usefulness" (298). This condition is also reflected by Whalley's own feelings about life: "[he] met, as it were incidentally, the thought of death. He pushed it aside with dislike and contempt. He almost laughed at it; and in the unquenchable vitality of his age only thought with a kind of exultation how little he needed to keep body and soul together" (214). 16

The three stages in Captain Whalley's development, which have been mentioned above, are spread irregularly over the time of his command of the *Sofala* and become shorter in gradual succession. The first, beginning with the conclusion of the contract, seems to be the longest although it is not possible to determine its exact duration from the text. It causes Whalley's final separation from his former societal ties and his definition of a new and absolute goal. The second stage is characterized by the captain's progressing blindness and can thus be identified as a parallel to the middle section of many anthropological scenarios, which symbolizes initiatory death. The final stage comprises no more than the few moments, on the way from Van Wyk's jetty to Pangu Bay, between the *serang's* increasing insecurity about the overdue sight of land and the Sofala's stranding, which includes Whalley's final transition.

New Beginning

The reason why Whalley himself intensely feels his own isolation is mainly to be seen in the necessity for him to return from a half-begun retirement, in which his continued merchant voyages in his own barque *Fair Maid* only served as a pastime, 17 back to serious work for a living. This return, then, also marks the beginning of his separation from his former life in a manner perceptible for himself. 18 Another call for help from his daughter, whose husband has failed in business first and then has been confined to a wheelchair for good, finally even forces Whalley to sell the *Fair Maid*.

That is the only way in which he can meet Ivy's request with part of the proceeds. The larger part he invests in a partnership with the engineer Massy, whose steamer *Sofala* he commands from now on. Thus he wants to earn his living and at the same time preserve the small remainder of his fortune, a mere five hundred pounds, and if necessary secure it for Ivy in full.

The disposal of the barque is a distinct turning-point after which the captain is finally and radically separated from his former life:

What to the other parties was merely the sale of a ship was to him a momentous event involving a radically new view of existence. He knew that after this ship there would be no other; and the hopes of his youth, the exercise of his abilities, every feeling and achievement of his manhood, had been indissolubly connected with ships. He had served ships; he had owned ships; and even the years of his actual retirement from the sea had been made bearable by the idea that he had only to stretch out his hand full of money to get a ship. He had been at liberty to feel as though he were the owner of all the ships in the world. The selling of this one was weary work; but when she passed from him at last, when he signed the last receipt, it was as though all the ships had gone out of the world together, leaving him on the shore of inaccessible oceans [...]. (184-85)

This separation completes the picture of the man isolated for the purpose of an existential transformation that has already become discernible and consequently forms the real beginning of the captain's development as noticeable in the story. As with Marlow in "Youth", it comprises the spheres of individuation, socialization and revelation, which, however, take a partly inverted turn in Whalley's case.

Through his partnership with Massy, Whalley's detachment is further enhanced as he has to work in a steamship he little likes and as his seeming arrogance as a ship's commander sets him apart not only in the eyes of the engineer harassed by inferiority complexes. In truth, however, his behaviour results from two causes which emphasize his isolation. On the one hand, he continues to observe a professional code determined by meticulous correctness and conscientiousness, which has become obsolete and conveys to the people around him an impression of presumptuous pedantry; on the other hand, he concentrates the greater part of his energies on an attempt to circumvent the consequences of a reverse of fortune that struck him shortly before the beginning of the story's events and leads to his refusal to prolong the expiring partnership contract with Massy as intended.

The discovery of his diminishing eyesight and the additional, in some respects total separation from the world surrounding him which is preparing through it at the same time jeopardize his life plan, revised on entering into commitment with Massy in an absolute trust in his unbroken vitality and now aimed primarily at self-realization as a father standing up for his child at any time. And they also mean giving up his own moral values, strictly adhered to during his entire lifetime. For Whalley has to conceal his affliction since otherwise Massy would be entitled to keep his share for another year after the expiration of the contract – too long to survive without income and to entrust himself to Ivy's care in time, who could not keep him without a financial contribution of his own.

Therefore he tries to continue commanding the *Sofala*, relying on the eyes of the Malay boatswain whom he has brought on board with him. In so doing, however, he irresponsibly imperils the ship and her crew, as is proved by the hair's breadth crossing of the bar outside the Batu Beru River. And since perfection in his professional skills, correctness, and absolute integrity have so far been among Whalley's most outstanding characteristics, 19 what becomes visible behind his desperate deception is also the continuing disappearance of his former personality, which has begun as early as his resumption of serious work with the *Fair Maid*.

To begin with, the transformation of the old captain shows only superficially in his abandonment of life-long habits. He denies himself good cigars, for which he has a soft spot, 20 and no longer drinks any wine21 so as to use as little money for himself as possible and to be able to go on relieving his daughter. Not later than the sale of his own ship meant to be his "last command" (170), however, we see the beginning of the direct disintegration of his former self; 22 it continues with the conclusion of the contract with Massy23 and escalates into the total loss of his own past and of his life's achievement. 24

At the same time Whalley in this phase redefines his purpose in life by now understanding himself as a father living and working exclusively for Ivy's support: "As it happens, my life is necessary; it isn't my own, it isn't – God knows" (292), he declares to Mr. Van Wyk during one of their meetings. 25

Visitation

When his eyesight begins to fade, the old captain enters into a new stage corresponding to the middle phase of many initiation rituals. The darkness which increasingly surrounds him and the intensified isolation which it entails, in ritual contexts often symbolize initiatory death or the embryonic state as a preliminary stage of a renewed existence.26 Because of the slow progress of the blindness, it is the second variant which here offers itself as an obvious parallel, with which Whalley's perception of his own state as a "living grave" (328) is in perfect keeping. Just as much, the fact that Whalley can see less and less may be understood as a reminiscence of anthropological prohibitions to see, which occur quite often and also become effective in the middle phase. 27 Finally, Whalley's handicap is also remotely in parallel with initiatory wounds: even before discovering the truth, Massy observes a change in Whalley, who appears weakened to him, "as though he had received a secret wound" (272). And doubtlessly blindness represents, just like those real injuries or their ensuing scarves, an unalterable bodily mark.

At the same time, blindness as a very salient symbol also stands for intensified mental seeing, and that is also true for Captain Whalley: "You begin to see a lot of things when you are going blind" (300), he says to Van Wyk during his confession, and the narrator in another passage makes a similar comment: "In the steadily darkening universe a sinister clearness fell upon his ideas" (324). Thus, also the ground for new insights has been prepared for the man who has meanwhile been characterized several times as resembling a neophyte.

In this phase the constant waning of his former personality goes hand in hand with a changing view of life and of men in the old captain, which is exclusively caused by his diminishing strength of vision and leaves him isolated, not only physically as before, but more and more spiritually so, too. At the beginning he has a "large, tolerating certitude" (289) both regarding human nature28 and the state of the world as caused by men. 29 And Van Wyk's reflection makes it clear that this is not an unfounded, naive optimism: "With all his trust in mankind he was no fool; the serenity of his temper at the end of so many years, since it could not obviously have been appeased by success, wore an air of profound wisdom" (290).

But Whalley's composed certitude is more and more hollowed out by his progressing blindness ("this — visitation", 301) and his accompanying fear of discovery until it finally turns into its opposite: "In the illuminating moments of suffering he saw life, men, things, the whole earth with all her burden of created nature, as he had never seen them before" (324).

It is true that this is not a very precise description of his new point of view, but faced with his formerly optimistic perspective, his attitude must necessarily have adopted a negative quality. 30 In addition, Whalley's apprehensive insecurity results in a situation where, "as if in a nightmare of humiliation, every featureless man seemed an enemy" (303). Paradoxically, only the *Sofala* is excepted from this fear, the formerly disliked steamship31 that now becomes his "last friend": "he was not afraid of her; he knew every inch of her deck; [...]" (303).

This observation, therefore, proves that it is not only Whalley's attitude towards men that has changed, an aspect which may in a way be attributed to the sphere of an inverted individuation, but that an inverted socialization has equally taken place, by which the captain has been completely secluded from the human society around him. It is true that this process arises more or less inevitably from Whalley's visitation, that he does not turn away from society on the grounds of an act of will prompted by critical refusal; yet at the same time there are also hints of social rejection, at least with regard to his immediate microcosm. For one thing there is Sterne's attempt to oust him from office, which, if successful, would amount to a direct de-socialization; and for another there is the hateful attitude of the owner of the *Sofala*.

Massy feels wrongfully taken advantage of by his captain who is not willing to renew the expiring contract and much less willing to invest in the ship that badly needs new boilers an additional part of the fortune Massy supposes to be his. When the engineer leaves the captain's cabin after his penultimate attempt to persuade Whalley, therefore, "he enveloped in the same hatred the ship with the worn-out boilers and the man with the dimmed eyes. [...] The old fraud! He longed to kick him out" (321). But Massy is crafty enough to keep that waiting, though he, too, has found out Whalley's secret some time ago. And this confirms his function as the one who ultimately decides on the captain's path.

Whalley's attitude towards life likewise changes in the course of this phase. It turns from his former positive hope for a long life useful to his daughter to a definitive death wish: "I was ready for her sake to live forever. I half believed I would. I've been praying for death since" (301-02).

Finally, Whalley's religious attitude undergoes a far-reaching change in this phase. The man who formerly, in a simple devoutness, believed firmly in the benevolent guidance of his fate by a kindly God[32] begins increasingly to realise – but cannot accept – that this God seems to turn against him. On becoming aware of his gradually progressing blindness he first feels as if God had abandoned him[33], so that his prayers, formerly a matter of course to him,[34] seem to lose their meaning: "He lived on without any help, human or divine. The very prayers stuck in his throat. What was there to pray for?" (302).

This feeling is intensified by the fact that even his hope for deliverance from his troubles, for "a manner of going out of which he need not be ashamed" (291) is not fulfilled: "death seemed as far as ever" (303), although "he had prayed for death till the prayers had stuck in his throat" (324-25). At last this impression clarifies into a certainty of divine punishment, against which he rebels[35] because he feels it to be incompatible with his loving care for his daughter, which, in his understanding, is ordained by the same God ("I suppose the blessed know the secret of God's dealings with His created children. [...] I don't. I know only the child He has given me", 304) and because it appears unjust to him in spite of his beginning insight into some misguided behaviour on his own part: "The punishment was too great for a little presumption, for a little pride" (324).

Ultima ratio

The once more accelerated final part in the transformation Whalley undergoes before the reader's eye is limited to the time after the *Sofala* has regained the open sea. As far as the symbolic frame of the underground journey is concerned, it may be significant that Whalley brings nothing back with him – no 'elixir' that could renew the world and no certitude of personal salvation either –, so that the outlines of a failure of his journey begin to appear.

Nevertheless the ship reaches the open sea unharmed; Whalley, with the help of his *serang*, first overcomes a number of obstacles which are put in his way in the shape of rocks hardly awash – but which he knows just as well as his assistant – before he ultimately fails because of another one which Massy sets up by deliberately deflecting the ship's compass. In this way the latter expects an 'unproblematic' running aground which would put him in possession of the insurance money and rid him of his permanent worries about the ship; and he would no longer have to show any consideration for a partner, whose blindness he has also discovered, it is true, but which he has not as yet employed to blackmail him because he has for some time been toying with the idea of using it to have Whalley appear quasi automatically responsible for a premeditated shipwreck.

In falsifying the *Sofala's* course by means of his jacket hung up near the compass with iron parts in its pockets, Massy confirms his role as a 'mentor' who ultimately determines the course of events on Whalley's way. While, through him, the steamer gets caught in reef-infested waters, an imminent conclusion of events seems to be indicated by the fact that the still unsuspecting Whalley's thoughts wander back to the past after dwelling for a while on the ship's name. 36 He remembers his daughter's childhood, the hopes he and his wife had for her, and begins to long for her love – in other words, in his heart of hearts to hope urgently for a successful sustaining of his deception until the end of his present voyage, which would bring him to her together with the money invested in the *Sofala* and would thus also mean self-realization as a father.

Simultaneously, the *serang* is more and more alarmed at not being able to make the overdue landfall. And when he finally asks the captain, "Tuan, do you see anything of the land?" (328), he pushes him headlong into his final crisis:

The horror of incertitude had seized upon Captain Whalley, the miserable mistrust of men, of things – of the very earth. He had steered that very course thirty-six times by the same compass – if anything was certain in this world it was its absolute, unerring correctness. Then what had happened? Did the Serang lie? Why lie? Why? Was he going blind, too? (328)

What is remarkable here is Captain Whalley's fear-stricken insecurity as a reflection of certain forms of ritual frightening found in many anthropological scenarios as a preliminary to the initiation proper and meant to cause insecurity concerning the oncoming events. The same effect has already become visible in the captain before: "Sometimes he was seized with a sudden vertigo and an overwhelming terror [...]" (324); its repetition in the present situation clearly points to an increasingly critical development of events. Furthermore, the crisis-like quality of the situation is given prominence by the fact that Whalley is irresolute for the first time and that, again for the first time in the story, he thinks of giving up:

Captain Whalley steadied the trembling of his limbs by an effort. Should he stop the engines at once and give himself away? A gust of irresolution swayed all sorts of bizarre notions in his mind. The unusual had come, and he was not fit to deal with it. (328-29)

Yet the thought of Ivy makes him stick to his "falsehood" (324) yet another time as if in a last desperate effort ("No, he must not give himself away after having gone so far for her sake", 329) – a "falsehood" into which he had initially drifted rather unwittingly because of his increasing blindness, downright unable and unwilling to believe in such a stroke of fate. 37 But when his groping hands touch Massy's iron-laden jacket and cause it to fall to the ground in his attempt to bend far forward and read the compass himself, he gives up once and for all: "Captain Whalley fell on his knees, with groping hands extended in a frank gesture of blindness" (329). With this gesture and his subsequent rush to stop the engines he makes plainly visible for everybody in his vicinity what he has so far kept secret: "He ran himself – hands forward, a blind man" (329).

All the same, he is at least spared the humiliation of this

disclosure, for the ship simultaneously hits a reef at full speed. The impact, reiterated because of the ship's speed and her unstopped engines, devastates the superstructures and leaves Captain Whalley, bleeding and with torn clothes, in a heap of debris:

Captain Whalley picked himself up and stood knee-deep in wreckage, torn, bleeding, knowing the nature of the danger he had escaped mostly by the sound [...] (330)

Thus, his outward appearance shows the typical signs reminiscent of initiatory wounds and a ritual change of clothes, which point to a transformation of a corresponding nature. The same effect is achieved by the cloud of steam resembling a white fog (a symbol of transition) that shrouds the *Sofala's* deck and, consequently, the captain: "the ship had gone clear of the reef and lay still, with a heavy cloud of steam issuing from the broken deck-pipes, and vanishing in wispy shapes into the night" (330); however, the fleetingness of this 'fog' indicates that the event symbolized by it cannot be fully equated with what it usually stands for, thus pointing to a special form of transformation or passage which does not happen for the rest of life in the generally accepted meaning, but will immediately dissolve into nothing without leaving any traces.

After these events, Whalley's thoughts for the moment appear surprisingly clear and his previous insecurity seems to have yielded completely. He instantly knows where the steamer is at that moment ("Amongst the reefs to the eastward", 331) and seems to have a clear-cut idea of what he wants to do – his order to the first officer shows that he does not intend to save himself: "Boats, Sterne.

Even one will save *you all* in this calm" (331, italics added). This somewhat premature hint – the insight occasioning his plan only comes to Whalley some time later – certainly makes him appear sure of his intentions again and therefore must have prompted Conrad to insert it here, but it is inconsistent with his following behaviour towards Massy. For when the latter, losing his head, implores him to keep his manipulation of the compass to himself, the captain is initially filled with feelings of revenge ("Mr. Massy, you shall get five years for this", 331) – which, however, he will only be able to realise if he saves himself, too. It is only when the shipowner, in the following argument, confronts him with his own subsequent exposure and points out that he will achieve nothing in this way, the insurance money and consequently his own investment intended for Ivy getting lost forever, that Whalley gets a clear picture of what will ultimately determine his actions:

Again he had a flash of insight. He was indeed at the end of his tether. (332) Whalley is further encouraged in his decision born from this insight ("I shall stay on board", 332) by a final religious perception. While as yet he has never stopped hoping his impression as to his growing blindness might be wrong or that he could protect himself from the consequences by denying its existence,[38] he now becomes aware with an irrefutable and revelation-like clearness that "God had not listened to his prayers" (333).

In realizing his decision – he puts the iron parts Massy had used to deflect the compass into his own pockets and lets himself be pulled down by the sinking steamer – Whalley, then, finally turns away from a society and a divine order of the world by which he finds himself abandoned and cornered since they apparently would not let him achieve his life's aim. And as he can perceive no other way out, he chooses what from his point of view is the last possible and at the same time the most radical form of abandonment that can be imagined, suicide.

But it is only by appearance that he thus draws an absolutely unavoidable conclusion; on closer inspection, his thoughts reveal that in the choice of his course he is exclusively following a *personal* moral code that allows of no alternative: "it was unseemly that a Whalley who had gone so far to carry a point should continue to live. He must pay the price" (333) – 'the price' is self-imposed, not one which the world with which he is at variance exacts from him. Therefore, his step remains a deliberate and willed abandonment, for it is only 'a Whalley' who is not suited for this world.

Conclusion

At the same time, however, the price paid by Whalley may also be objectively seen as such since his action likewise amounts to a sacrificial death. 39 Thus, a structural shift of the story's events becomes evident as compared with the pattern underlying it. For, other than in actual anthropological surroundings, where the passage into another form of existence is the final step after a completed transformation, Captain Whalley's final passage is at the same time still part of his development because it unexpectedly makes possible his self-realization: Only because he does not adhere to his initial idea of revenge and therefore cannot be exposed in his own reprehensible behaviour, can the court examining the accident attribute it to an unusual set of the current and exonerate the captain from any fault. In consequence, not only is his reputation kept intact, but the insurance becomes payable, too, ensuring that his share invested in the *Sofala* falls to his daughter 40 as he had always wanted it to do.

Moreover, Whalley's sacrificial death parallels the idea contained in many initiation myths of the necessity of self-destruction as a precondition for entrance into another, purified form of existence. What is only symbolically imagined there, however, in a way takes place in reality in his case. He literally destroys himself by going down with the steamer, and the form of his death with its inherent symbolism of a supreme baptism at the same time evinces a kind of rebirth. So he, too, experiences the most radical change of his existence that can be imagined and will thereafter – if only in people's memories – endure 'purged' by the court's judgement. The tarnish of deception thus has forever been kept away from his name, and Massy will never be able to confide to anybody Whalley's secret discovered by him – unless he wants to do what is unthinkable in a man of his disposition, risk his own share of the insurance money even after collecting it.

Chapter 8

Heart of Darkness and Apocalypse Now: A Comparative Analysis of Novella and Film

In the opening scenes of the documentary film "Hearts of Darkness-A Filmmaker's Apocalypse," Eleanor Coppola describes her husband Francis's film, "Apocalypse Now," as being "loosely based" on Joseph Conrad's Heart of Darkness. Indeed, "loosely" is the word; the period, setting, and circumstances of the film are totally different from those of the novella. The question, therefore, is whether any of Conrad's classic story of savagery and madness is extant in its cinematic reworking. It is this question that I shall attempt to address in this brief monograph by looking more closely at various aspects of character, plot, and theme in each respective work.

The story of Heart of Darkness is narrated by its central character, the seasoned mariner Marlowe, a recurring figure in Conrad's work. "Apocalypse Now" features a corollary to Marlowe in Captain Willard, a U.S. Army special forces operative assigned to go up the Nung river from Viet Nam into Cambodia in order to "terminate the command" of one Colonel Walter Kurtz whom, he is told, has gone totally insane.

It is fitting that Marlowe's character should be renamed, as Willard differs from Marlowe in several significant ways: 1) He is not the captain of the boat which takes him and a party of others up the river; 2) He does not reflect the deep psychological and philosophical insights that are a signal feature in Marlowe's character, and 3) He is sent on his mission specifically to kill Kurtz, unlike Marlowe who is simply piloting others in the capacity of captain of a steamboat. However, Willard does communicate Marlowe's fascination (growing, in fact that he holds the rank of captain, tying in with Marlowe's occupation.

As to the character of Kurtz, it is worth noting that while significant discrepancies exist between the depictions of Conrad and Coppola, the basic nature of the man remains fairly similar. The idea of company man turned savage, of a brilliant and successful team-player, being groomed by "the Company" for greater things, suddenly gone native, is perfectly realized in both novella and film. In the film, Kurtz is portrayed by Marlon Brando, the father of American method actors, who lends weight (both physically and dramatically) to the figure of the megalomaniacal Kurtz.

Brando's massive girth is all the more ironic for those familiar with Heart of Darkness who recall Conrad's description: "I could see the cage of his ribs all astir, the bones of his arms waving. It was as though an animated image of death carved out of old ivory had been shaking its hand with menaces at a motionless crowd of men..." [1]. One could speculate that Coppola's Kurtz is a graphic analogy of the bloated American war machine dominating and perverting the innocent montegnards of Cambodia; however, after viewing Eleanor Coppola's documentary, one finds that the casting was more based on a combination of Coppola's wanting to work weight problem. (It should also be noted that the cult-like following of Kurtz in Sharer (New York: Doubleday & Co., 1978), p. 135,

Heart of Darkness is brilliantly and subtly updated by Coppola in a foreshadowing scene in which missives to Willard from headquarters are intercut with scenes of newspaper clippings about Charles (Manson.)

Also present in Cappola's film is the loveable, addle-headed harlequin/fool figure who meets Marlowe's boat upon arrival at Kurtz's station. This role is rendered in grand, demented style by Dennis Hopper, replete with a plethora of cameras (he is an American photojournalist) to update his fool's motley. Much of his dialogue is taken directly from Conrad, although his character does not flee the scene as does his doppelganger in Heart of Darkness.

Regarding plot, as stated earlier, Coppola's rendering of Heart of Darkness diverges wildly from Conrad. Conrad's story depicts a turn of the century riverboat captain transporting members of an unnamed "Company," an ivory trading concern, up a snake-like river winding its way into relieve him of his independently-stockpiled ivory. The Company has judged Kurtz to be a renegade whose methods are "unsound." Coppola's film gives us Willard, an Army captain who is sent by Army intelligence up a similar river in Viet Nam to kill a certain Colonel Kurtz. Again, Colonel Kurtz is considered by the parties in charge to be insane, his methods unsound (a direct dialogue echo from the text.)

This last fact, however, that Willard is from the beginning an assassin, is a fundamental difference between the film and the book. It changes the whole psychological dynamic between that of Marlowe and Kurtz. In Conrad, Marlowe is in awe of Kurtz, comes to identify with him in some dark recess of his own psyche; Willard, on the other hand, is more impressed with Kurtz's credentials than moved by his force of mind and will. His mission to kill Kurtz gives him some measure of pause, but his military protocol mentality ultimately rules the day.

Compared with Marlowe's deep, searching ruminations on the dark, enigmatic Kurtz, Willard is a government-issue automaton. Add to this the fact that the first two thirds of the movie "Apocalyp0se Now" are concerned with the Viet Nam war and have absolutely nothing to do with the plot of heart of Darkness, and it seems as if there is an unmendable rift between the film and its purported inspiration. To be fair, however, it is important to mention that the two plots do converge at the point just before the boat parties arrive at Kurtz's station, when a thick fog envelops each boat and a rain of arrows showers down on the passengers. From here we witness the death of the black helmsman by a spear, the greeting of the fool figure, and, finally the meeting with the mad Kurtz. Which brings us to the question of theme. The dominant theme of Heart of Darkness is man's vulnerability to his own darker nature and the various ways in which this terrible, savage, proto-man can be unleashed; power, the jungle, "the Company," all serve as catalysts for the emergence of this hidden, voracious id-thing within us all, most realized in Kurtz.

In "Apocalypse Now," Coppola is right on target in exploring this theme, his choice of Viet Nam in the sixties providing all the requisite elements: power, the jungle, and "the Company" are all present, the latter being represented by the U.S. Army, or perhaps the U.S.A. as a whole.

This last touch is ingenious, as it calls up a whole series of speculations regarding the various forms of imperialism. In Conrad, set at the turn of the century, the imperialism is traditional, overt. In Coppola, the U.S. presence is just as overt, yet the pretense upon which it is based is more ideological, geopolitical.

Both situations provide the possibility for endless abuse of power by foreigners in a primitive jungle setting, a setting which tends to bend their minds and release their dormant savage energies. Heart of Darkness depicts gun-crazy members of "the Company" firing wildly upon anything and everything as they progress up the river. Likewise the men in the PBR in "Apocalypse Now," even more so, in fact, due to the circumstances of the Viet Nam war.

The ultimate extreme of man's dark side, as explored in Conrad and Coppola, is madness. The embodiment of this madness is Kurtz, and it is explored more thoroughly, in fact, in Coppola. One might argue that no credit is to be given to Coppola for this, that so many men went mad in Viet Nam, that the war was madness itself.

But the way in which Kurtz's madness is portrayed must be examined: the way Brando is filmed in perpetual half-shadow, as if darkness is pouring over him in some black ooze; the strange, nonsensical yet at the same time compelling ruminations he shares with Willard; the scene in which he beheads one of Willard's men and presents the trophy to

Willard in full camouflage make-up. These are examples of the filmmaker's craft and should not be overlooked.

To sum up, the question must be answered as to whether Conrad's Heart of Darkness has survived the passage of seventy-five years and a cinematic treatment by Francis Ford Coppola, I would say yes, in its basic thematic elements, it has. Much has changed, but the basic feel of the novella, the brooding, mysterious jungle energy, its maddening influence over those who would try to tame it, and Kurtz, whose soul went mad, whose last words were "The horror, the horror," all remain relatively in tact. I wonder what Conrad would have thought.

Chapter 9

A Personal Remembrance as Metafiction

Joseph Conrad wrote three novels in collaboration with Ford Madox Ford: The Inheritors (1901); Romance, A Novel (1903); and The Nature of a Crime (1909, 1924). Each of them has a metafictional thrust in it, varying from plotting a suicide to collaborating on the writing of a biography of Oliver Cromwell. These metafictional moments seem inevitable in works that were the product of two writers who incessantly discussed with each other every aspect of the writing of fiction.

What happened in their life together, appropriately enough, made its way into their fiction. And their metafictional quality makes these novels more interesting to modern readers than they would otherwise be. This metafictional matrix also adds a dimension to Ford's Joseph Conrad: A Personal Remembrance (1924). Its major action is the quest for the New Form of the novel.

This is a heroic quest that grew out of Ford's and Conrad's conviction that "the only occupation fitting for a proper man in these centuries is the writing of novels" (Remembrance 186) because great works of art... put their fingers upon the disease spots of nations or describe the diseases of civilisations. A great work of art is a precise diagnosis of human estates, and this is why great works of art are so frequently disliked. They are passionless; they state without comment; and, just as we dread the surgeon who declares that we are doomed by a mortal disease, so we dread the writer who tells us dispassionately what is the matter with us.

This dangerous quest for the truth and a form in which to render it is as heroic as any task one can undertake and confers immortality on the writer who succeeds. Why? Because "a great talent occupies itself with the deep places of the mind and frames its projections of those secrets in projections of kingdoms that are the kingdoms not merely of to-day" (Thus 95). So although the writer must die, the work need not. The Elizabethan poets and dramatists, more than anyone else in the English tradition, have made this, indisputably, a fact of literary life.

The quality of permanence in Conrad's work, consequently, led Ford to present him as an Elizabethan poet. Ford also shows that Conrad felt that plays like The Duchess of Malfi and Hamlet read like novels and that playwrights like Webster and Shakespeare- "the greatest novelist as a delineator of character" (62)-wrote like novelists. So Conrad's business, like theirs, was to hypnotize his audience into "seeing moonlight, laurel hedges, palaces, cracks in walls or forest glades" when on the bare page and on the bare stage none of these things were to be found (March 468). And, as with the Elizabethans, "the human heart as recorded in Mr. Conrad's pages is the human heart of an immense number of men in all ages and in all climes" (94). Ford's memoir is inescapably of a piece with his earlier and later essays about his collaborator because they too show Conrad to be an Elizabethan poet writing modern fiction.

The Inheritors and The Nature of a Crime lead inevitably to Joseph Conrad: A Personal Remembrance where Conrad steps forth as an "Elizabethan Gentleman Adventurer." Like that memoir each of these novels is metafictional in its rendering of a writer's adventures. The Inheritors (1901), for instance, has a struggling writer as its central character. Arthur Echingham Granger is an impoverished aristocrat who wants to be a novelist in the Jamesian tradition. But he gets involved in puffing the powerful and promoting their interests in a literary atmosphere of writers and their sponsors, collaborators and editors, critics and publishers2-publishers who found journals like the Hour to serve the financial interests of men like the Duc de Mersch. Granger, aligned with this group, betrays them for the love of an unloving Fourth Dimensionist ("Fate" is the name she gives herself) who wipes out their world by using him to implement the plot she constructs to destroy them.

It involves Granger's betraying his honour for her love and destroying himself as a writer in the process. He loses the world of the past and has no place in the world of the future. He fails to achieve the artistic integrity of Jenkins, a painter who never makes his fortune but whose work is unimpeachably his own. And he fails to achieve the artistic acumen of Lea, a critic whose sense of merit is unswayed by fad or funds. The whole of the novel indicts the "System for the Regeneration of the Arctic Regions" as a replay of the Congo Free State;3 and de Mersch is the scoundrel behind the one as King Leopold was the "vampire" behind the other (Portraits 65).

This is a subject that obviously interested the author of Heart of Darkness; and although Conrad wrote very little of The Inheritors-perhaps two thousand of its seventy-five thousand words at most-Ford is explicit in A Personal Remembrance about Conrad's making it a much better book: he gave "to each scene a final tap; these, in a great many cases, brought the whole meaning of the scene to the reader's mind" (144).4 And Conrad's engagement with The Inheritors had the further happy result of turning his attention to "political and revolutionary subjects," which he explored with great success in the writing of The Secret Agent and Under Western Eyes as well as in Nostromo.

When we think about The Inheritors today in the context of the Ford/Conrad collaboration, the novel's metafictional aspects outweigh its interest as a political roman a clef in its own day.6 Granger's betrayal of his honour is acute because he and Churchill, a fundamentally decent politician, agree to collaborate on the writing of The Life of Cromwell. Churchill is already well along with the project when he invites Granger to be part of it. Granger's betrayal of Churchill for the love of Fate, who presents herself as his "sister"-his betrayal, then, of friendship for incest-also takes place as a collaboration. Her plot knocks out the past and brings in the future. Both of these collaborations-the honorable as well as the dishonorable one-bear some of the marks of the Ford/Conrad collaboration. For Conrad was better at the structure and plotting of novels (at what Ford called "architectonics"') and Ford was better at realizing a plot in colloquial English (at making "prose seem like the sound of someone talking"8).

Echingham Granger helps execute the schemes laid down by Churchill in his Cromwell and by Fate in her plot to bring down Churchill's government. And we note, furthermore, how the plot of The Inheritors, with its "worm at the very heart of the rose" (319), is like Conrad's plots in which the centre cannot hold. The Greenland scheme reminds us of something insubstantial on which everyone and everything depends, like the San Tome mine in Nostromo or the attack on the Greenwich Observatory in The Secret Agent.

And Granger, though inherently more capable than they, reminds us of such pawns as Donkin's hapless James Wait in The Nigger of the "Narcissus" and Verloc's feebleminded Stevie in The Secret Agent. Almayer's folly is rewritten in de Mersch's folly as the heart of darkness moves from the tropics to the Arctic.

The Inheritors, then, not only can be read as metafiction; it is best read as metafiction. It reminds us that Ford's collaboration with Conrad so intensely preoccupied his imagination that he more or less consciously made it the subtext of this novel. The same thing happened in The Nature of a Crime. Conrad said it was "fantastic" that he and Ford could "have believed, for a moment, that a piece of work in the nature of an analytical confession... could have been developed and achieved in collaboration!" (Nature 6). Yet, although Conrad wrote even less of it than he did of The Inheritors, he agreed to its publication under both his and Hueffer's names.

The unnamed narrator of The Nature of a Crime is an embezzler-a master of plots-whose masterplot can continue only if the unnamed woman to whom he writes will continue to talk and write to him. This is analogous to the Ford/Conrad collaboration. Conrad can continue as a novelist if Ford is there for him. More than anything else, Ford was important to Conrad as someone to speak to, as someone to listen to him.' The collaboration led, as Bernard Meyer remarked, to a "broader emotional attachment" between them. The result of this for Conrad was inspiring: it animated his career in the most dramatic way.

The result of this "broader emotional attachment" was Ford's "quasi-catalytic effect upon Conrad's creative energy." During what Meyer calls the "Hueffer decade" Conrad wrote "Heart of Darkness," Lord Jim, Nostromo, The Secret Agent, A Personal Record, "The Secret Sharer," Under Western Eyes, "Falk," "Amy Foster," "The End of the Tether"-virtually all of his finest work. Meyer thinks it is questionable whether Conrad alone, without Ford's moral support, "would have possessed the daring to explore man's `forgotten and bestial instincts' with the audacity manifested by him during the `Hueffer decade."' (Brebach, Making 29)

That judgment gains weight when we remember that Ford helped Conrad with the ending of "Heart of Darkness";10 wrote half of a chapter of Nostromo (Part II, Chapter V, "The Isabels")11 when Conrad was too depressed to do so for T P's Weekly; provided Conrad with the plot of The Secret Agent and details on anarchists for Under Western Eyes;12 gave Conrad the idea for A Personal Record, took dictation for it and published it as "Some Reminiscences" in the English Review;13 took down parts of The Mirror of the Sea in shorthand;14 carried out "book surgery" on The Rescue;15 encouraged Conrad's work on Chance, which profited from their previous work on The Nature of a Crime;16 provided Conrad with the germ for "Amy Foster,"" and helped him rewrite "The End of the Tether" when parts of the original perished in a fire.18 Ford also helped Conrad dramatize his story "Tomorrow," which was performed as One Day More at the Royal Theatre in June 1905.19

What the embezzler/plotter in The Nature of a Crime does in his letters to his beloved/collaborator is discuss in detail the making of plots and the drawing of character. He does so by revealing how he has embezzled money from the estate of his ward, Edward Burden, and how, when chance saves him from suicide, he will return that money. In a word, he tells her how he cooked the books and how, now, he is going to uncook them. His plot is Conradian in its use of a centre that cannot hold. The plot's centre is the embezzler-his accounts are about to be audited and the scheme by which he enriched himself is about to be exposed-who will kill himself by biting into a poison ring. This does not happen, however, because Edward Burden decides that it would be ungenerous to submit his gentlemanlike guardian to such an ungentlemanly act. So Burden lifts the burden of the unnamed narrator's having to kill himself.

Now Burden himself has led a double-life. About to come of age and marry on his twenty-fifth birthday, he comes clean too, admitting that he has had a lover prior to his fiance, Annie Avrey. This intensifies the plotting of the novel by giving us, so to speak, the nature of another hidden crime. And it leads Burden's guardian to see himself and his beloved as playing Tristan and Isolde to Edward and Annie's ordinary Darby and Jane. He and she are dramatically superior human beings. So just as Granger and Churchill collaborate to realise the Life of Cromwell in The Inheritors, the plotter/embezzler/lover and his confidante collaborate to realise the perfect love-story of Tristan and Isolde (without the inconvenient deaths) by being perfect-if, unavoidably, Platonic— lovers.

The situation of the writing of this novel duplicates, in part, the situation of its plot. Ford tells us that he wrote it to read to Conrad: "We wrote and read aloud one to the other" (Nature 11). This itself duplicates the way the collaboration began with Ford reading "Seraphina" to Conrad (Remembrance 16). And Conrad tells us that he got tired of The Nature of a Crime-though it eventually helped him in the writing of Chance20— and told Ford to bring it to an end.

I seem to remember a moment when I burst into earnest entreaties that all of those people should be thrown overboard without much ado. This, I believe, is the real nature of the crime. Overboard. The neatness and dispatch with which it is done in Chapter VIII were wholly the act of my collaborator's good nature in the face of my panic. (Nature 7)

The letter-writer who writes for his beloved so that she can read about him after he dies likewise quickly ends the correspondence when his burden is lifted in his last letter.21 Casting his analysis of this novel in a deconstructive mode, Eric Meyer centers it on the poison ring which recalls to him Derrida on "Plato's Pharmacy" where the pharmakon is both beneficent and maleficent-the drug can both heal and kill. The threat of killing himself becomes the letter-writer's source of new life in The Nature of a Crime.

"Like the pharmakon, writing becomes a cure for itself that sickens to heal, that kills to make well," says Meyer (504). And he goes on to point out that this combination is more memorably realized when John Dowell takes life from Florence's death and tells the saddest story at his own expense in The Good Soldier (1915), which is the story of Edward Ashburnham's suicide. And, as Dowell goes on to claim of Edward Ashburnham, "he was just myself ' (291). So if we follow this thread from The Nature of a Crime to The Good Soldier, we can see that just as Conrad's collaboration with Ford led to his greatest fiction, Ford's collaboration with Conrad did the same for him. Their more intense life as novelists is encapsulated in the intense plotting of the letter-writer to make his way back to life once he escapes the sentence of death.

If we see that The Inheritors and The Nature of a Crime are not only novels in which collaborations are underway (to finish a life of Cromwell and to live the Tristan and Isolde story) but novels that also centre on Conrad's trademark of a decentered plot and that discuss writing in detail-if we see these things clearly we immediately recognize the intensity of Ford's metafictional preoccupation in writing them. And we see, perhaps more importantly, when Ford came to write his memoir of Conrad and centre it on the affair of their writing Romance, that that memoir had to be metafictional too.

These novels, then, lead inevitably to Joseph Conrad: A

Personal Remembrance (1924), which is metafiction in the form of memoir. One reviewer noted that it is, "in part, a textbook for novelists" ("Biography" 866). And another that "there can be no better textbook" for "the writer or student of writing" (Farrar 83). Indeed, A Personal Remembrance is a novel about writing a novel. "Le centre," Louis Cazamian pointed out, "est la composition de Romance" (553).

To take the implication of these remarks to their logical conclusion is to read the memoir as metafiction: the romance of writing Romance. Its major action is a quest for the New Form of the novel, which grew out of Ford's and Conrad's conviction that "the writing of novels was the one thing of importance that remained to the world and that what the novel needed was the New Form" (Remembrance 30). A Personal Remembrance presents the search for this one important thing as a heroic quest that confers immortality.

Ford presents his hero as an "Elizabethan Gentleman Adventurer" (19)22 in order to give him a distinct identity. He does this to counteract the public perception of Conrad as "Slav," "Oriental," and "Romantic," which Ford sees as totally inappropriate. His Conrad "was practical... the last thing he was was Slav" (53). He deals effectively with his grocer, his publisher, and his insurance agent. He gets what he wants without fomenting revolutions. And his style is not, as H. G. Wells thought, "Oriental" (48). He seeks words like "serene" and "azure" to express his meaning precisely in the cadences of the English language (173). And Conrad has not a romantic attachment to the past.

Rather he presents himself as a traditional English Gentleman only to promote the goal of his quest, for "all revolutions are an interruption of the processes of thought and of the discovery of a New Form... for the novel:" (58). That form insists on "rendering" and "constatation": "Never state, present" (Ford, "Joseph Conrad" 77). Thus Conrad shows himself in his novel-writing to be like the Elizabethan playwrights who wrote like novelists. And with even greater subtlety than they- "they could not," for instance, "prize honour quite so highl[y]" as he did (72)—Conrad emerges as "the finest of the Elizabethans" (70). Thus, "Lord Jim is all of all of us" ("Joseph Conrad" 323). Ford's memoir insists on such metafictional motifs as these to reincarnate Conrad as an Elizabethan poet who creates a New Form for fiction.

The romance of writing Romance is also a love-story, as we would expect a romance to be. Joseph Conrad and Ford Madox Ford agree to work together as collaborators to rewrite Ford's novel-in-manuscript, "Seraphim," and turn it into Romance. They bring to this union their strengths and weaknesses as human beings; thus they take each other for better or worse, not really knowing (as the title of Part I indicates) "qui dort dans l'ombre."23 Each as they meet is a character in shadow to the other because they do not, at the beginning, know each other at all well.

The course of their collaboration reveals Conrad as one of a "new class of mental adventurers," like the Elizabethans, plundering Mediterranean civilizations (March 460). At the same time, Conrad cherishes a love of England and an ideal of fidelity that he admired in Marryat's fiction and that reminds Ford of Sir Francis Drake as well as of Christopher Marlowe. "For, if this country have any civilisedness at all, any tradition, or any craving for self-respect, it is because its real inner standard, its poetic view of life, comes still from the poets who made feasts at the Mermaid" ("Literary Portraits-XLI": 848).

Collaboration further reveals to Ford Conrad's highly developed talent as a navigator in the world of fiction. Ford finds in his mariner a master of the architectonics of fiction as well as of exotic lands and troubled seas. Ford's Conrad is, consequently, ideally suited to tell the story of John Kemp, a young English sea adventurer, the hero of Romance, who is "kidnapped by pirates and misjudged by the judicial bench of our country" and who is, additionally, "a political refugee, suspect of High Treason and victim of West Indian merchants" (Remembrance 42). Macmillan's reader summarized the plot this way:

It turns on the adventures of a young Englishman, of good family, in the West Indies early in the nineteenth century. Being forced to fly his country for some trouble with smugglers (though entirely guiltless) he falls in with some Spanish kinfolk, through whom he gets involved (though again guiltless) with a gang of pirates. The story is too complicated to follow in detail, but there is the necessary amount of love-interest, and,... an almost unnecessary amount of adventure. The hero gets very nearly hanged for his pains on his return to England, through a series of unfortunate, and not very possible, mistakes, but escapes at the last moment by the skin of his teeth. (Higdon 275)

Ford shows himself ideally suited to be Conrad's collaborator because he is "the finest stylist in the English language of to-day" (Remembrance 32). And although Ford acknowledges the precariousness of this estimate of his style, W. E. Henley, to whom the estimate is attributed, did warn Conrad against collaboration lest he ruin Ford's style (Conrad, Collected Letters 2:107). Conrad nonetheless pushed the collaboration. And Ford complemented Conrad's sense of "constructive beauty" (Remembrance 30) with his own sensitivity to words, his pensive approach to achieving the New Form of the novel, his tenaciousness in sticking to a task undertaken, and his determination to complete that task in the manner agreed upon (178-85).

Ford shows moreover that like their Elizabethan predecessors who looked "over each other's shoulders" (March 471) he and Conrad could work together effectively. He shows this by dramatizing his taking down The Mirror of the Sea in shorthand as Conrad dictated it (Part I); by his writing The Inheritors, which Conrad called "a damn good book" (Part II);24 by his reordering the opening of The Rescue when Conrad could not manage it (Part III); by his giving Conrad the subject of The Secret Agent as well as incidental details on anarchists (Part IV); and by his working with Conrad on the ending of "The End of the Tether" (Part v).25

These five parts in which these five works are discussed are nonetheless focused with impressionistic intensity on the writing of Romance. That project, which began Ford's and Conrad's working together, resulted in something more than this novel and The Inheritors and The Nature of a Crime. It made possible the other works that Ford and Conrad wrote independently of each other. And the writing of Romance also produced, Ford claims, "a third artist" who combines the best of both of them: "The third had neither [Conrad's] courage nor his gorgeousness; he himself had none of [Ford's] literary circumspection or verbal puritanism. So the combination was at least... different" (Remembrance 46). Different enough to write a novel that neither could write alone. Different enough to remind us that Romance, A Novel is a romance indeed. If it does not end with a marriage, it does end with an offspring as well as a successful quest.

Part I, "C'est toi qui dort dans l'ombre" of Joseph Conrad: A Personal Remembrance introduces the subject of the book as the affair of writing Romance. It also introduces Conrad and Ford as the characters who work out that affair. Part 11, "Exellency, A Few Goats," by way of their collaboration on The Inheritors, shows how the proper ending of a novel should be written, giving The Inheritors as a bad example and Heart of Darkness and "Youth" as good examples. Part III, "It Is Above All to Make You See," shows how a proper beginning should be written for a novel by way of Ford's rearranging the beginning of The Rescue for Conrad.

This part also goes on to treat of the structure, colour, and texture that make up the middle of a novel by a discussion of general effect, impressionism, selection, speeches, conversations, surprise, style, cadence, structure, philosophy, progression d'effet, and language. Just how these techniques are translated into fiction is rendered impressionistically in the story of Mr. Slack, "your neighbour," who builds and paints his greenhouse and who has a dipsomaniacal wife whose incapacitation nudges him into the arms of Millicent, "your daughter," whom he gets with child, having won her affections with the present of a bangle bracelet. In short, Mr. Slack's story is a novel within a novel that illustrates how the New Form of the novel can be achieved.

Part IV, "That, Too, Is Romance...," returns to the story of writing Romance with Ford and Conrad going to Bruges and

Knocke to complete it. This part also applies the techniques of the New Form to completing Romance, emphasizing again, first, Conrad's doing what Ford could not do in writing the fourth part of the novel; second, Conrad's writing the inspired beginning of that part which supersedes Ford's uninspired attempt at the same; and, third, their working at the Pent to achieve a progression d'effet in the ending of Romance.

Part V, "The End," shows their success in achieving this by beginning with the passage that ends Romance. In "The End" the ending of Romance is achieved and so too is the end of Joseph Conrad's life. Both are encapsulated in the rewriting of the ending of "The End of the Tether," which involves disaster (a fire that destroys a manuscript installment), tenacity (working together to rewrite the ending), and a journey (by train to London, followed by another by motor to Canterbury). "The End," then, is a journey's end for life and writing.

"The End" is also given over to the "reverses" that made up Conrad's life as a writer-with the accidental burning of the installment of "The End of the Tether" acting as an exemplum of these reverses. And as one reversal follows another the reader begins to wonder what Ford is up to in ending his metafictional memoir in this way. Then suddenly Ford makes himself clear by telescoping a trip he took with Conrad to Canterbury with a trip that Conrad took there with an interviewer shortly before he died.

> And he stopped the car in Postling Gap that looks over the lands of the Pent, right away over the Stour Valley that is like the end of a bowl, over the Channel, to France on a clear day. He said, "This is the view I love best in the world!" That was his last Wednesday but one and the writer hopes that he will never speak with anyone who saw Conrad later. (267)

Like Chaucer before him, Conrad ends his quest at the Falstaff Inn in Canterbury. Shortly after his happy vision comes a happy death. For though Conrad suffered many reverses-and some of them are vividly described in A Personal Remembrance-during his life's pilgrimage, none of them kept him from his goal:

> He surely could look back on life, so much of it passing

in that country that he loved, and could say with his dying breath that all his reverses had been temporary but that his achievements truly had all such permanence as is vouchsafed to us men.... That is to be granted what we Papists call the cross of the happy death. (267)

Like Chaucer, Conrad reaches Canterbury again; his quest, though painful, has been successful; thus he has a happy death. This folding of Conrad into Chaucer's narrative seems an apt ending for a novel that revels in metafictional moments and celebrates progressions of effect; an apt ending, indeed, for a novel that has as its subject-and is itself-a romance. "This too is Romance," says Ford repeatedly in "The End." And we "conclude with a Bravo! for Mr. Ford," exclaims Thomas Moult, The Bookman's reviewer. "This passion of his for romance is irresistible" (176). So too is Joseph Conrad: A Personal Remembrance when it is read for what it is-memoir as metafiction.

Ford is manifestly not on an ego-trip for which Conrad paid the fare in his memoir. Romance "was written-where it is splendid-by Joseph Conrad," Ford told the City Editor of The World; "the rest of it was by, sir, Yr. Obedient servant Ford Madox Ford" (Naumburg 180). That is the message of Joseph Conrad: A Personal Remembrance. The memoir is not the work of "a fat patronizing slug upon the Conradian lettuce," as "The Londoner" suggested (49). Like Jessie Conrad, who thought that Ford's book "revile[d]" Conrad (Circle 65), this reviewer simply did not read Ford's memoir well enough to understand it. Like her he was "singularly lacking in imagination" (McFee 500). They did not see that it was plain to see that Ford relentlessly presents Conrad as the older and better writer in his biography. Thus "the sensitive perfection" of the fictional memoir is everywhere in evidence (English Review 865).

Ford was not able to say the same of Richard Curle's Joseph Conrad: A Study (1914). He found that that book showed no understanding of Conrad's personality and poetic achievement.26 He would later find G. Jean-Aubry's two-volume compendium on Conrad's life similarly limited (see

Harvey 247-48). Curle and Jean-Aubry write books that embalm "Conrad in a grand tomb. Ford shows us the living man" (McFee 500).

Indeed, Ford could not write about a poet without writing about his "brainwave" ("Literary Portraits-XXXV": 653). And Ford's Conrad is "a very great poet of today." Conrad had agreed with Ford "that a poem was not that which was written in verse but that, either prose or verse, had constructive beauty" (30). Curle's book only manages for Ford to be a "patient, laborious, and honourable study" that will make the critic himself "a distinguished ornament of that British school of letters which... must always remain outside the great comity of European civilization" ("Literary Portraits-XLI": 849).27

Ford's Curle is incapable of being a secret sharer with Conrad as Ford himself was. Indeed, that story in which the young captain first saves Leggatt by taking him aboard his ship and Leggatt then saves the captain and his ship by letting his hat float on the surface of the sea as a mark to steer by-that story could be read as an allegory of the Ford/Conrad collaboration, which ended only shortly before "The Secret Sharer" was composed in August and September 1910. Ford and Conrad, like Leggatt and the young captain, parted company after having each given the other skills to navigate the lonesome waters of their respective literary enterprises." Neither the young captain nor Legatt, however, like Conrad and Ford themselves, were without limitations.

YET Ford admired Conrad precisely because he rose above his own human failings to become a great artist-specifically, a great novelist in the tradition of the Elizabethan dramatists. Ford further demonstrated the unique value of placing Conrad in an English tradition when he wrote, in 1927, The English Novel from the Earliest Days to the Death of Joseph Conrad. There Ford says once again that "the plays of Shakespeare were novels written for recitation" (43); and there, literally, he pays Conrad the ultimate compliment: "the conception of novel-writing as an art began for Anglo-Saxondom with Joseph Conrad" (33). What Ford does here he anticipates in Joseph Conrad: A Personal Remembrance. The "radiance which Ford's admiration and love pour upon" Conrad, consequently, can hardly be missed (Dial 338). His awe of Conrad's talents "infuses every page". Typhoon, Ford told Richard Hughes-whose In Hazard he praised as the masterpiece of an "inhuman" writer- "Typhoon was written by a great writer who was a man.21 "Typhoon is at one and the same time a tremendous poem of pure humanity and a tremendous tour de force of pure writing".

The perfection of Joseph Conrad: A Personal Remembrance requires Ford's telling the one telling truth about Conrad: "he was a great man, but... only a mortal man" (McFee 500). Thus he gives us a Conrad who "lives, works and suffers" (Howland 666). That Conrad, that modern man, is the Elizabethan poet. The "radiance which Ford's admiration and love" (Dial 338) pour upon Conrad can hardly be missed in his characterization of Conrad as "a very great poet of to-day writing about things which are very engrossing to a nation brought up upon the English Bible and Shakespeare".

What England needs more than anything to-day [and Conrad can give it] is a return to Elizabethan standards-is a return to a frame of mind that had only just left behind Papistry, the large sense of honour, the large sense of cosmopolitanism, the large senses of those attributes that are called loyalty, self-sacrifice, and chivalry. These are the fine things of life, and, although Mr. Conrad does not preach them, nevertheless in the work that he has created we recapture a whole dimension in which these things have their values again as they had them in [1588].' ("Literary PortraitsXLI": 549)

This sense of Conrad's estimable place in the English tradition makes Ford's fictional memoir of him for John Farrar "a record of a personality which has seldom been equaled as interpretative biography" (83). The reader "soon finds he is getting a clearer conception of Conrad the man than any other book or essay has given him" (New Statesman xvi). "Fidus Ford," Joseph Collins writes, "has made us his debtors for showing Conrad as he appeared to him" (176). "The inner and spiritual truth" of Conrad's personality "shines out" (Current Opinion 178). And Conrad's "personality ultimately makes his art endure" ("An Impression" 727). Ford agreed: "What the artist wishes to do-as far as you are concernedis to take you out of yourself As far as he is concerned, he wishes to express himself" ("Literary Portraits-VIII": 2). Because of his unshakable belief in the presence of personality in the artistic process, Ford gave us Conrad as he knew him-as "the greatest English poet of today."31 And his book is, in Christopher Money's words, "one of the most thrillingly intelligent tributes ever paid to a great writer" (519).

The method is unsound: the aesthetic dissonance of colonial justification in Kipling, Conrad, and Greene - authors Rudyard Kipling, Joseph Conrad and Graham Greene

In his 1970 Charles Eliot Norton Lectures published as Sincerity and Authenticity, Lionel Trilling contends of Joseph Conrad's Heart of Darkness:

Today it is scarcely possible to read Marlow's celebration of England without irony; to many, especially among the English themselves, it is bound to seem patently absurd. The present state of opinion does not countenance the making of discriminations among imperialisms, present or past, and the idea that more virtue might be claimed for one nation than another is given scant credence. But this was not always the case. Having the choice to make, Conrad himself elected to become English exactly because he believed England to be a good nation. (110)

Trilling's notion that one can discriminate among imperialisms, claiming virtue for some and not for others, is a perfect starting point for a discussion of the imperial justifications of Conrad, Rudyard Kipling, and Graham Greene, all of whom saw in Britain's empire a justifiable endeavor. In their three fictions, Kipling's Plain Tales From the Hills, Conrad's Heart of Darkness, and Greene's The Heart of the Matter, these authors discriminate among possible motivations for the colonial project, critiquing their predecessors' justifications and offering their own. Further, having inherited a fictional tradition from Kipling, Conrad and Greene also link what they consider to be of value in the colonies to what they consider to be of value in their predecessors' texts, believing as well that more virtue might be claimed for some fictional techniques than for others. In this essay, I will present Kipling's, Conrad's, and Greene's valuations, both cultural and aesthetic, as they are presented in these colonial fictions.

Plain Tales from the Hills, Kipling's first collection of stories, brought colonial India home to England: those individuals who went out to India were for the British reading public suddenly endowed with faces, vices, virtues, and love affairs and disappointments, their administrative, military, and patriotic roles constituted as full lives. At one stroke, Kipling created for the English reading public the culture of Anglo-India: what the British in India do for leisure; what they value; where the best and where the worst posts are; how love and friendship differ in Anglo-India as compared to at home.(1) Though introducing a new culture is no small task, for the Victorians it could never be a solitary one.

True to his Victorian fellows, Kipling sought, in capturing that culture, to justify its existence as well. Faced with such a task, where better to turn than Matthew Arnold, who had done the same for England itself nearly 20 years earlier. Thus Kipling invokes the famous Arnoldian binary from Culture and Anarchy:

We may regard this energy driving at practice, this paramount sense of the obligation of duty, self-control, and work, this earnestness in going manfully with the best light we have, as one force. And we may regard the intelligence driving at those ideas which are, after all, the basis of right practice, the ardent sense for all the new and changing combinations of them which man's development brings with it, the indomitable impulse to know and adjust them perfectly, as another force. And these two forces we may regard as in some sense rivals. (107)

Between the "intelligence driving at... ideas" and "the obligation of duty," Kipling situates Indian colonial culture. Not content with Arnold's pendulum swinging back and forth between the two, however, he adds to the binary a middle term. In the last story of his collection, Kipling brings Arnold's two forces together in the figure of McIntosh Jellaludin.(2) Mcintosh is a Hellenist:

He was, when sobre, a scholar and a gentleman. When drunk, he was rather more of the first than the second.... On those occasions the native woman tended him while he raved in all tongues except his own. One day, indeed, he began reciting Atalanta in Calydon, and went through it to the end, beating time to the swing of the verse with a bedstead-leg. But he did most of his ravings in Greek or German. The man's mind was a perfect rag-bag of useless things. (330)

He is also a Hebraist who at one point in his life served society, though in what capacity the reader never learns: "'The public are fools and prudish fools. I was their servant once'" (335). Most importantly, Mcintosh has a knowledge of a middle way, of an alternative that partakes of both opposing qualities:

"I do not refer to your extremely limited classical attainments, or your excruciating quantities, but to your gross ignorance of matters more immediately under your notice. 'That, for instance'; he pointed to a woman cleaning a samovar near the well in the centre of the Serai. She was flicking the water out of the spout in regular cadencejerks.

"There are ways and ways of cleaning samovars. If you knew why she was doing her work in that particular fashion, you would know what the Spanish Monk meant when he said-

'I the Trinity illustrate, Drinking watered orange-pulp - In three sips the Arian frustrate, While he drains his at one gulp' and many other things which are now hidden from your eyes. However, Mrs. Mcintosh has prepared dinner. Let us come and eat after the fashion of the people of the country - of whom, by the way, you know nothing." (331)

This passage includes references both to the Hellenism of McIntosh's book learning and to the Hebraism, the "energy driving at practice," about which the narrator knows nothing. We later learn that Strickland, whom we've been brought by the narrator to respect for his awe-inspiring knowledge of the natives he rules, is for Mcintosh an "ignorant man" (332). Unlike Strickland, Mcintosh does not merely know how the natives will act, but he also understands why they act.

McIntosh's understanding of the significance of the cleaning of the samovar and the sipping in Browning's poem represents a marriage of the most esoteric knowledge with the most mundane of daily actions; the rhythmic cleaning is as informed by a theology or cosmology as is the three sips of the Spanish Monk. Mcintosh alone sees to the heart of matters, an ability that, far from precluding an attention to ordinary practice, in fact entails a knowledge of the ideal in and through "practice."

Kipling makes much of this ability in the Plain Tales collection. Figures who embody one or the other side of the dyad are undercut, just as Strickland in all his practical glory is undercut by Mcintosh. Mrs. Hauksbee, the clever-est woman in India, who helps several people stick to the straight and narrow, is herself bested at the beginning of the short story sequence in "Three and - an Extra," when she acts without the backing of an approved ideal.

Trejago in "Beyond the Pale" brings doom upon himself and his lover: the practicality that makes his intrigue possible prevents him from fully acknowledging the cultural laws he has transgressed. On the other hand, those who err on the side of Helenism, who attach too much meaning to everyday events, are equally suspect: the "Boy" of "Thrown Away" who commits suicide over a "cruel little sentence, rapped out before thinking" (19), or Aurelian McCoggin, whose love of "isms" is cured by an attack of aphasia. Only a handful of figures manage to inform their practical doings with the knowledge of a higher sphere.

In "His Wedded Wife," the Worm, who joins a "high-caste regiment" in which "you must be able to do things well... to get on with them," does nothing well except read, keep to himself, and write home. The members of the regiment refuse to accept him until he inadvertently advertises his acting talents, by dressing as a neglected wife and coming upon the regiment as a fury "rushing out of the dark, unannounced, into our dull lives" (160). The revenge is successful because his play-acting speaks to the regiment's deep feelings of complicity, haunting even those in no way concerned in this particular matter. Janoo in "In the House of Suddhoo" respects the spiritual hold the seal-cutter has on Suddhoo, though she understands it is all a sham, and that respect assures her revenge as well: "Unless something happens to prevent her, I am afraid that the seal-cutter will die of cholera - the white arsenic kind - about the middle of May" (154). Finally, Moriarty in "In Error" is saved by his illusion that Mrs. Reiver is a saint whose respect he must earn: the "error" has no foundation in reality, but his belief in that self-constructed ideal has the amazing practical result of curing his alcoholism.

Yet this ability to get to the heart of the matter, though it involves a knowledge of the ideal, is anchored in an English practicality. In "To Be Filed for Reference," when Mcintosh turns scholar during one of his drunken binges, he speaks either Greek or German, the former the language of scholars and the clergy, the latter the language of idealists. At these moments, the narrator tells us, he is not a "gentleman," nor, the reader may add, an "English gentleman." The ability to get to the heart of matters includes both a spiritual astuteness and a practical knowingness, but what these two opposing qualities have in common is a directedness, a doggedness that Kipling identifies with Englishness, an ability to recognize things as they really are. The story "In the House of Suddhoo," a tale of spiritualism, includes an account of the honour of an English gentleman, the narrator, whose principles and kindness have put him at the centre of conflicting moral and legal claims:

> Now, the case stands thus. Unthinkingly, I have laid myself open to the charge of aiding and abetting the seal-cutter in obtaining money under false pretenses, which is forbidden by Section 420 of the Indian Penal Code. I am helpless in the matter for these reasons. I cannot inform the Police. What witnesses would support my statements?... I dare not again take the law into my own hands, and speak to the seal-cutter; for certain am ! that, not only would Suddhoo disbelieve me, but this step would end in the poisoning of Janoo, who is bound hand and foot by her debt to the bunnia.... And thus I shall be privy to a murder in the House of Suddhoo. (154)

Yet for all his confusion, he nonetheless is able, in his

directedness, to appreciate the complexities of his own case. In "Lispeth" the native girl taken from the hills and raised according to British tradition is "killed" not by an English gentleman but by an Englishman whose conduct is ungentlemanly and by a Chaplain's wife who advises lying in preference to a "fuss or scandal" (5).

While their actions may be very "English," they are not those of a true English gentleman and lady. Rather, Lispeth is the only one in the story to embody such traits, expecting a forthrightness of which the Chaplain's wife and the Englishman are incapable. In the same way, Moriarty is proud of his "very good reputation" and worries that his alcoholism will "undermine that reputation," but "reputation" is not enough to work his cure: he controls his alcoholism only in order to show himself worthy of the finest of English ladies.

It is the doggedness of the English, allowing them to get to the heart of matters, that qualifies the British for the role of colonial administrators.(3) In "The Bronckhorst Divorce-Case," Strickland, the man with great practical knowledge of native life, is called in to show that Bronckhorst's accusations against Biel, which have been confirmed by native witnesses, are a total fabrication. Strickland manages to scare the natives into recanting their testimony. Thus one Englishman, Strickland, corrects through intimidation the wrongs of another Englishman, Bronckhorst, who has bribed the natives to lie, while a third Englishman, Biel, is provoked by Strickland to thrash Bronckhorst but allows him to go free of charges of "fabricating false evidence": "Biel came out of the Court, and Strickland dropped a gut trainer's whip in the verandah.

Ten minutes later, Biel was cutting Bronckhorst into ribbons behind the old Court cells, quietly and without scandal" (252). But all this occurs outside the courthouse, the place where such claims should be weighed. None of the three is an English gentleman, for they manage to denigrate, sidestep, and tamper with that justice housed in the British courthouse, a justice the narrator cannot report since his story follows Biel: just when "the Judge began to say what he thought," the text cuts away to Biel's punishment of

Bronckhorst behind the courthouse. Such merely practical "virtues" are outside the purview of true English justice. English justice is also at stake in one of the stories that perfectly embodies the union of the practical and the ideal, the tale of "The Bisara of Poree," a magic charm in a silver box that brings good only to those who obtain it dishonestly.

Churton, the present owner of the charm, is suffering because he bought the object unknowingly; his chief complaint is that "his decisions were being reversed by the upper Courts more than an Assistant Commissioner of eight years' standing has a right to expect" (264). Magic, a spiritual practicality, and English administrative justice are thus closely linked. With the aid of the charm, Churton is able to administer justice against a fellow Englishman named Pack, who steals the charm, a justice well deserved in Churton's eyes since he had not been "brought up to believe that men on the Government House List steal - at least little things" (266).

In his practical endeavor to bring about justice, he is aided by another Englishman, who holds the knowledge of the powers of the Bisara of Poree. Together, practical action and the knowledge of esoteric matters ensures justice.

This English trait that Kipling defines and locates at the centre of the colonial project in the Plain Tales is Conrad's leaping-off point in Heart of Darkness: Conrad examines Kipling's justification, finds it lacking, and offers one of his own. The first section of the story heavy-handedly presents itself as an answer to Kipling's Plain Tales, taking up as it does the question of the practical colonial endeavor redeemed by the Idea:

> These chaps were not much account, really. They were no colonists; their administration was merely a squeeze, and nothing more, I suspect. They were conquerors, and for that you want only brute force.... The conquest of the earth, which mostly means the taking it away from those who have a different complexion or slightly flatter noses than ourselves, is not a pretty thing when you look into it too much. What redeems it is the idea only. An idea at the back of it; not a sentimental pretence but an idea; and an unselfish belief in

the idea - something you can set up, and bow down before, and offer a sacrifice to. (Heart 7)

Marlow has enlisted the aid of his aunt in his efforts to secure a position, and his aunt in turn represents Marlow to her influential friend as one of the new "gang of virtue," those who go out to the colonies motivated not by profit but by a commitment to a transcendent idea: "'weaning those ignorant millions from their horrid ways.'" The gang of virtue bring to the practical colonial endeavor an intelligence that supplies "those ideas which are, after all, the basis of right practice."

Clearly, Marlow distances himself from the redeeming idea at the outset, but the first section of Heart of Darkness is nonetheless ruled by it.(4) Critics rightly emphasize how central the Idea's role in the colonial process is to the story, but they often fail to recognize that Conrad emphasizes the Idea informing practical action. As Hunt Hawkins states, Conrad judges the colonial project on the basis of "two explicit criteria - efficiency and the 'idea'" (288).

Conrad's initial critique of Kipling is, however, aesthetic: he objects to the way in which Kipling embodies his colonial justification in the Plain Tales. Moreover, it appears that the aesthetic shortcomings of the Plain Tales lead Conrad to note the potential ethical or moral dangers of the defence of colonialism Kipling offers. Through the reactions of those listening to Marlow's story, Conrad shows that Kipling's "message" in the Plain Tales is at odds with the effect they produce in their readers. Those characters in the Plain Tales who successfully embody the spiritually informed pragmatism of the English, who are thus ideal colonial administrators, are not the characters who most engage the reader.

Even a casual reader of the Plain Tales will come away with a memorable impression of Strickland, the adventurous undercover policeman, and of Mrs. Hauksbee, the cleverest woman in India. In terms of effect, the practical characters win the day, though the spiritual characters have a haunting quality that also makes them linger in the reader's mind. "The Gate of Sorrows," an eerie story that is so pervasively depressing it nearly sinks the entire volume with its weight, puncturing a hole in the stories' offhand narrative charm, is powerful, as is the sudden and harrowing reassertion of spiritual right and race purity at the end of "Beyond the Pale."(5) But Moriarty or Churton or the narrator of "In the House of Suddhoo" do not leave the same lasting impression on the reader. They are all intriguing characters, but they fade from memory until specifically recalled to one's attention, unlike Mrs. Hauksbee and Strickland. Those characters who embody the English ability to get to the heart of matters, valorized by Kipling and aligned with British justice in its colonies, do not demand the attention their privileged status seems to require.(6)

Conrad conveys this perceived shortcoming of Kipling's collection almost from the start in Heart of Darkness, when Marlow's narrative is not met with a warm welcome. The narrator notes of Marlow's jarring first line, tossed into the silence - "'And this also... has been one of the dark places of the earth'" - "It was accepted in silence. No one took the trouble to grunt even," suggesting a company that acquiesces to the inevitable: hearing another of Marlow's yarns (Heart 5). Near the end of the first section, the reader again is reminded that Marlow may not have completely captivated his audience: "There was not a word from anybody.

The others might have been asleep." While this description may betoken an awed silence or breathless interest, it may just as easily be a straightforward account of the truth: the others present are sleeping and therefore not listening. The reader can be sure only that the narrator is listening to Marlow's tale, and he is interested in Marlow's discourse on the informing idea only because it matches his own sense of Empire as well as his own tendency to see the world in terms of the Spirit moving in the real; two beliefs upon which he expounds in the prologue.

As it is with Kipling, however, Conrad's story of pragmatic idealism may not be an engaging one. Marlow chooses initially to tell the story of Moriarty and Churton, without regard for the interests of his listeners who might be more engaged by the likes of Strickland or Mrs. Hauksbee. The moral value of Kipling's project aside, Conrad's point here is that the fiction fails aesthetically, and this failure leads Conrad to question the very nature of Kipling's justification. The aesthetic dissonance of Kipling's collection triggers its ethical dissonance.

In the second section of Heart of Darkness, Conrad makes it clear that the impression made by such stories of the ideal informing practice is strongly at odds with the set of values those stories are intended to convey. Kipling never makes it possible for his readers to experience his own high regard for those who make ideas the basis of their practice. We share Kipling's regard for an ideal-informed practice only as an idea extracted from the text, not one experienced firsthand inside Kipling's narratives. Twice in the second section of Heart of Darkness, the listeners are again brought into the frame of the narrative, and in both instances their responses provide an occasion for Marlow to break the flow of the narrative for a more direct idea-driven form of address:

"The inner truth is hidden - luckily, luckily. But I felt it all the same; I felt often its mysterious stillness watching me at my monkey tricks, just as it watches you fellows performing on your respective tight-ropes for - what is it? half a crown a tumble"

"Try to be civil, Marlow," growled a voice, and I knew there was at least one listener awake besides myself.

"I beg your pardon. I forgot the heartache which makes up the rest of the price. And indeed what does the price matter, if the trick be well done? You do your tricks very well." (Heart 34-35)

"I couldn't have felt more of lonely desolation somehow, had I been robbed of a belief or had missed my destiny in life.... Why do you sigh in this beastly way, somebody? Absurd? Well, absurd. Good Lord! mustn't a man ever - Here, give me some tobacco...."

There was a pause of profound stillness, then a match flared, and Marlow's lean face appeared, worn, hollow, with downward folds and dropped eyelids, with an aspect of concentrated attention; and as he took vigorous draws at his pipe, it seemed to retreat and advance out of the night in the regular flicker of the tiny flame. The match went out.

"Absurd!" he cried. "This is the worst of trying to tell.... Here you all are, each moored with two good addresses, like a hulk with two anchors, a butcher round one corner, a policeman round another, excellent appetites, and temperatures normal - you hear - normal from year's end to year's end. And you say, Absurd! Absurd be - exploded! Absurd! My dear boys, what can you expect from a man who out of sheer nervousness had just flung overboard a pair of new shoes!" (Heart 48)

Indeed, in the second of these two examples, his listener's response leads Marlow on a digression that takes him far ahead of his story. In both examples, the synthesis of the practical (the dangerous particulars of the uncharted river, the new shoes, the butcher around the corner) with the ideal (the inner truth and the stolen belief) forces Marlow out of the flow of the story itself. This idealistic pragmatism, this attempt to get to the heart of matters, can appeal to readers only as an extra-narrative datum, a disembodied notion beyond the borders of the narrative, as in Kipling's story sequence.(7)

In the third section of his story, Conrad rejects Kurtz and, in doing so, rejects Kipling's justification for such an approach to the colonial enterprise. As Marlow makes clear, Kurtz's exalted ideals have freed him of constraint, opening the way for "forgotten and brutal instincts": "There was nothing either above or below him, and I knew it. He had kicked himself loose of the earth. Confound the man! he had kicked the very earth to pieces. He was alone, and I before him did not know whether I stood on the ground or floated in the air" (Heart 67).

In fact, the entire third section consists of Conrad's rejection of Kurtz, as one by one he is abandoned by all those who have been waiting so eagerly to meet him. First, the Russian, who had been helping Kurtz at great personal risk to himself, decamps. Then, of course, the manager, looking after his own interests, declares that Kurtz has "done more harm than good to the company" (Heart 63). His native worshippers flee at the sound of the steamer's whistle, and even the manager's boy casts him off: "Suddenly the manager's boy put his insolent black head in the doorway, and said in a tone of scathing contempt: 'Mistah Kurtz he dead'" (Heart 71).

Finally, back in Europe, Marlow slowly divests himself of what is left of Kurtz, his report, which he gives to the journalist friend, and "some family letters and memoranda," which he gives to Kurtz's cousin (Heart 74). And in lying to Kurtz's Intended, Marlow, who held to Kurtz longest, is unable to render him "that justice which was his due" (Heart 79).

If Kipling's practical idealism provides such unsteady ground for the colonial project, what then redeems it? In the second section of the story, Conrad offers what he sees as the only real justification for empire: the spiritualism of Arnold and Kipling is rejected in favour of the rich wilderness that surrounds Marlow. Portrayed throughout the story as a dark, unknowable force to be reckoned with, the wilderness, the land and its richness is justification enough for the colonial endeavor:

"H'm. Just so," grunted the uncle. "Ah! my boy, trust to this - I say, trust to this." I saw him extend his short flipper of an arm for a gesture that took in the forest, the creek, the mud, the river - seemed to beckon with a dishonouring flourish before the sunlit face of the land a treacherous appeal to the lurking death, to the hidden evil, to the profound darkness of its heart. It was so startling that I leaped to my feet and looked back at the edge of the forest, as though I had expected an answer of some sort to that black display of confidence. (Heart 33)

According to Conrad, the justification for colonialism is the land itself. Its treacherousness requires enormous skill and concentration - the accountant working in the most stressful of climates, Marlow piloting the ship up an unknown river, the native monitoring the boiler - yet such concentration pays great dividends. Kurtz's great material accomplishment, the collection of large amounts of ivory, is belittled by the manager as "mostly fossil," which Marlow glosses as ivory the natives have buried (Heart 63). But his repetition of the phrase transforms ivory into a rich mineral deposit that the land has been made to yield. For Conrad, the colonial endeavor has only one objective: raw material, the natural resources so plentiful in Africa.(8)

Phil Joffe writes that "the disillusioned Conrad, in the last year of his life, wrote of his 'distasteful knowledge of the vilest scramble for loot that ever disfigured the history of human conscience and geographical exploration'" (78). But the target of Conrad's critique in Heart of Darkness is not this attempt to tap the richness of the land, but the hypocrisy, the Lie that masks this motivation. As Born writes: "The profit motive for oneself is neatly excluded from this altruistic strand of imperial ethical progress. We can usefully recall here Orwell's telling remark 'that Kipling does not seem to realise, any more than the average soldier or colonial administrator, that an empire is primarily a money-making concern'" (110).(9) The colonial enterprise becomes morally dangerous when the profit motive is clouded by all sorts of grand ideals; Kurtz is Conrad's object lesson of the "horror" of that sort of colonialism.

Heart of Darkness does not denigrate a colonial endeavor motivated by the richness of the untapped land. The ethical control in such an enterprise is the work ethic itself: only those who know their jobs and do them efficiently can effectively tap these riches. The natives left to die on the hillside are the victims of an inefficient and poorly managed colonial enterprise, one that excavates and blasts a hill for no reason: "They were building a railway.

The cliff was not in the way or anything; but this objectless blasting was all the work going on" (Heart 16). Seen in this light, the manager's strictures on Kurtz's behaviour, though heartless in their zealous concern only for profit, embody the sort of practical moral safeguard Conrad sees as part of the redeeming nature of work, the ethic of the work ethic: "'Mr. Kurtz has done more harm than good to the Company. He did not see the time was not ripe for vigorous action. Cautiously, cautiously - that's my principle. We must be cautious yet. The district is closed to us for a time. Deplorable! Upon the whole, the trade will suffer'" (Heart 63).(10)

Conrad takes up the issue of materialism and idealism in his discussion of the Russo-Japanese war in "Autocracy and War," where he seems to occupy a position similar to Kipling's ideal-driven pragmatism: "The trouble of the civilised world is the want of a common conservative principle abstract enough to give the impulse, practical enough to form the rallying-point of international action tending toward the restraint of particular ambitions" ("Autocracy" 111).

He also seems vehemently opposed to the rule of material interests: "Germany's attitude proves that no peace for the earth can be found in the expansion of material interests which she seems to have adopted exclusively as her only aim, ideal, and watchword" (113). Yet Conrad's stance in this essay is far more realistic, more expedient, than the two statements just quoted might suggest.(11) Conrad notes that Germany's material interests are dangerous only insomuch as they have been "adopted exclusively as her only... ideal."

Here is the Conrad of Heart of Darkness. Immediately following his rousing endorsement of a Politik driven by the Ideal, he concedes that "the true peace of the world will be a place of refuge much less like a beleaguered fortress and more, let us hope, in the nature of an Inviolable Temple. It will be built on less perishable foundations than those of material interests. But it must be confessed that the architectural aspect of the universal city remains as yet inconceivable - that the very ground for its erection has not been cleared of the jungle" ("Autocracy" 107). Indeed, Conrad acknowledges that hope for immediate peace may be found in the pursuit of material interests, however distasteful they may be, though not according to the example set by Germany, but according to the one set by the world's democracies:

Democracy, which has elected to pin its faith to the supremacy of material interests, will have to fight their battles to the bitter end, on a mere pittance - unless, indeed, some statesman of exceptional ability and overwhelming prestige succeeds in carrying through an international understanding for the delimitation of spheres of trade all over the earth, on the model of the territorial spheres of influence marked in

Africa to keep the competitors of the privilege of improving the nigger (as buying machine) from flying prematurely at each other's throats. ("Autocracy" 107)(12)

As the tone alone makes clear, this option does not thrill Conrad; as it is in Heart of Darkness, here his distaste for the cure is palpable.(13) But it is a cure nonetheless, and the example he cites is none other than colonized Africa. Further, the statesman who will create delimited "spheres of trade all over the earth" has in fact much in common with the manager of Heart of Darkness.(14) Despite a lack of stature, ability, or force of personality, the manager holds absolute authority over the region he controls:

He was obeyed, yet he inspired uneasiness. That was it! Uneasiness. Not a definite mistrust - just uneasiness - nothing more. You have no idea how effective such a... a... faculty can be. He had no genius for organising, for initiative, or for order even.... He originated nothing, he could keep the routine going - that's all. But he was great. He was great by this little thing that it was impossible to tell what could control such a man. He never gave that secret away. (Heart 22)(15)

Further, Conrad aligns this greatness with trade - "'He was a common trader... nothing more'" - and presents the manager as a representative of delimited spheres of trade, influence, and action (Heart 22). The manager views the Russian as a threat to ordered spheres of trade: "They approached again, just as the manager was saying, 'No one, as far as I know, unless a species of wandering trader - a pestilential fellow, snapping ivory from the natives'" (Heart 32), and "'It must be this miserable trader - this intruder,' exclaimed the manager.

'He must be English,' I said. 'It will not save him from getting into trouble if he is not careful,' muttered the manager darkly" (Heart 39). He insists at all times on respecting the boundaries of spheres of action: "'Well, I must defer to your judgment. You are captain,' he said, with marked civility" (Heart 43); "'The district is closed to us for a time'" (Heart 63); and "'It is my duty to point it out in the proper quarter'" (Heart 63). The manager is no paragon, as Marlow's hatred for him makes clear,(16) but in a world in which "the conscience of but very few men amongst us, and of no single Western nation as yet, will brook the restraint of abstract ideas as against the fascination of a material advantage" ("Autocracy" 110), his pragmatic, compartmentalized rule is the safest option.

Like Conrad does with Kipling, Graham Greene's The Heart of the Matter begins where Conrad's narrative leaves off, embodying in its first section his materialist justification for the colonial enterprise. Though reference to it is subtle, set far in the background of Greene's narrative, the land and its allure are at the heart of Scobie's desire to stay in West Africa:

He said aloud, "You know I like the place." "I believe you do. I wonder why." "It's pretty in the evening," Scobie said vaguely. (Matter 17)

The narrator registers for the reader the inadequacy of Scobie's reply, which seems an odd, insufficient reason for staying, particularly in light of his wife's desire to leave and his overwrought feelings of responsibility for her. But what seems at first like an off-hand comment gets picked up in the narrative, taking on a seriousness that the first comment never even vaguely suggests:

In the evening the port became beautiful for perhaps five minutes. The laterite roads that were so ugly and clay-heavy by day became a delicate flower-like pink. It was the hour of content. Men who had left the port for ever would sometimes remember on a grey wet London evening the bloom and glow that faded as soon as it was seen: they would wonder why they had hated the coast and for a space of a drink they would long to return.

Scobie stopped his Morris at one of the great loops of the climbing road and looked back. He was just too late. The flower had withered upwards from the town; the white stones that marked the edge of the precipitous hill shone like candles in the new dusk. (Matter 26)

The days in the colony are harsh, and the nights, as Scobie's wearisome duels with Louise suggest, hardly restful. But evening is "the hour of content." Scobie, as he himself acknowledges, is seeking "peace" "content[ment]," and the land at evening provides these for him. Though not exactly Conrad's image of the rich, untapped, colonized land, the land as presented in book 1 nonetheless is the reason for Scobie, representative of British law in the colony not coincidentally, to stay in West Africa: for him it has a value that ensures his continued presence there.

Also like Conrad, Greene aligns the value of the land, in this case its temporary beauty that gives Scobie a brief nightly repose, with work: "He had nearly everything, and all he needed was peace. Everything meant work, the daily regular routine in the little bare office, the change of seasons in a place he loved" (Matter 59). The throw-away tag, "a place he loved," emphasizes the connection: the land provides peace, and Scobie longs only to work (in) that land. Further, this notion that the land itself, the very physicality of it, imparts "peace" to Scobie suggests that Greene also recognizes the motivation, as suggested in "Autocracy and War," for Conrad's turn to materialism: that the land, both in what it yields and in its partition, may offer the only viable chance for peace in the context of the present state of the world.

Greene rather ingeniously transplants Conrad's justification for the colonial project to the West African world and the life of his British police captain, Scobie, for the purpose of critiquing it, in the same way that Conrad critiqued Kipling.

Just as Conrad first noted the aesthetic discord of Kipling's programme in Heart of Darkness, so too does Greene identify an aesthetic dissonance in Conrad's colonial justification that reveals its ethical dissonance. A number of critics have concurred with F. R. Leavis's censures of Conrad's style in The Great Tradition:

There are, however, places in Heart of Darkness where we become aware of comment as an interposition, and worse, as an intrusion, at times an exasperating one. Hadn't he, we find ourselves asking, overworked "inscrutable," "inconceivable." "unspeakable" and that kind of word already? - yet still they recur. Is anything added to the oppressive mysteriousness of the Congo by such sentences as: "It was the stillness of an implacable force brooding over an inscrutable intention." The same vocabulary, the same adjectival insistence upon inexpressible and incomprehensible mystery, is applied to the evocation of human profundities and spiritual horrors. (177)(17)

At times in Heart of Darkness, Conrad's attempt to demonstrate the importance of the land to the colonial project is quite heavy-handed. The story begins with the frame narrator's description of the scene before him and his vision of the Roman triremes on the Thames and goes on to include descriptions of the mining operation at the outer station, of the dense jungle surrounding the two-hundred-mile trek inland, of the river itself and the challenge it poses to navigation, and even of the "defensive attack" launched by the natives loyal to Kurtz, which is presented as a rejection by the jungle itself of the Nellie and its crew.

Some of the description and evocation serves a distinct scene- and mood-setting purpose, but too often the attempt to present a distinct impression is overwrought. For instance, in the scene quoted earlier, the manager gestures towards the forest, improbably causing Marlow to leap to his feet: "It was so startling that I leaped to my feet and looked back at the edge of the forest, as though I had expected an answer of some sort to that black display of confidence. You know the foolish notions that come to one sometimes" (Heart 33). Or the description of the trip upriver, which begins with an effective evocation of the imposing fullness of the jungle:

Going up that river was like traveling back to the earliest beginnings of the world, when vegetation rioted on the earth and the big trees were kings. An empty stream, a great silence, an impenetrable forest. The air was warm, thick, heavy, sluggish. There was no joy in the brilliance of sunshine. (Heart 34)

The heaviness of the air requires such "adjectival insistence," but the description trails off into the passage Leavis singles out for its heavy-handed repetition: "This stillness of life did not in the least resemble a peace: It was the stillness of an implacable force brooding over an inscrutable intention" (Heart 34). This passage may be excused as Marlow's, not

Conrad's, rhetoric, but such an excuse fails to account for the strange scene of Marlow's "foolish notion." Conrad's tale falls short only when he continues to detail an impression he's already managed to capture.

Greene's criticism of Conrad in book 1 of The Heart of the Matter is later repeated in his African journal.(18) He does not adopt Conrad's method of introducing the question of aesthetic merit by including the responses of an "audience" within the frame of his tale. Instead, within the narrative itself he introduces a motif of aesthetic appreciation, which he then links to excess. Louise's love of poetry, which is shared by the newcomer Wilson, thus becomes a symbol of excess.(19) Wilson is introduced at the beginning of the novel as someone who loves to read poetry but, because he fears it will call undue attention to himself, he hides his interest. And, indeed, Louise's interest in poetry becomes the objective correlative of the club's dislike for her pushy, whining, and patronizing airs: "'Literary Louise has got him" (Matter 31). This mutual aesthetic appreciation eventually plunges Wilson headlong into excesses of romantic love as he tries to play the avenging, protective lover, a role Louise either ignores or ridicules.

Greene is guilty of some excess himself in his heavy-handed, incremental revelation of Wilson's spying. He punctuates the first book with hints concerning the identity of the new spy who has been sent out to report on the colonial administration:

"You ought to have been a policeman, Father."

"Ah," Father Rank said, "who knows? There are more policemen in this town than meet the eye - or so they say."

"Who says?" (Matter 68)

"Been in to see the Commissioner about a pass. There are so many passes one has to have in this town, sir. I wanted one for the wharf...."

When Wilson had gone, Scobie went in to the Commissioner. He said, "I was just coming along to see you, sir, when I ran into Wilson."

"Oh, yes, Wilson," the Commissioner said. "He came in to have a word with me about one of their lightermen."

"I see." The shutters were down in the office to cut out the morning sun. A sergeant passed through carrying with him, as well as his file, a breath of the Zoo behind. The day was heavy with unshed rain: already at 8.30 in the morning the body ran with sweat. Scobie said, "He told me he'd come about a pass."

"Oh yes," the Commissioner said, "that too." (Matter 73)

"Then the special man they have sent from London...."

"You must come back when I'm clearer, Yusef. I don't know what the hell you are talking about."

"They have sent a special man from London to investigate the diamonds - they are crazy about diamonds - only the Commissioner must know about him - none of the other officers, not even you."

"What rubbish you talk, Yusef. There's no such man."

"Everybody guesses but you."

"Too absurd. You shouldn't listen to rumour, Yusef." (Matter 92-93)

She said, "Oh, Wilson's been attentive."

"He's a nice boy."

"He's too intelligent for his job. I can't think why he's out here as just a clerk."

"He told me he drifted." (Matter 95)

Though several of these passages serve to characterize Scobie's peculiar blindness, neither the episode with Father Rank nor that with Scobie and the commissioner, in which Scobie seems aware that something's amiss, clearly work to that end. Yet, if the passages are meant to tip the reader off to Wilson's true role in the colony, and to some extent they do have that purpose since the reader has no other means of reaching that conclusion, they are hardly notable for their subtlety.

Between Wilson's earlier paranoia and the fact that the novel begins with his arrival, the reader takes Father Rank's meaningful comment as the first hint. The following passages at first confirm the reader's suspicions and finally vex the reader. The insistent and repeated hints as to Wilson's "real" role in the colony enact a narrative excess akin to Conrad's.

Moreover, the diamonds, which are at the heart of Wilson's spying, connect this excess to the "natural resources" that the colonies yield.

Greene's perception of Conrad's excess, the one source of aesthetic dissonance in Heart of Darkness, leads him to note the danger of Conrad's excessively materialistic take on imperialism.(20) In book 3, the natural profuseness of the land is invoked and, in each case, identified with illogic:

"You must promise. You can't desire the end without desiring the means."

Ah, but one can, he thought, one can: one can desire the peace of victory without desiring the ravaged towns. (Matter 221). They kissed as formally now when they met as a brother and sister. When the damage was done, adultery became as unimportant as friendship. The flame had licked them and gone on across the clearing: it had left nothing standing except a sense of responsibility and sense of loneliness. Only if you trod barefooted did you notice the heat in the grass. (Matter 230)

They would imagine, he thought with amazement, that I get something out of it, but it seemed to him that no man had ever got less. Even self-pity was denied him because he knew so exactly the extent of his guilt. He felt as though he had exiled himself so deeply in the desert that his skin had taken on the colour of sand. (Matter 235)

Then he realized what it was - a diamond, a gem stone. He knew nothing about diamonds, but it seemed to him that it was probably worth at least as much as his debt to Yusef. Presumably Yusef had information that the stones he had sent by the Esperanca had reached their destination safely. This was a mark of gratitude - not a bribe, Yusef would explain, the fat hand upon his sincere and shallow heart. (Matter 236)

Oh God, he thought, I've killed you: you've served me all these years and I've killed you at the end of them. God lay there under the petrol drums and Scobie felt the tears in his mouth, salt in the cracks of his lips. You served me and I did this to you. You were faithful to me, and I wouldn't trust you. (Matter 247-48)

The land - the grass, the sand - and its resources - diamonds, petrol - are only referred to in conjunction with a reality that defies logic: Yusef's sincere yet shallow heart, desiring the end without desiring the means, having more than one's share yet left with nothing. All describe situations that are possible and yet, at the same time, wholly illogical. Greene suggests that the colonial project, tied to the land and its natural resources, motivated by the very real desire for mineral/material wealth - in other words, a colonialism based on the real and not on the ideal - creates a situation that lacks rationality because it lacks an Idea, and it exists in an atmosphere of illogic, a world in which cause and effect are out of whack and prediction is an impossibility.

A colonialism based on reality is damned to the perverse and quirky workings of that reality, and the final book of The Heart of the Matter is full of thwarted predictions. Scobie attempts to spare his wife suffering when in fact she has known about his affair all along. Although he hoped by his death to help Helen forget him, as it turns out, in death Scobie has more hold over her mind than he did in life: "'You can't love the dead, can you? They don't exist, do they?... She put her hand out beside her and touched the other pillow, as though perhaps after all there was one chance in a thousand that she was not alone, and if she were not alone now she would never be alone again" (Matter 270-71).

Scobie is certain of his own damnation, but Father Rank insists at novel's end, "'For goodness' sake, Mrs. Scobie, don't imagine you - or I - know a thing about God's mercy'" (Matter 272). Scobie embraces an all too real, meticulously planned, material solution to his problems, which fails to achieve any of its goals. The one aspect of his suicide that seems to go as planned, the material one - the dosage is enough, the climate makes it impossible to perform a post-mortem - betrays Scobie: the "colour of the ink," under Wilson's trained scrutiny, gives him away (Matter 269). For Greene, the colonial project that is motivated by very realistic material goals is even more unpredictable in its results on all levels than is that motivated by the Idea. The search for smuggled diamonds, as nearly every intelligent person in the colony concedes, is a farce, involving large merchant ships on which a handful of tiny gems could be hidden anywhere.

Scobie is appointed commissioner one-half year too late, and would have, in effect, nullified the entire series of tragic events the novel narrates. Scobie's appointment is based on the "good impression" he makes in an interview in which he entirely loses his cool and acts like a man guilty of the worst corruptions. A colonial administration based in reality alone is at the mercy of a myriad of forces, all unguided: natural, psychological, political, economic, and so forth.

Greene himself sees the empire as nothing more than an outlet for those forces that English life and England itself cannot contain: thwarted ambitions, restless longings, boredom. The colonies serve not so much as a safety valve for England or as a dumping ground for undesirables, but as a haven for those whose needs are not met at home. Book 2 of The Heart of the Matter is populated with such figures. Perrot imagines himself on the frontiers of the empire, far from the decadence of the "big city," protecting the empire's borders from alien invasion - a hard thing to imagine when home is an island:

Scobie said, "If they ever joined the Germans, I suppose this is one of the points where they'd attack."

"Don't I know it," Perrot said, "I was moved here in 1939. The Government had a shrewd idea of what was coming. Everything's prepared, ye know.... We're stripped for action here." (Matter 111-12)

Scobie reads to Fisher A Bishop among the Bantus, a missionary tale that he transforms into a pirate tale set in the West Indies in order to relieve the boy's boredom. Helen Rolt is intrigued by the story, the first indication that in the wake of her extraordinary ordeal at sea, she too is looking for an adventurous and romantic alternative to her now-safe existence, a desire she repeatedly expresses during her stay in the colonies with Scobie: "'If you knew,' she said, 'how tired I get of all your caution. You come here after dark and you go after dark. It's so - so ignoble'" (Matter 178). The colonies offer

Father Rank the opportunity to be "useful": "'They were very generous in Northampton.

I only had to ask and they'd give. I wasn't of any use to a single living soul, Scobie. I thought, in Africa things will be different.... I wanted to be of use, that's all'" (Matter 183). Finally, Harris defines the colonies as the fit place for boys who never quite fit in, who were not quite happy at school. He says: "'I wonder if Wilson was happy there.... I don't suppose he was... or why should he have turned up here?'" (Matter 148). The colonies exist because they meet a need that home cannot, a restlessness that Greene never particularizes because it varies with different individuals.

The need to roam, to confront the unknown, to make a name, to experience adventures, all of which spurred on the late Renaissance explorers, the Victorian expeditions to the poles, the twentieth-century astronauts and kept them from staying at home - such impulses are not limited to a celebrated or noted handful, and the colonies, according to Greene, exist to provide an outlet for those others.(21) Scobie's tremendously strict Catholicism leads him to choose his own damnation in order to save Louise and Helen as well as God himself from the suffering his acts are inflicting on them.(22) Clearly, such an immense project, immense in the assumptions it questions of God and man, requires a breadth, a large playing field, that England cannot provide.

Indeed, Patrick McCarthy states that for Scobie "in the context of the West African colony it [Catholicism] acts as a seditious force because it undermines the pretence of law and duty. Scobie likes the colony because 'human nature hasn't had time to disguise itself.' The poverty and misery of the colony present man as God sees him" (225-26). This then for Greene is the only valid justification for empire: an extensive stage on which to follow and achieve vast aspirations.

Kipling inherited a Victorian mandate: in describing the Anglo-Indian culture, he felt obligated to justify its existence. He found in Arnold a schema with which to represent Anglo-Indian life. But as Conrad recognized, Kipling failed to realise that schematization fully in Plain Tales from the Hills. Why?

One can only speculate. In adopting another's schema, did Kipling ignore the power of his own first-hand contact with Anglo-Indian life, his lived experience in the colony, which in turn then took on a life of its own in his short story sequence? If such is the case, Greene's response to Conrad can be read as an odd return to Kipling's own view of the matter. Greene, like Kipling and unlike Conrad, believes the colonial endeavor can only be justified with recourse to the Idea.

In the face of the purposelessness of Conrad's hyperrealism, Greene returns to an intellectual construct reminiscent of Kipling's Arnoldian borrowing, though he rejects that specific, as well as imported, schema. In this respect, Greene is closer to Kipling. Yet unlike Kipling, both Conrad and Greene encounter the project of empire as artists first. Conrad's initial response to Kipling in the opening section of Heart of Darkness is an aesthetic critique leveled at Kipling's failed fictional embodiment of an idea. Greene's first critique of Conrad is similarly an aesthetic one. In this respect, responding first as artists, Greene is much closer in spirit and approach to Conrad than he is to Kipling.

Chapter 10

To Sup on Horrors: Christopher Hampton's Film

In Joseph Conrad's famed preface to his 1897 novella "The Nigger of the Narcissus" he wrote, "My task which I am trying to achieve is, by the power of the written word,. before all, to make you see" (xiv). In 1913 D.W. Griffith said, "The task I am trying to achieve is above all to make you see" (McFarlane 4). It is significant to notice how the statements by Conrad the novelist and Griffith the filmmaker seem to echo one another. Conrad stated that his task as a novelist was "to make you see." Griffith likewise affirmed that his task as a filmmaker was "to make you see" (McFarlane 3,4).

At first glance, it seems that both artists were saying virtually the same thing. Yet the written image, i.e., a metaphor on the printed page which the reader "sees" with the eye of the imagination, is not the same thing as the visual image which the filmgoer sees on the movie screen. In sum, the different methods of seeing, to which Conrad and Griffith are referring, are a vivid reminder that fiction belongs to the print medium while motion pictures are essentially a visual medium.

Because fiction and film are two fundamentally different artistic mediums, literal fidelity to a literary source is rarely, if ever, possible when a fictional work is adapted to the screen. Yet, as we shall see in the course of this article, screenwriter-director Christopher Hampton endeavored to remain as faithful to his literary source as possible in adapting Conrad's Secret Agent for film.

Joseph Conrad's Secret Agent (1907) has often been called the first modern spy novel. It is also a stark tale of madness, murder, and despair. In fact, John Griffith writes that the novel vividly depicts Conrad's "dark view" of modern society, dealing as it does with "urban alienation and degeneracy" (206). Indeed, when Conrad's stage version of his novel failed to attract an audience during its brief run in London in 1922, Conrad felt that his dark, brooding tragedy was too grim for the theater audience of his day. He confided to his agent, J.B. Pinker, at the time, "To make an audience of comfortable, easy-going people sup on horrors is a hopeless enterprise" (Houze 84).

Conrad biographer John Batchelor suggests that the play's failure was mainly due to Conrad's lack of experience as a dramatist. Still, Conrad was perhaps correct in thinking that the gruesome storyline of his play contributed to its failure. Indeed, Christopher Hampton recalls in his introduction to the published screenplay of The Secret Agent (1996) that, when he sought, to finance the film, "several potential investors reeled back, appalled at the darkness of the story" (Screenplay ix). Nevertheless, Hampton was eventually able to raise $7 million to make the film.

Hampton's film continues to be available on videocassette, while the screenplay is available in book form. For the record, the finished film adheres very strictly to the screenplay as published.1

Hampton's adaptation is significant for sticking to Conrad's period setting, whereas Sabotage (1936), the film version of the same Conrad novel directed by Alfred Hitchcock, was updated to the 1930s, the time when the Hitchcock film was made.2

The Secret Agent takes place in the asphalt jungle of a big city; London in the novel is portrayed as a grimy, hostile wilderness, little different from the jungle of Conrad works like Heart of Darkness. It thus makes one wonder just how "civilized" modem society really is. In the novel, Cedric Watts observes, "London is described predominately as dark, dank, slimy, and oppressive" (29). As a matter of fact, Conrad describes London in the course of the novel as a colossal aquarium, with streets "drowned in cold rain" (Novel 100). Hampton picks up on this imagery when he describes in the screenplay the atmosphere of several of the exterior scenes as being characterized by "mud and slime" and "a driving cold rain" (Screenplay 3, 46).

In Hampton's script, as in Conrad's book, Winnie Verloc (Patricia Arquette) weds Adolf Verloc (Bob Hoskins), the proprietor of a soft-core pornographic book shop, which masquerades as a stationery store. Although Verloc is several years her senior, Winnie marries him in order to provide a secure home for her mentally retarded younger brother Stevie (Christian Bale).

Winnie is unaware that Verloc's disreputable occupation as a small-time pornographer is merely a front for his clandestine activities as an anarchist. He is really working secretly in London for a foreign power: In the novel Conrad implies that it is Russia. But Hampton states explicitly in the screenplay that "the Russian imperial flag is fluttering" outside the embassy that employs Verloc as a secret operative (Screenplay 19). Verloc is ordered by his contact at the embassy to blow up the Greenwich Observatory. (Conrad based his story on an actual attempt by terrorists to bomb the Greenwich Observatory in London in 1894).

Inspector Heat, the chief adversary of Verloc and his band of terrorists, finds anarchists an inscrutable group to fathom. The revolutionary whom Heat finds it most difficult to understand is the one known only by the code name "the Professor" (Robin Williams), who supplies Verloc with explosives for his terrorist plots.3 The Professor is a true fanatic, one whose goal in life is the total destruction of the present social order because he believes that it has outlived its usefulness. In harmony with this ambition, the Professor is determined to create the perfect detonator with which to trigger his bombs, in order to fashion the most efficient instrument of destruction possible.

The Professor vows that he will never be arrested because he carries with him at all times the means of his own self-destruction: a rubber bulb hidden in his pocket, which is actually a detonator with which he can blow himself to kingdom come if he is cornered by the police. The Professor, possessed as he is by a single-minded dedication to violence and destruction, is one of the most fascinating characters in the movie.

Conrad punctuates the novel with several flashbacks; Hampton for the most part follows Conrad's lead in his script by inserting flashbacks throughout the movie. But Hampton places one key episode in chronological order, at the beginning of the film, which Conrad presents as a flashback much later in the book. He does so presumably because the scene in question tells us a good deal about Winnie's relationship with her younger brother and helps to establish their characters for us.

This particular scene shows Winnie and Stevie accompanying their mother to the retirement home where she has decided to take up residence. The aging woman moves out of the Verloc household voluntarily because she does not want Mr. Verloc's charity to be strained by having to support two dependents-Winnie's mother and younger brother-in addition to his wife.

In the course of the cab ride to the charity home, the driver of the decrepit hackney coach beats his emaciated horse for not moving fast enough. Stevie is moved with horror and compassion at the animal's plight. The cabbie explains that life is no easier for him than it is for his horse since he must work long hours to support his family. Hampton draws on Conrad's dialogue throughout this scene, as he often does in the script. Thus Stevie's interchanges with both the cab man and with Winnie are taken over virtually verbatim from the novel.

For example, Stevie says to the cabbie, "You can come in my bed if you like, and your horse as well. I'll ask Winnie" (Screenplay 14). This is Stevie's bizarre-but well-meant-method for trying to console both the driver and his horse. And he adds, "It's a hard world, Winnie. Hard on horses and for poor people" (Screenplay 16). Winnie is touched by Stevie's compassion for the unfortunates of this world and seeks to smooth his ruffled feelings. In essence, this scene displays the close bond that exists between brother and sister; indeed, Winnie's devotion to Stevie underlies her deep determination that no harm shall come to him. But harm does come to Stevie, as the story unfolds, when Verloc involves the hapless Stevie in his conspiracy to set off a bomb at the Greenwich Observatory.

Throughout the film, Stevie shows a sincere reverence for Verloc, for the fatherless lad implicitly sees Verloc as a father-figure. Similarly, Winnie Verloc views her husband as a surrogate father for Stevie. Early in the film Winnie reflects that they "might be father and son" as she watches Verloc and Stevie set off on a walk together (Screenplay 27). Ironically, as James Ray points out, Winnie is unaware at that moment that Verloc's purpose in taking the lad for a stroll is to "prepare Stevie for his role in the bombing" (71).

Following the book, the film details how Verloc, without Winnie's knowledge, gives Stevie a package containing a time bomb, supplied to him by the Professor. Verloc instructs Stevie to deposit the parcel at the Greenwich Observatory; the hapless Stevie follows Verloc's instructions to the letter-except that he stumbles over an exposed tree root in the yard outside the Observatory, accidentally sets off the bomb prematurely, and is himself blown to fragments. Winnie had assured Verloc that the boy "would go through fire for you" (Novel 184), and, as Catharine Rising wryly remarks in her book on Conrad, Stevie finally did.

It was unfortunate that Winnie knew nothing of Verloc's nefarious profession as an anarchist and that she furthermore was unaware that Verloc had involved her beloved brother in his activities. But she was simply living by her golden rule that "things do not stand much looking into"-a conviction based on the questionable assumption that what you don't know can't hurt you (Novel 177). Consequently, Winnie had never bothered to inquire into her husband's private activities, and hence she only learned the truth about Verloc's covert conspiracies after Stevie died in his futile effort to carry out one of Verloc's terrorist plots. (We see Stevie's death in flashback when Verloc recounts what happened in Winnie's presence).

When Winnie finally discovers what happened to Stevie, she realizes with deep anguish that, as Rising puts it, "Verloc has ended her supreme illusion: that he and Stevie might be father and son" (110). As a matter of fact, when Winnie learns of Stevie's death, there is a flashback to her watching Verloc and Stevie walking down the street side by side when she murmured to herself, "Like father and son." She repeats these words to Verloc when she confronts him about Steve's fate: "I thought you were like father and son. But you were just taking him away from me to murder him" (Screenplay 60).

Crazed with grief. Winnie wreaks revenge on Verloc for the death of her beloved brother by murdering him with a carving knife. Paul Kirschner points out that one of Conrad's vividly imagined scenes could easily be transferred to the movie screen. Kirschner mentions the stabbing scene in The Secret Agent as a premier example of one of Conrad's vividly realized scenes which could be transplanted virtually intact to the cinema.

As Conrad composed the episode in the novel, the carving knife is prominent from the beginning of the scene: Verloc is pictured employing the knife to carve the meat and cut the bread, as he devours his supper. When he is finished, Verloc lies down on the living room couch, and Winnie moves toward him with murder on her mind:

He was lying on his back and staring upwards. He saw partly on the ceiling and partly on the wall the moving shadow of an arm with a clenched hand holding a carving knife. It fluttered up and down.. Mr. Verloc, the Secret Agent, turning slightly on his side with the force of the blow, expired without stirring a limb, in the muttered sound of the word 'Don't' by way of protest. (Novel 266-67)

Krischner sums up the scene by saying that although Conrad had probably never seen a film when he wrote The Secret Agent in 1906, "a director would not be hard put to translate this sequence into terms of a shooting script" (348). Needless to say, Christopher Hampton modeled the stabbing scene in his film adaptation of The Secret Agent on Conrad's depiction of the episode in the novel. Winnie's actions at this juncture are described in the script in the following terms:

She looks at him, stretched out on the sofa.... She crosses the room with the carving knife concealed behind her back.... She brings the knife from behind her back. Verloc, finally realizing what Winnie means to do, says, "Don't." But "Winnie plunges the knife into his chest."(Screenplay 64)

Verloc is completely surprised by Winnie's murderous intent and does not have time to defend himself against her onslaught. In summary, the stabbing scene is superbly shot and edited and provides a shocking dramatic highpoint for the film. Hampton is careful to incorporate into the film a visual symbol that is taken right from the novel.

Immediately after Winnie learns of Stevie's horrible death in the movie, "her right hand moves across and begins playing with the golden ring on her left. It glitters as it catches the light" (Screenplay 56).

Winner now views her wedding ring as the emblem of her failed marriage. She had tried to create a family with Verloc and herself as Stevie's surrogate parents. But her husband has destroyed their surrogate son-her brother. Furthermore, Knoepflmacher observes that, when Winnie defiantly clutches the carving knife in the murder scene, she plans to use it "to sever once and for all the stifling bonds represented by the gold circlet of her wedding ring," bonds that have bound her to Verloc, her despised husband (53).

Still in the grip of madness and despair, Winnie shortly afterward decides to end her life by throwing herself into the sea from the deck of a channel steamer. Just before she leaps to her death, "she looks down at the wedding ring. It is difficult to ease it off her finger, but she eventually manages it and lays the ring down beside her on the wooden bench. Then she rises and begins to move toward the rail" and jumps overboard (Screenplay 66).

Winnie discards the ring just before her suicide as a way of totally repudiating the marriage that has brought her anguish and despair. Hampton's strong sense of visual storytelling is clearly on display in the deft symbolism of the ring just described.

The novel concludes with the Professor walking down a crowded London thoroughfare, ruminating about the destruction caused by the explosives that he supplies for the acts of terrorism perpetrated by his fellow anarchists. "Nobody looked at him," Conrad writes, "He passed on unsuspected and deadly, like a pest in the street full of men" (Novel 311).

Hampton gives a shocking twist to Conrad's ending. In the film "the Professor is engulfed in throngs of passers-by," as he takes out of his pocket a rubber bulb; it is the detonator that he keeps hidden there. Just as he squeezes the bulb, the sound track cuts off.

"In the ensuing perfect silence, a thin smile begins to spread across the Professor's wintry features; and there is a freeze frame" (Screenplay 75-76). The Professor, who has called himself a force for ruin and destruction, destroys himself and many of the hapless pedestrians who surround him on the pavement in a final gesture of madness.

Although Caryn James praises Patricia Arquette's "stirring performance" as Winnie Verloc, she criticizes the movie as a whole for lacking in suspense (28). Edmund Eugene notes that Hampton "adheres religiously to both letter and the spirit of the novel," but likewise faults the film for being neither suspenseful nor intriguing (81). On the contrary, once Verloc sets in motion his plan to blow up the Greenwich Observatory, the film proceeds at a lively pace. Moreover, it is highlighted by some engrossing and gripping scenes, such as the hideous death of Stevie (shown in flashback), Winnie's vengeful killing of Verloc, and her ultimate suicide.

Hampton feels that too often in the past filmmakers have tried to dilute Conrad's uncompromising vision of the dark side of the human condition in bringing his work to the screen. "We like our great writers to be optimists about human nature," he explains, "and Conrad was not. His eye was very bleak" (Rosenthal 35). For his part, Christopher Hampton believes that the sensibilities of contemporary audiences are in tune with Conrad's pessimistic view of mankind. In the present film Hampton has faithfully portrayed Conrad's somber vision of life, as it is reflected in this tragic tale, with spare, unvarnished realism.

In sum, Hampton's Secret Agent is a faithful rendering on the screen of the Conrad original, and therefore deserves a prominent place among the better screen versions of Conrad's fiction. As James Welsh has written in these pages of Hampton's Secret Agent, "Adaptations of this order inspire some hope and confidence" in the future of the

Moral Conditions for Genocide in Joseph Conrad's Heart of Darkness 1, The Scholars may differ in their moral assessment of Joseph Conrad's fiction, but they all seem to agree that morality is a legitimate lens for interpreting the novels.

The problem, of course, is specifying Conrad's orientation toward morality, for as scholars consistently observe, unstable knowledge and unreliable perception are persistent themes in Conrad's corpus.2 Not surprisingly, there has been much confusion on the topic of Conrad's moral vision.

Given Conrad's rejection of certain knowledge, Ian Watt claims that Conrad develops a flexible moral paradigm, what he dubs "subjective moral impressionism" (1980, 174). This theoretical approach has found its most recent formulation in John G. Peters's Conrad and Impressionism, which articulates an impressionist epistemology that allows Conrad to maintain "moral values" and thereby "avoid the abyss of ethical anarchy and epistemological solipsism" (2001, 135).

Like Watt and Peters, Mark Wollaeger intelligently examines Conrad's moral vision in relation to his obstinate epistemological questionings: "A skeptic himself, Conrad nevertheless remained consciously devoted to a moral perspective on life and literature" (1990, 14).

Less optimistic, however, is H.M. Daleski, who sees in the fiction a "pervasive moral nihilism" (1977, 24), a view that Dwight H. Purdy shares when he calls the later novels "morally repellent" (1984, 7). In this same tradition is Patrick Brantlinger, who writes about the "moral bankruptcy' of Conrad's "literary project" (1996, 96).

MORE ARTICLES OF INTEREST

'Heart of Darkness' and late-Victorian fascination with the primitive and the...

Colonizers, Cannibals, and the Horror of Good Intentions in Joseph Conrad's...

Joseph Conrad

"Signifying nothing": Conrad's idiots and the anxiety of modernism - Joseph...

"Speech Was of No Use": Conrad, a New Journalism, and the Critical...

In the following pages, I want to demonstrate why the moral interpretation of Conrad's texts is problematic at best and completely misguided at worst. Put simply, to determine whether Conrad's "literary project" is moral or not, the scholar must be strategically positioned to make such a judgment. In other words, the scholar must have an implicit or explicit set of criteria to determine what constitutes a true moral vision. Moreover, this scholar must be in possession of a reliable epistemology that gives him/her access to true moral criteria.

Significantly, it was when Conrad was working through the ideas central to Heart of Darkness that he rejected the concept of morality. For instance, in a letter to his dear friend R.B. Cunninghame Graham dated January 31, 1898, approximately one year before Conrad completed the novella, Conrad says: "There is no morality, no knowledge and no hope; there is only the consciousness of ourselves which drives us about a world that whether seen in a convex or a concave mirror is always but a vain and fleeting appearance" (1969, 71).

This rejection of morality is not a one-time affair, for only five months after Heart of Darkness had completed serialization with Blackwood's Magazine, Conrad makes a similar observation in a letter to Edward Garnett: "I still have some pretensions to the possession of a conscience though my morality is gone to the dogs.

I am like a man who has lost his gods" (1986, 2:198). This is a very curious remark. Conrad is certainly not endorsing an inhumane philosophy rooted in moral nihilism; as a possessor of a conscience, he believes in taking personal and political responsibility for one's actions. The problem is that something intrinsic to morality makes socially responsible and politically just action impossible. So, for Conrad, to have a conscience means rejecting morality; or conversely, being moral conflicts with having a conscience.

Of course, this strict morality/conscience dichotomy begs the question: what is Conrad's definition of morality? As I will argue in this essay, however, such a question is incoherent. For Conrad, the problem is not defining true morality; rather, the problem is that morality is an empty signifier, a semiotic vacuity that dominant political powers can strategically manipulate in order to justify crimes against humanity.

Put differently, Conrad rejects morality, not because it is an essential concept that leads necessarily to social injustice, but because it is such an amorphous concept that political powers can so easily exploit in order to justify some of the most heinous crimes against humanity, specifically genocide.

Therefore, instead of claiming that Conrad details a clear but extremely negative concept of morality in his fiction, I examine how he portrays a charismatic political figure who appropriates morality in order to justify crimes against humanity. Specifically, I discuss how an intelligent imperialist like Kurtz can strategically construct a political system that makes a crime like genocide a moral imperative.

I. "Mind the Gap"

To illustrate the insurmountable difficulties of the moral interpretation, I examine Heart of Darkness, specifically Kurtz's report to the International Society for the Suppression of Savage Customs. It is my contention that scholars have consistently misinterpreted what little we have of this document precisely because they have interpreted it through a moral lens.

The document begins with an observation about the superior development of white Europeans, who "'must necessarily appear to them [savages] in the nature of supernatural beings-we approach them with the might as of a deity'" (Conrad 1996, 66). Given European "superiority," white colonizers could by "'the simple exercise of'" their "'will... exert a power for good practically unbounded'" (66).

Such "altruistic sentiment" leads Marlow into a state of euphoria, that is, until the concluding postscript, which reads: "'Exterminate all the brutes!'" On reading this line, Marlow is horrified. How could a simple exercise of will exerting a power for good lead to a call for genocide? For Marlow, the problem with Kurtz's call to exterminate the brutes is that it seemingly contradicts the content of the preceding "altruistic sentiment."

Chapter 11

Achievement Without Success

After finishing "'The End of the Tether'", Conrad took Jessie to London for 'a week of what to rustics of our sort was a Whirl-(with a capital W)' [1] where they saw something of the Galsworthys. Back at work again Conrad made yet another attempt to tackle *The Rescue,* [2] but with as little success as before. In desperation he sent it off to Hueffer's 'friendly hands for the only real work of Rescue that will ever be found in its text'. [3] It is not known what, if anything, Hueffer did to it.

At the same time he started work on another story, telling Hueffer: 'I believe it will end in something silly and saleable as "Youth" seems to be in a measure.' [4] He had previously told Galsworthy that with his 'head full of a story, I have not been able to write a single word—except the title, which shall be, I think: *Nostromo*: the story belonging to the "Karain" class of tales...'. [5] His original conception of this novel thus seems to have been totally different from its final form.

1903 was to be a year of worry and bad health, but also of some achievement. In February Conrad told Ernest Dawson that he had been 'rather seedy and somehow very wretched'. [6] He was of course still very worried about money and in March he wrote to Hueffer:

I just only begin to pick up. I had two days in bed. As it was to be expected I found myself in a hole on my return with a stiff letter from Watson [his banker]—d'un ton très rogue—indeed.

However, it's no use. He must put up with me up to that point. I've no doubt he will take good care I don't go beyond.

Damn! Anyhow if I can finish N. in three months I am

saved for a time. And if then I can finish *Rescue* by December next I am saved altogether. The question is—Can I make the effort—is it in me?

But he went on:

I have begun to write at a good rate enough for a sick man and I shall improve on that no doubt. [23 March 1903]

On 26 May he told Elsie Hueffer that 'despair of ever accomplishing anything good has dulled my nerves and I plod on drearily and caring but very little'. He persevered and in August was able to tell Pinker that he had written about 42,000 words of *Nostromo*. [7] He continued:

I have never worked so hard before—with so much anxiety. But the result is good. You know I take no credit to myself for what I do—and so I may judge my own performance. There is no mistake about this. You may take up a strong position when you offer it here. It is a very genuine Conrad. At the same time it is more of a Novel pure and simple than anything I've done since *Almayer's Folly*....

But it's a miserable life anyhow. Have you sent anything to Watson this month? I daren't draw a cheque. But I felt too sick of everything to write you before. Moreover, my salvation is to shut eyes and ears to everything—or else I couldn't write a line. And yet sometimes I can't forget—I remember the tradesmen, and all the horrors descend upon me. Damn! Try to help me out to the end of this and then we will see how we stand. [22 August 1903, *LL., I,* 316]

He also wrote to Galsworthy:

Dearest Jack,

The book is, this moment, half done [it turned out to be no more than a quarter] and I feel half dead and wholly imbecile.

If you want to do your part by a man, for whom you have done so much already, then do not fail to come down here the first day you can spare.

To work in the conditions which are, I suppose, the outcome of my character mainly, is belittling—it is demoralising. I fight against demoralisation, of which fight I bear the brunt and my friends bear the cost. All this is very beautiful and inspiriting to think about, and elevating and encouraging and—I can't think of any more pretty words....

I didn't write to you because, upon my word, I am ashamed to write to anybody. I feel myself strangely growing into a sort of outcast. A mental and moral outcast. I hear of nothing—I think of nothing—I reflect upon nothing—I cut myself off—and with all that I can just only keep going, or rather keep on lagging from one wretched story to another—and always deeper in the mire.

We are so glad to hear your father is really better. Remember us all round, pray, as kindly as you know.

And do come. The prospect of your going abroad fills me with dread. Why? Nerves?

Don't you think I ought to apologise for this silly letter? I do! I do!

[22 August 1903, *LL., I,* 317]

He continued to plod on but then had a relapse. At the end of November he wrote once more Galsworthy:

I've been ill again. Just got down, shaky, weak, dispirited. No work done. No spring left to grapple with it. Everything looks black, but I suppose that will wear off, and anyhow, I am trying to keep despair under. Nevertheless I feel myself losing my footing in deep waters. They are lapping about my lips.

My dear fellow it is not so much the frequency of these gout attacks, but I feel so beastly ill between, ill in body and mind. It has never been so before. Impossible to write—while the brain riots in incoherent images. It is sometimes quite alarming. [30 November 1903, *LL., I,* 322]

To crown the year he wrote to Miss Capes in December:

My mind struggles with a strange sort of torpor, struggles desperately while the sands are running out. That is the most terrifying thought of all. They are running out—and there is nothing done; nothing of what one desires to do. [26 December 1903, Keating Collection]

And to Meldrum:

It has been a most disastrous year for my work. If I had written each page with my blood I could not feel more

exhausted at the end of this twelvemonth. [26 December 1903]
It might be thought that Conrad was exaggerating his disorders. He was certainly no stoic, but these letters reflected his state of mind as is shown by a letter which William Rothenstein wrote to Gosse eighteen months later. 'Of course he is terribly hysterical—indeed last year I feared for his reason'; and, after referring to Conrad's 'morbid excitable mind', Rothenstein added, 'I am terribly sorry for him, but it is very hard at times to be patient—natures like his demand as a right, if one once gives affection, a very great deal of one's time and energy.' [8] How far his ills were psychologically induced is another matter. As Jessie pointed out, Conrad almost invariably went down with gout after a period of stress or a crisis, which suggests a psychological element. However there are not adequate grounds for doubting a physical basis, and Conrad's bad teeth (he was apparently very loth to visit the dentist) indicate a possible cause of his gout.

The new year started with a misfortune which did not seem serious at first but which affected the rest of Conrad and Jessie's life. In January Conrad took Jessie to London to consult a doctor because he was worried about her heart. [9] He was reassured on this, but as Jessie was coming out of John Barker's after doing some shopping she 'slipped the cartilage of both knees at once and fell on the pavement, hurting very badly the knee already damaged by an accident I had at the age of sixteen'. [10] The result of this accident was that Jessie remained a partial cripple for the rest of her life, despite a number of operations.

On top of this came a further disaster. Conrad's bankers, Watson and Co., failed. He thus 'lost a good friend for he did back me up through all these years', [11] as he told Wells, and was faced with the necessity to pay off his overdraft. In the same letter he told Wells that he had 'started a series of sea sketches and have sent out Pinker on the hunt to place them. This must save me. I've discovered that I can dictate that sort of bosh without effort at the rate of 3,000 words in four hours. Fact. The only thing now is to sell it to a paper and then make a book of the rubbish. Hang! So in the day *Nostromo* and, from

11 to 1 a.m., dictation.' [12] The sea sketches were the beginning of *The Mirror of the Sea*.

He also said that, on Sidney Colvin's advice, he had started to write a play in one act, based on the short story "'To-morrow'". He called the play *One Day More*. Although Conrad never apparently showed much interest in the theatre, disparaged it as a medium of expression—proclaiming his "ineradicable mistrust of the theatre as the destroyer of all suggestiveness' [13] —and frequently inveighed against actors, he had some years earlier confessed his desire, like so many novelists and poets, to write a play. In a letter to Cunninghame Graham he had said:

> I haven't seen a play for years, but I have this one [*Admiral Guinea*, by Henley and Stevenson]. And that's all I can say about it. I have no notion of a play. No play grips me on the stage or off. Each of them seems to me an amazing freak of folly. They are all unbelievable and as disillusioning as a bang on the head. I greatly desire to write a play myself. It is my dark and secret ambition. And yet I can't conceive how a sane man can sit down deliberately to write a play and not go mad before he has done. The actors appear to me like a lot of wrong-headed lunatics pretending to be sane. Their malice is stitched with white threads. They are disguised and ugly. To look at them breeds in my melancholy soul thoughts of murder and suicide,—such is my anger and my loathing of their transparent pretences. There is a taint of subtle corruption in their blank voices, in their blinking eyes, in the grimacing faces, in the false light, in the false passion, in the words that have been learned by heart. [6 December 1897, *LL.*, *I*, 213]

It is not known why Conrad felt this astonishing hostility towards actors or on what he based it. He confessed in the letter that he had not seen a play 'for years' and so he presumably had little or no experience of the English theatre. In a letter to Garnett he shows that he knew the work of Scribe and Sardou [14] and he may well have frequented the theatre while he was based on Marseilles. *

This was not a solitary outburst and he seems to have persisted in his dislike of actors and acting throughout his life;

more than ten years later he told Garnett: 'Though I detest the stage I have a theatrical imagination—that's why perhaps I detest the stage—that is the actors who mostly, poor souls, have no imagination.' [15] And four years before he died he wrote to Curle: 'The Movie is just a silly stunt for silly people—but the theatre is more compromising since it is capable of falsifying the very soul of one's work, both on the imaginative and on the intellectual side—besides having some sort of inferior poetics of its own which is bound to play havoc with that imponderable quality of creative literary expression, which depends on one's individuality.' [16] Despite this prejudice he persisted in his ambition to write a successful play.

Although there was no longer any specific collaboration, Hueffer was still very close to Conrad, both in his personal life and in his work. He had helped Conrad with *One Day More* by extracting all the dialogue from "'To-morrow'". [17] It is clear that he also gave considerable help to Conrad with six of the 'sketches' which were subsequently collected together as *The Mirror of the Sea*. In a letter to Hueffer Conrad wrote:

> I saw Pinker the other day. No word yet from Harvey as to sketches. Halkett offered to take six at 5 guineas per thousand. Halkett really is a last resource and I told Pinker not to throw the thing away in haste.
>
> But still Halkett's proposal means 90 guineas of which (I told Pinker again) I must have 30 when—and if—the affair is concluded, *pour votre Seigneurie*.
>
> As to the book form (which Harvey already is ready to take) a small calculation will fix our proportions; for I suppose we cannot now finish the whole together. Can we? [29 May 1904]

Hueffer gives an account of how he helped Conrad:

> *The Mirror of the Sea* and *A Personal Record* were mostly written by my hand from Conrad's dictation. Whilst he was dictating them, I would recall incidents to him—I mean incidents of his past life which he had told me but which did not come freely back to his mind because at the time he was mentally ill, in desperate need of money, and, above all,

sceptical as to the merits of the reminiscential form which I had suggested to him. The fact is I could make Conrad write at periods when his despair and fatigue were such that in no other way would it have been possible to him. He would be lying on the sofa or pacing the room, railing at life and literature as practised in England, and I would get a writing pad and pencil and, whilst he was still raving, would interject: 'Now then, what was it you were saying about coming up the Channel and nearly running over a fishing boat that suddenly appeared under your bows?' and gradually there would come "'Landfalls and Departures'". [18]

Even Jessie concedes Hueffer's help in this case, saying:

F. M. H. has made the most fantastic claims with regard to my husband's various plots, yet *The Mirror of the Sea* owes a great deal to his ready and patient assistance—not perhaps to the actual writing, but that book would never have come into being if Joseph Conrad had had no intelligent person with whom to talk over these intimate reminiscences. [19]

Their intimacy during this period was such that when Conrad was asked for a story by the Northern Newspaper Syndicate he wrote to Hueffer: 'I was going to fling it [the letter] into the paper basket. Still —if you have something written that you do *not* care for *in the least* send it on. I'll put in a few of my jargon phrases and send it on. As I remarked—nothing matters—and we are intimate enough to say anything to each other.

You may as well have this modest cheque. If the thing shocks you tear the sweet note up.' [20] Hueffer also claims to have helped with *Nostromo,* but it is difficult to discover how far he did so. Certainly Conrad seems to have been prepared to call on Hueffer if necessary because, in the early stages of *Nostromo,* he wrote to him: 'I do not doubt of your assistance in my efforts. You must run down and see me soon.' [21] And he told Pinker: 'If people want to begin printing (serial) say in Sept[er] you may let them safely—for you know that, at the very worst, H. stands in the background (quite confidentially you understand). But there's no reason to anticipate anything of the kind. If I am to break down it will be after this infernal thing is finished.'[22] Moreover, Hueffer sold to Keating fifteen pages of manuscript of the *Nostromo* text written in his own hand. This fragment comes early in Part III,[23] and Hueffer would have had to have known the story very well indeed to have written the passage himself; he may have done so, but it is more likely that he took it down from Conrad's dictation.

The first five papers of *The Mirror of the Sea*, a little more of *Nostromo*, and three articles for the *Daily Mail* were all written while the Conrads were still in London after Jessie's accident.[*] The Conrads' rooms in Gordon Place were very close to the Hueffers, and during this period the two families apparently shared household expenses, the Conrads usually going to have their meals with the Hueffers although Jessie says that she 'never felt at home and welcome there'. There was an influenza epidemic raging at the time and both households were prostrated, including Conrad. Hueffer tells how, his German cook having been taken off in an ambulance with influenza, he did the cooking himself without Conrad being aware of the change as long as he imitated Johanna's plain German cooking. Then one day he decided to do a *civet do lièvre à la Parisienne*:

> Conrad inspected it as he always did, carefully and with his monocle screwed into his eye. He rubbed his hands and with enthusiasm unfolded his napkin. When, with head on one side and a look of pleased anticipation, he had tasted it, he started slightly. He said:
>
> 'My dear faller.—The admirable Johanna has of course surpassed herself.—But—eh—my gout!—*Une telle succulence, mon cher.*—Tebb [his doctor] says the greatest abstinence.—' He added that—if there remained a little of the admirable saddle of Lamb of the night before—a small slice, cold, with a leaf of salad.—
>
> I went down wearily into the kitchen, put the remains of lamb on the dumbwaiter, washed a lettuce and beat up some dressing.—I imitated Johanna from then on.

The Conrads returned to the Pent some time in March and both of them retired to bed.[26] Jessie was laid up for a month with her knee.

For the next five months Conrad worked hard at *Nostromo,* which he finished on 30 August [27] amid the usual dramatic circumstances:

Phoo! I am weary. For more than a month I have been sitting up till three a.m.—ending with a solid 36 hours, (in the middle of which I had to wire for the dentist and have a tooth drawn!!...) It broke!!...!! Till at 11.30 I broke down just after raising my eyes to the clock.

Then I don't know; two blank hours during which I must have got out and sat down—(not fallen) on the concrete outside the door.

That's how I found myself; and crawling in again noted the time; considerably after one.

But I've finished. There's no elation. No relief even. Nothing. Moreover I've yet a good fortnight's work for the book form.... I am weary I! weary.[28]

(3)

In the Author's Note to *Nostromo,* Conrad mentioned that 'after finishing the last story of the *Typhoon* volume it seemed somehow that there was nothing more in the world to write about'.[29] All his substantial work had hitherto been based on his own experience or on hearsay within a context which he knew well and he presumably felt that he had now exhausted this source. He therefore began to search further afield and, during the period of his greatest achievement, his novels were to range over areas of which he had had virtually no personal experience.

In the same Author's Note he continued: 'This so strangely negative but disturbing mood lasted some little time; and then, as with many of my longer stories, the first hint for *Nostromo* came to me in the shape of a vagrant anecdote completely destitute of valuable details;'[30] this was the story of a man having stolen singlehanded a lighter full of silver on the Tierra Firma seaboard during a revolution. Conrad says that he had first heard the story in 1875 or '76 when he was in the Gulf of Mexico and that he had later discovered an account of the exploit in the memoirs of a seaman which he had picked up outside a second-hand bookshop.

The book to which Conrad was evidently alluding has recently been tracked down; it is *On Many Seas: the Life and Exploits of a Yankee Sailor*, by Frederick Benton Williams, edited by his Friend William Stone Booth. * Frederick Benton Williams is the pseudonym of Herbert Elliot Hamblen and *On Many Seas* is an account of his youthful adventures as a seaman from 1864 to 1878.

In Chapter XXXII Hamblen describes his association with a 'swarthy, piraticallooking fellow' named Nicolo who told him one night how he had been entrusted with a lighter full of silver during a revolution; Nicolo had killed the two other members of the crew, then scuttled the lighter near the shore and had since been growing rich slowly. † Conrad used a few details from this story, but transformed the character of Nicolo which was that of an 'unmitigated rascal' [31] into that of Nostromo. It appears most likely that Nicolo's exploit had never occurred but, somewhere along the line, had been invented;[32] in view of this and of Conrad's tendency to disguise his indebtedness to books, his claim to have heard the anecdote himself in the Gulf of Mexico must be treated with circumspection.

In the Author's Note he goes on facetiously to say that his principal authority for the history of Costaguana is Don José Avellanos's fictitious History of Fifty Years of Misrule. And, until recently, it had been generally assumed that, apart from a few details picked up here and there, the whole South American background to the novel was the product of Conrad's imagination. The remarks of two of his closest friends are typical.

Galsworthy wrote that *Nostromo* was Conrad's 'most sheer piece of creation. For by his own confession, very much of his work was based intimately on his own adventures and experiences; and *Nostromo* creates a continent which he had only glimpsed.' [33] While Richard Curie has said: 'His [Conrad's] power of visualisation was immense. For example, he built up the whole atmosphere of *Nostromo*, which breathes the very spirit of South America, from a few days upon the coast.' [34] Conrad had told Curle:

As to *Nostromo*. If I ever mentioned twelve hours it must relate to Puerto Cabello where I was ashore about that time. In La Guayra, as I went up the hill and had a distant view of Caracas, I must have been two and a half to three days. It's such a long time ago! And there were a few hours in a few other places on that dreary coast of Venezuela. [22 July 1923]

When he was grappling with the novel, Conrad complained to Cunninghame Graham: 'I am dying over that cursed *Nostromo* thing All my memories of Central America seem to slip away. I just had a glimpse twenty-five years ago,—a short glance. That is not enough pour bâtir un roman dessus. And yet one must live.' [35] Perhaps Cunninghame Graham then advised that Conrad should turn to books to supplement his memories and suggested some titles or perhaps Conrad had already decided to fill in the gaps and stimulate his imagination with some reading about South America. At all events it is clear that at some point he carefully studied George Frederick Masterman's *Seven Eventful Years in Paraguay*, [36] Edward B. Eastwick's *Venezuela*, [37] probably one or more of Sir Clements Markham's books on South America, [38] and possibly some others.

From Masterman, Conrad took most of the names of his characters, including Gould, Decoud, Corbelàn, Mitchell (Michell in Masterman), Fidanza (Nostromo's surname), Barrios and Monygham. Masterman was a doctor and Conrad based his account of Dr Monygham's torture and confession on that of Masterman himself; [39] the character and career of the tyrannical dictator, Francisco Solano Lopez, supplied Conrad with material on which to draw for the Montero brothers [40] and for the ruthless Guzman Bento. [*] There are also a number of other small details.

From Eastwick, Conrad took some more names; there are names of geographical features like Mt. Higuerota and of people, like Sotillo, General Guzman Blanco, whom Conrad turned into Guzman Bento, while the reigning beauty of Valencia is Antonia Ribera. Her surname is used for that of the benevolent President of Costaguana and although Conrad said that Antonia Avellanos was modelled on his first love [41] there is a very close correspondence between her character and appearance and that of Antonia Ribera. Eastwick's Antonia was, like Conrad's, emancipated and Europeanised; her opening remark to Eastwick was ' Caballero, are you married?' to which he, taken aback but hopeful, replied: 'Sometimes.' [42] 'The other young ladies of Sulaco stood in awe of' the 'character and accomplishments' of Antonia Avellanos.

'She was reputed to be terribly learned and serious.' [43] Eastwick found that Antonia Ribera 'talked like a bookworm, like a politician, like a diplomatist, like a savant'. [44] In appearance Antonia Avellanos was a 'tall, grave girl, with a self-possessed manner, a wide, white forehead, a wealth of rich brown hair, and blue eyes', [45] while Eastwick said of the other Antonia: 'her eyes were dark blue, her hair a rich brown, her nose Grecian, her eyebrows arched'. [46]

Eastwick describes Puerto Cabello in some detail and Conrad evidently used this to revive his own memories in order to base the topography of the port of Sulaco on that of Puerto Cabello. The latter is situated in the Golfo Triste, which became the Golfo Placido in *Nostromo* and is protected by a spit of land, like the peninsula of Azuera, on which was situated an unused lighthouse. Opposite the spit are the reefs of Punta Brava, which became the cape of Punta Mala.

It is 'protected from all winds, on the east, north, and south' by the land and from the west by a group of islands as well as the mainland. 'In short, there is perhaps no harbour in the world where the sea is at all times so calm as at Puerto Cabello.' [47] The customs houses at Sulaco and Puerto Cabello are similarly situated, and for some of the topography of the town of Sulaco Conrad draws on Eastwick's description of the inland town of Valencia. It is fascinating how even the most insignificant detail would be picked up and used by Conrad. At one point, at a reception, when Eastwick was presented with a yellow flower there was much delight at his exclamation of '*Viva la Amarilla*' because yellow was, unknown to him, the colour of the political party in power; in *Nostromo* the most exclusive club of Sulaco is called the Amarilla. [48]

Through the reading of these books, written at first hand

by intelligent, observant men, Conrad was able to immerse himself in the authentic atmosphere of the South America of the middle of the nineteenth century. The points of view of the authors, particularly that of Eastwick, would have been sympathetic to Conrad. For instance:

Those who think that the overthrow of a bad government implies the inauguration of a better will do well to ponder over these remarks, and the more they reflect upon them and study the history of the events to which they refer, the less will be their sympathy with the revolutionary principles which are spreading so rapidly in Europe.

But although this knowledge of Conrad's sources invalidates the assumption that he created Costaguana out of his head it in no way detracts from the far more important aspects of his achievement. There is no question of plagiarism because these books only supplied the raw material with which he built the edifice. A comparison between the sources and what Conrad made of them serves above all to underline the transmuting power of his imagination.

For instance, there are mundane allusions in Eastwick to the uncompleted railroad from Puerto Cabello to San Felipe; from this hint Conrad creates the scene of the inauguration of that 'progressive and patriotic undertaking', the National Central Railway, with all its philosophical overtones, [50] the description of the trains passing old Viola's house, [51] and Nostromo's magnificent dash to the construction camp on an engine. [52] Equally interesting are the modifications which Conrad added to Eastwick's topographical descriptions; Douglas Hewitt his stressed the significance of Conrad's emphasis on the isolation, the inaccessibility of Sulaco [53] and there is no parallel to this in Eastwick or Masterman. In fact all the important elements of *Nostromo* are to be found either not at all in Conrad's sources (although the possibility of an undiscovered source cannot be ruled out) or else in the merest embryo.

Nostromo is Conrad's most ambitious feat of imagination and is worthy of comparison with the most ambitious of all great novels, *War and Peace*. Hitherto Conrad had written primarily about men in communion with themselves, and in relation to one another or within the restricted society of a ship's crew, although it is true that 'Heart of Darkness' contains an implied criticism of colonialism and commercial exploitation of backward peoples and wider issues are broached in the Patusan section of *Lord Jim*.

In *Nostromo* he maintained his concern with the individual and with personal relations but extended his range to include public as well as private life. He chose a far larger canvas than he had used before or was to use again; it is as large as that of any great novel except *War and Peace*. On it he placed not only the lives and fates of an array of characters but the physical and political composition of a whole country, creating it with the most meticulous though selective detail. The account of Mrs Gould's travels through the Occidental Province is an example of the care with which he built up the visual background to the events:

She saw them on the road carrying loads, lonely figures upon the plain, toiling under great straw hats, with their white clothing flapping about their limbs in the wind; she remembered the villages by some group of Indian women at the fountain impressed upon her memory, by the face of some young Indian girl with a melancholy and sensual profile, raising an earthenware vessel of cool water at the door of a dark hut with a wooden porch cumbered with great brown jars.

The solid wooden wheels of an ox-cart, halted with its shafts in the dust, showed the strokes of the axe; and a party of charcoal carriers, with each man's load resting above his head on the top of the low mud wall, slept stretched in a row within the strip of shade.[54]

The frequent allusions to light show the extent to which Conrad must have projected himself visually into Costaguana, while the topographical description of the surroundings of Sulaco, shut off from the sea by the vast Golfo Placido and dominated by the Cordillera, where 'the white head of Higuerota rises majestically upon the blue',[55] has such precision that it remains imprinted photographically upon the mind throughout the book. Conrad allows himself an assortment of devices to develop his subject. There is no narrator as there was in his previous long novel, *Lord Jim*. Instead most of the book is written anonymously and directly in the third person, although the anonymity is occasionally broken by phrases like 'those of us whom business or curiosity took to Sulaco... can remember' or '... as I am told'. [57] Then on one important occasion Conrad uses the garrulous and portentous Captain Mitchell to relate the events and on another Decoud describes them in a long letter to his sister.

Without a narrator to perform the task of analysis and comment Conrad uses the characters to comment on each other and to reflect events. The sardonic Dr Monygham and the sceptical Decoud are particularly exploited in this way, and Captain Mitchell is used to impart unconsciously an ironic tone. Although they can often be taken as reflecting the author's view Dr. Monygham and Decoud are characters in their own right; they reveal themselves as well as others by their comments and it is always necessary to take the com mentator's own character into account when assessing the comment. Conrad does not, however, rely on this method alone, but frequently intervenes with impersonal judgments and reflections.

It is perhaps the lack of a narrator which exposes the weakness of Conrad's characterisation, because far more is demanded of the characters than when Marlow is there as Master of Ceremonies. It is evident that most of the characters, in particular the leading ones, exist for what they represent rather than for what they are. Although they play important roles in the development of the themes and are in that respect vivid and real, their psychology is on the whole crude, blurred, or even unconvincing. It is with the minor, picturesque characters such as Sotillo, General Montero, and Mitchell that Conrad succeeds best.

For instance, magnificent figure though Nostromo is, his psychology is rudimentary. He is summed up in a few words and the comments upon him of the other characters, as well as those of the author, tend to be repetitive. So do his own actions and words. Conrad himself does not seem to have been satisfied with him. He agreed with Cunninghame Graham's criticism, although it must be admitted that he would not have been likely to dispute the point in this context:

> I don't defend Nostromo himself. Fact is he does not take my fancy either. As to his conduct generally and with women in particular, I only wish to say that he is not a Spaniard or S. American. I tried to differentiate him even to the point of mounting him upon a mare, which I believe is not or was not the proper thing to do in Argentine: though in Chile there was never much of that nonsense. But truly N. is nothing at all,—a fiction, embodied vanity of the sailor kind,—a romantic mouthpiece of the 'people' which (I mean 'the people') frequently experience the very feelings to which he gives utterance. I do not defend him as a creation. [31 October 1904, *LL., I*, 338]

Nostromo might be looked on as an exception, but Gould too, on whom depends so much of the effect of the book, is far from clear. His thoughts, feelings, and actions as well as the opinions of other characters on him accumulate into a pile of separate entities but never coalesce into a vital organism.

Apart from this weakness of characterisation and from the melodrama of the last two chapters presented in appropriately magazinish language the book is almost without blemish. The writing is otherwise on a consistently high level and perhaps Conrad's greatest sustained achievement; it has none of the purple passages or philosophical effusions that sometimes mar his work. He shows a wonderful versatility of style and mood ranging from deep seriousness and irony to scenes of superb comedy such as those between Sotillo and Mitchell.

The complexity of intention expressed through such a diversity of character and incident demanded an exceptionally intricate structure if the peaks of significance were not to be submerged by the flood of detail. Aside from the epilogue, the events take place in a period of a little over eighteen months, although there are numerous references to the past, particularly to the tyranny of Guzman Bento, in the biographical flashbacks of the important characters. Conrad deliberately flouts chronological narration in *Nostromo* and it is here that the 'unconventional grouping and perspective... wherein', he claimed, 'almost all my "art" consists' [58] is most in evidence. He uses the device of the time-shift to gain an effect of irony. Thus, in Part I, the day of President Ribiera's subsequent flight across the mountains is described before the festivities in Sulaco at which he inaugurates a new era for Costaguana 'emerging after this last struggle, he hoped, into a period of peace and material prosperity'. [59] The irony is pointed at the end of the ceremony:

As the mail-boat headed through the pass, the badly timed reports announced the end of Don Vincente Ribiera's first official visit to Sulaco, and for Captain Mitchell the end of another 'historic occasion'. Next time when the 'Hope of honest men' was to come that way, a year and a half later, it was unofficially, over the mountain tracks, fleeing after a defeat on a lame mule, to be only just saved by Nostromo from an ignominious death at the hands of a mob. It was a very different event.... [60]

Part II is again concerned with events leading up to Ribiera's flight and it is not for almost another hundred pages that we are abreast of the day of his escape. Thenceforth the time-shifts are largely mechanical and dictated by the need to follow the various threads of the plot until we come to the most important of all chronological breaks: just when the book seems to be building up to an exciting climax [61] Conrad jumps to a time some years later and makes Captain Mitchell, in the role of unofficial guide to the sights of Sulaco, tell the story of the dramatic events which led to the defeat of the Monteros and the establishment of the Occidental Republic. Then the thread is picked up again.

Apart from showing that Conrad had no intention of writing an exciting tale of action, the effect of these time-shifts is almost to abolish time in *Nostromo*. In fact it seem to have been Conrad's aim to approach the simultaneity of visual experience which a painting offers. The elimination of progression from one event to another also has the effect of implying that nothing is ever achieved. By the end of the book we are virtually back where we started; it looks as if the future of Costaguana will be very similar to her past.

Unlike some great works, *Nostromo* is not a book whose subject can be summed up in a sentence. Conrad wrote in Curle's copy that it had been his 'ambition to render the spirit of an epoch in the history of South America'. And in this he succeeded, creating a world compounded of tragedy and farce, brutality, pathos, idealism, and venality. But his claim was too modest because the life described in Costaguana transcends a particular epoch or continent and contains an element of the universal. It is thus not too much to claim that *Nostromo* is an investigation of the motives of human behaviour, in which idealism is set against scepticism, illusion against disillusion, and responsibility against irresponsibility. Every category of human activity which Conrad considered important, except the arts,—it is significant that religion is only dealt with in its temporal aspect—is portrayed and analysed.

Because of the title as well as the prominent part that Nostromo plays, it would be natural to assume that the book is concerned primarily with the fate of Nostromo. But although Nostromo is constantly alluded to—it is in this indirect manner that Conrad first builds up his reputation as he did that of Kurtz in 'Heart of Darkness'—he is barely concerned with the most important issues of the book and Conrad has specifically stated that he was not intended to be the hero.

In a letter to Ernst Bendz, a Swedish professor who had written a study of Conrad's work, he said:

> I will take the liberty to point out that Nostromo has never been intended for the hero of the Tale of the Seaboard. Silver is the pivot of the moral and material events, affecting the lives of everybody in the tale. [7 March 1923, *LL., II*, 296]

Even this statement needs modifying because although the silver is the thread which binds the book together it has only a superficial or formal connexion with some of the most important moral events.

In its crudest aspect, the desire for gain, the silver only influences the lives of Nostromo and of one other character, Major Sotillo, who is killed during his frantic search for the sunken lighter. But even in the case of Nostromo the theft of the silver is more the effect than the cause of his downfall. The theme of the corruptive power of riches is broached in the first chapter, in the story of the two gringos hunting the forbidden treasure on Azuera ('The poor, associating by an obscure instinct of consolation the ideas of evil and wealth...' [62]), and that story is frequently alluded to throughout the book, serving the same purpose as the recurring phrases in *Lord Jim*. This theme is worked out in the fate of Nostromo.

From the start Nostromo is presented as dependable and resourceful. Whenever there is a job to be done it is Nostromo who is sent for; Captain Mitchell, the pompous and stupid representative of the O.S.N., has developed a mania for 'lending' his illustrious Capataz de Cargadores. But above all Nostromo is 'incorruptible'; this is insisted on again and again. He has built up his reputation for resourcefulness and incorruptibility until, as Decoud says, he is 'the next great man of Sulaco after Don Carlos Gould'. [63] And it is his reputation alone about which he seems to care. In Decoud's words: 'The only thing he seems to care for... is to be well spoken of.... He does not seem to make any difference between speaking and thinking.' [64] And again: 'He is more naive than shrewd, more masterful than crafty, more generous with his personality than the people who make use of him are with their money.... It is curious to have met a man for whom the value of life seems to consist in personal prestige.' [65]

Nostromo does indeed possess these qualities but they are, as Decoud says, the expression only of 'his enormous vanity, that first form of egoism which can take on the aspect of every virtue'. [66] Dr Monygham also penetrates to the springs of Nostromo's conduct: 'I believe him capable of anything—even of the most absurd fidelity'. * Nostromo has been impelled by vanity to win his reputation and if this is endangered his reliability, fidelity, and incorruptibility are also endangered. It is only those such as Don Pepe, a sort of South American Singleton, mounting guard over the mine, General Barrios in his raddled way and, one should add, Captain Mitchell, whose incorruptibility and fidelity can be relied on because in their case these qualities derive from a belief, from their concept of service, and are not merely an expression of their egoism.

Nostromo resents being entrusted with the removal of the silver from Sulaco because he realises that his reputation is at stake and is afraid that he may fail. [67] Similarly, he cannot tolerate being taken for granted by the 'hombres finos' because it belittles his reputation. That is why he proclaims that he is determined to make the removal of the silver 'the most famous and desperate affair of my life'. [68]

Thus when he has partially failed in his mission he begins to disintegrate and 'the confused and intimate impressions of universal dissolution which beset a subjective nature at any strong check to its ruling passion had a bitterness approaching that of death itself.... The facts of his situation he could appreciate like a man with a distinct experience of the country.... He was as if sobered after a long bout of intoxication. His fidelity had been taken advantage of.' [69] He imagines the world on which his reputation depends collapsing and himself a hunted man. 'He had been betrayed!' [70]

Returning to the Great Isabel, where he has left Decoud with the hidden silver, 'He descended the ridge and found himself in the open solitude, between the harbour and the town. Its spaciousness, extended indefinitely by an effect of obscurity, rendered more sensible his profound isolation. His pace became slower. No one waited for him; no one thought of him; no one expected or wished his return. 'Betrayed! Betrayed!" he muttered to himself. No one cared.' [71]

Although Nostromo's imagination has run away with him and his world, though threatened, has not collapsed, the spell has been broken and he persists in the feeling that he has been exploited and must henceforth look after his own interests. He can no longer rely on his reputation. It is at this point, after his created world has begun to crumble, that the silver takes hold of him:

'There is something in a treasure that fastens upon a man's mind. He will pray and blaspheme and still persevere, and will curse the day he ever heard of it, and will let his last hour come upon him unawares, still believing that he missed it only by a foot. He will see it every time he closes his eyes. He will never forget it till he is dead—and even then-Doctor, did you ever hear of the miserable gringos on Azuera, that cannot die? Ha! Ha! Sailors like myself. There is no getting away from a treasure that once fastens upon your mind.'

Thus, although he goes on to transcend even his own past achievement and saves the Occidental Province in his great ride to Cayta, his thoughts remain with the silver. And when he realises that, with the death of Decoud, he is the only person who knows that the silver has not been sunk in the lighter, he decides not to disclose its whereabouts but to use it to enrich himself. And at this moment the San Tomé mine 'appeared to him hateful and immense, lording it by its vast wealth over the valour, the toil, the fidelity of the poor, over war and peace, over the labours of the town, the sea, and the Campo'. [73] Thenceforth Nostromo is corrupted:

A transgression, a crime, entering a man's existence, eats it up like a malignant growth, consumes it like a fever. Nostromo had lost his peace; the genuineness of all his qualities was destroyed. He felt it himself, and often cursed the silver of San Tomé. His courage, his magnificence, his leisure, his work, everything was as before, only everything was a sham. But the treasure was real. He clung to it with a more tenacious, mental grip. But he hated the feel of the ingots. Sometimes, after putting away a couple of them in his cabin—the fruit of a secret night expedition to the Great Isabel—he would look fixedly at his fingers, as if surprised they had left no stain on his skin. [74]

Retribution comes in the end. When Nostromo is dying, shot in error by his devoted admirer, Old Viola, he tells Mrs Gould with literal and symbolical truth, 'The silver has killed me'. [75]

Silver is both the symbol and the embodiment of those 'material interests' which are transforming Sulaco, capital of the isolated Occidental Province and once 'an inviolable sanctuary from the temptations of a trading world' protected by 'the prevailing calms of its vast gulf'. [76]

The power of the San Tomé mine or, in effect, of Charles

Gould who controls it, dominates the Occidental Province of Costaguana and even extends to the rest of the country, because Gould has used the wealth of the mine to finance a revolution which brought to power Don Vincente Ribiera, 'a man of culture and of unblemished character, invested with a mandate of reform by the best elements of the State'. [77]

Gould has not achieved this dominant position through the desire for enrichment or for power. Although the San Tomé mine has brought nothing but misfortune to his family, on the death of his father Gould is determined to accept its challenge: 'The mine had been the cause of an absurd moral disaster; its working must be made a serious and moral success.' [78] But 'after all his [Gould's father's] misery I simply could not have touched it for money alone' [79] and throughout the book there is no mention of Gould becoming rich or being interested in that aspect of the situation. As for power, Gould his always shunned it. He was no 'political intriguer' [80] and had supported Ribiera primarily in order to assure the unhampered working of the mine. 'He had persuaded himself that, apart from higher considerations, the backing up of Don José's hopes of reform was good business.' [81] Thus when the Ribiera regime is in danger and General Barrios's counter-stroke is planned, he holds himself aloof:

Charles Gould was not present at the anxious and patriotic send-off. It was not his part to see the soldiers embark. It was neither his part, nor his inclination, nor his policy. His put, his inclination, and his policy were united in one endeavour to keep unchecked the flow of treasure he had started singlehanded from the re-opened scar in the flank of the mountain. [82]

The successful working of the mine is sufficient justification in itself and his satisfaction is gained through the essentially Conradian formula of the idealisation of action:

It hurt Charles Gould to feel that never more, by no effort of will, would he be able to think of his father in the same way he used to think of him when the poor man was alive. His breathing image was no longer in his power. This consideration, closely affecting his own identity, filled his breast with a mournful and angry desire for action. In this his instinct was unerring. Action is consolatory. It is the enemy of thought and the friend of flattering illusions. Only in the conduct of our action can we find the sense of mastery over the Fates. As the chief engineer says later; 'Upon my word, doctor, things seem to be worth nothing by what they are in themselves. I begin to believe that the only solid thing about them is the spiritual value which everyone discovers in his own form of activity.' [84]

Gould finds a philosophy to express this belief:

What is wanted here is law, good faith, order, security. Any one can declaim about these things, but I pin my faith to material interests. Only let the material interests once get a firm footing, and they are bound to impose the conditions on which alone they can continue to exist. That's how your money-making is justified here in the face of lawlessness and disorder. It is justified because the security which it demands must be shared with an oppressed people. A better justice will come afterwards.

But Gould's belief in the value of action does not save him, as it did Marlow in 'Heart of Darkness'; it ends by enslaving him. Mrs Gould, on the other hand, distrusts material interests and progress from the start. In her conversation with the chairman of the railway board she looks back wistfully to the past. The chairman is speaking:

'... What an out-of-the-way place Sulaco is!—and for a harbour, too! Astonishing!'

'Ah, but we are very proud of it. It used to be historically important. The highest ecclesiastical court, for two viceroyalties, sat here in the olden time,' she instructed him with animation....

and the chairman replies:

'We can't give you your ecclesiastical court back again; but you shall have more steamers, a railway, a telegraph-cable—a future in the great world which is worth infinitely more than any amount of ecclesiastical past. You shall be brought in touch with something greater than two viceroyalties....'

But she nonetheless follows her husband in attaching a spiritual value to the mine. Her original impulse of enthusiasm is personal and derives from her devotion to Gould [87] and her desire for adventure. But she soon idealises the meaning of the mine:

> ... She had laid her unmercenary hands, with an eagerness that made them tremble, upon the first silver ingot turned out still warm from the mould; and by her imaginative estimate of its power she endowed that lump of metal with a justificative conception, as though it were not a mere fact, but something far-reaching and impalpable, like the true expression of an emotion or the emergence of a principle. [88]

Thus, in different ways, for both the Goulds 'each passing of the escort under the balconies of the Casa Gould was like another victory gained in the conquest of peace for Sulaco'. [89]

The Goulds, then, are idealists, although at opposite ends of the scale; he has become the victim of his ideal to the point of obsession whereas she has sunk her personality in the ideal of service. Around the Goulds there revolve the conflicting forces of idealism, scepticism, and brazen self-interest. Among the idealists there is Holroyd, the great power in San Francisco who is financing the mine. He has 'the temperament of a Puritan and an insatiable imagination of conquest'. [90] He 'attached a strangely idealistic meaning to concrete facts' and combines a 'lavish patronage of "the purer forms of Christianity"' [91] with ruthless exploitation of material interests. There is Mrs Gould's protégé, Giorgio Viola, the old Garibaldino, with his 'worship and service of liberty'. [92]

> The spirit of self-forgetfulness, the simple devotion to a vast humanitarian idea which inspired the thought and stress of that revolutionary time, had left its mark upon Giorgio in a sort of austere contempt for all personal advantage. [93]

There are Don José Avellanos and his daughter Antonia with their profound love of their country. Don José sees in Gould's power the means whereby his ideals may be realised. He 'was ruined in every way, but a man possessed of passion is not a bankrupt in life. Don José Avellanos desired passionately for his country: peace, prosperity, and... "an honourable place in the comity of civilised nations".'[94] Then, standing apart in his fanaticism, there is Antonia's uncle, Father Corbelàn, with his demands for the restitution of the confiscated church lands.

Self-interest is embodied in the crude lust for power of the Monteros, the squalid demagoguery of Gamacho and Fuentes, the equally crude desire for wealth on the part of Sotillo, and of the unfortunate Señor Hirsch, and, in disguised form, in Nostromo's conduct. Dr Monygham and Decoud, on the other hand, are both selfproclaimed sceptics. Dr Monygham's scepticism, or cynicism, has been forced on him, having its roots in a physical defeat when he had succumbed to atrocious torture during the tyranny of Guzman Bento; he had therefore lost faith in himself and others. This event placed him in the same situation as Jim and Razumov. He feels cut off from social communion with others and because of his uncouth behaviour is distrusted by them.

He is sustained only by his devotion to Mrs Gould, which is 'like a store of unlawful wealth'.[95] Decoud's scepticism, on the other hand, is a mental attitude; he 'recognised no other virtue than intelligence'[96] and 'had pushed the habit of universal raillery to a point where it blinded him to the genuine impulses of his own nature'.[97] He feels bound to explain 'away such impulses, or relate them to self-interest. Later he is able, like Dr Monygham, to attribute all his actions to one passion, his love for Antonia. 'I have no patriotic illusions,' he says; 'I have only the supreme illusion of a lover.'[98] He is confronted with Antonia's 'belief in the cause'[99] and with her accusation that he never sees 'the aim'.[100]

To Mrs Gould, Decoud ruthlessly analyses Gould's character:

'Don't you see, he's such an idealist.... It's a wonderful thing to say with the sight of the San Tomé mine, the greatest fact in the whole of South America, perhaps, before our very eyes. But look evenat that, he has idealised this fact to a point——... Are you aware to what point he has idealised the existence, the worth, the meaning of the San Tomé mine? Are you aware of it?'...

'What do you know?' she asked in a feeble voice.

'Nothing,' answered Decoud, firmly. 'But, then, don't you see, he's an Englishman?'

'Well, what of that?' asked Mrs. Gould.

'Simply that he cannot act or exist without idealising every simple feeling, desire, or achievement. He could not believe his own motives if he did not make them first a part of some fairy tale. The earth is not quite good enough for him, I fear. Do you excuse my frankness? Besides, whether you excuse it or not, it is part of the truth of things which hurts the—what do you call them?—the Anglo-Saxon susceptibilities, and at the present moment I don't feel as if I could treat seriously either his conception of things or—if you allow me to say so—or yet yours.' [101]

In Decoud's mind there is only one step from idealism to sentimentalism. He claims that both Gould and Holroyd are sentimentalists. [102] He tells Mrs Gould that her husband is a 'sentimentalist, after the amazing manner of your people' [103] and expounding his scheme for the Occidental Republic he says: 'I think he [Gould] can be drawn into it, like all idealists, when he once sees a sentimental basis for his action?'. [104]

It is Decoud who sees that Gould's idealisition of the mine has become an obsession. He speaks of 'this "Imperium in Imperio", this wealth-producing thing, to which his [Gould's] sentimentalism attaches a strange idea of justice. Unless I am much mistaken in the man, it must remain inviolate or perish by an act of his will alone. A passion has crept into his cold and idealistic life.' [105]

Gould has eventually reversed the order of values. Instead of the mine being justified by its service to 'law, good faith, order, security, [106] these ideals have become subordinated to the importance of the mine. He has become a monomaniac who can only think of the mine as identified with himself and plans to blow it up rather than let it fall into the hands of another. Decoud realises that the mine represents a tragedy in the personal relations of the Goulds, for Mrs Gould 'has discovered that he [Gould] lives for the mine rather than for her'. [107] It is Mrs Gould's 'mission to save him from the effects of that cold and overmastering passion which she dreads more than if it were an infatuation for another woman'. [108] She has found that her husband is becoming gradually estranged from her:

Mrs. Gould continued along the corridor away from her husband's room. The fate of the San Tomé mine was lying heavy upon her heart. It was a long time now since she had begun to fear it. It had been an idea. She had watched it with misgivings turning into a fetish, and now the fetish had grown into a monstrous and crushing weight. It was as if the inspiration of their early years had left her heart to turn into a wall of silver-bricks, erected by the silent work of evil spirits, between her and her husband. He seemed to dwell alone within a circumvallation of precious metal, leaving her outside with her school, her hospital, the sick mothers and the feeble old men, mere insignificant vestiges of the initial inspiration. [109]

She sees that 'the mine had got hold of Charles Gould with a grip as deadly as ever it had laid upon his father', [110] or, it might be added, as deadly as that which bound the ghosts of the two gringos to the treasure on Azuera. 'She saw clearly the San Tomé mine possessing, consuming, burning up the life of the last of the Costaguana Goulds.' [111] She only once tries to break down the wall and regain the intimacy of their early days together. [112] Otherwise she accepts her isolation fatalistically, but confesses at Nostromo's deathbed: 'I, too, have hated the idea of that silver from the bottom of my heart.' [113] Even she herself has been tainted by the silver because, persuaded by Decoud, 'for the first and last time of her life she had concealed the truth from her husband about that very silver. She had been corrupted by her fears at that time, and had never forgiven herself.' [114]

The silver, or the mine, happens to have been the cause of the tragedy, but the real cause is in Gould's obsessive character. He could have dedicated himself to something unconnected with wealth, with the same tragic consequences because:

A man haunted by a fixed idea is insane. He is dangerous even if that idea is in idea of justice; for may he not bring the heaven down pitilessly upon a loved head? To Decoud it seemed that 'every conviction, as soon as it became effective, turned into that form of dementia the gods send upon those they wish to destroy'. [116] But his scepticism leads him to a fate even more tragic than that of the Goulds. For when he is put to the ultimate test he fails. Alone on the Great Isabel his sense of his own personality disintegrates, as does that of Nostromo in similar circumstances. 'He had recognised no other virtue than intelligence, and had erected passions into duties. Both his intelligence and his passion were swallowed up easily in this great unbroken solitude of waiting without faith.' [117] Finally he can stand it no longer and shoots himself:

> He died from solitude, the enemy known but to few on this earth, and whom only the simplest of us are fit to withstand. The brilliant Costaguanero of the boulevards had died from solitude and want of faith in himself and others. [118]

Thus idealism and scepticism, faith and want of faith, both seem to lead to disaster. *Nostromo* is an intensely pessimistic book; it is perhaps the most impressive monument to futility ever created. Apart from Captain Mitchell with his comfortable old age secured by his seventeen shares in the San Tomé mine, no one achieves satisfaction; and Mitchell is certainly among those, like MacWhirr and Hermann, who have been 'disdained by destiny or by the sea'.

The fate of the individuals with whom *Nostromo* has been particularly concerned and of Costaguana as a whole are equally hopeless. Antonia Avellanos and Linda Viola both have the men they love taken away by death. Mrs Gould virtually loses her husband to the mine and is in the end disillusioned: 'She resembled a good fairy, weary with a long career of well-doing, touched by the withering suspicion of the uselessness of her labours, the powerlessness of her magic'. [119] She is engulfed by 'an immense desolation, the dread of her own continued life'. [120] Don José Avellanos dies 'vanquished in a lifelong struggle with the powers of moral darkness, whose stagnant depths breed monstrous crimes and monstrous illusions'. [121] Decoud dies 'a victim of the disillusioned weariness which is the retribution meted out to intellectual audacity' [122] just as Nostromo is the 'victim of the disenchanted vanity which is the reward of audacious action'. [123] This is the most deeply pessimistic judgement of all, because their 'audacity' has produced the two most constructive actions in the book. It is due to Decoud that the Occidental Republic is proclaimed and to Nostromo's ride to Cayta that it is established.

The country as a whole comes off no better. In an article on Anatole France written just after finishing *Nostromo* Conrad said: 'Political institutions, whether contrived by the wisdom of the few or the ignorance of the many, are incapable of securing the happiness of mankind'. [124] It is not surprising therefore that no section of the community seems to offer any hope for a permanently better future. The Democrats naturally get short shrift from Conrad, who goes out of his way to make their leaders, Gamacho and Fuentes, thoroughly disreputable and unscrupulous.

Don Juste Lopez, the conservative champion of parliamentary institutions, is made to appear pathetic and craven in his readiness to propitiate the villainous Pedrito Montero 'in order to save the form at least of parliamentary institutions'; [125] Conrad cannot even resist making him ridiculous by having half his beard blown off. Similarly, Ribiera, the 'hope of honest men', flees ignominiously from the Monteros; and it is significant that he is a particularly poor physical specimen, 'obese to the point of infirmity', 'almost a cripple'. [126] And at the end the fanatical Father Corbelàn is threatening the overthrow of the material interests which have made the Occidental Republic secure, justifying Dr Monygham's verdict of 'incorrigible' on the Costaguaneros. [127]

Then although at the end of the book justice and order have temporarily triumphed and Sulaco is 'growing rich swiftly', [128] material interests, which dominate the Occidental Republic, have their own form of tyranny. This has been foreshadowed from the start and is expressed in one of those sentences whose full significance only becomes apparent later:

The sparse row of telegraph poles strode obliquely clear

of the town, bearing a single, almost invisible wire far into the great campo—like a slender, vibrating feeler of that progress waiting outside for a moment of peace to enter and twine itself about the weary heart of the land. [129]

Thus when Mrs Gould asks: ''Will there never be any peace?' Dr Monygham prophesies:

There is no peace and no rest in the development of material interests. They have their law, and their justice. But it is founded on expediency, and is inhuman; it is without rectitude, without the continuity and the force that can be found only in a moral principle. Mrs Gould, the time approaches when all that the Gould Concession stands for shall weigh as heavily upon the people as the barbarism, cruelty, and misrule of a few years back. [130]

Mrs Gould cannot deny this, and her vision of the future is as black as Dr Monygham's because, although in the development of the San Tomé mine her husband had achieved a 'colossal and lasting success', [131] 'there was something inherent in the necessities of successful action which carried with it the moral degradation of the idea. She saw the San Tomé mountain hanging over the Campo, over the whole land, feared, hated, wealthy; more soulless than any tyrant, more pitiless and autocratic than the worst Government; ready to crush innumerable lives in the expansion of its greatness', [132] So much for Gould's hope of the mine becoming 'that little rift in the darkness' [133] which his father had despaired of seeing.

The future of Costaguana is as ominous as its past has been gory. Dr Monygham does 'not believe in the reform of Costaguana', [134] and this seems to be the conclusion implicit in the novel. To seek out a hopeful interpretation Robert Penn Warren, who has written perhaps the most perceptive essay on Nostromo and incidentally on Conrad, is forced to search beyond the limits of the book. But perhaps the most apt implied comment on the world of Nostromo is contained in 'Autocracy and War', an essay which Conrad wrote a few months after finishing the novel. After saying that, in a world dominated by industrialism and commercialism, there can only be an uneasy peace based on fear, he continues: 'The true peace of the world... will be built on less perishable foundations than those of material interests. But it must be confessed that the architectural aspect of the universal city remains as yet inconceivable—that the very ground for its erection has not been cleared of the jungle.' [135] A few paragraphs later he probes deeper:

The intellectual stage of mankind being as yet in its infancy, and States, like most individuals, having but a feeble and imperfect consciousness of the worth and force of the inner life, the need of making their existence manifest to themselves is determined in the direction of physical activity.

The idea of ceasing to grow in territory, in strength, in wealth, in influence—in anything but wisdom and self-knowledge is odious to them as the omen of the end. Action, in which is to be found the illusion of a mastered destiny, can alone satisfy our uneasy vanity and lay to rest the haunting fear of the future—a sentiment concealed, indeed, but proving its existence by the force it his, when invoked, to stir the passions of a nation. It will be long before we have learned that in the great darkness before us there is nothing that we need fear.

In *Nostromo* Conrad portrayed the world as he saw it, not as he hoped it might become; nor does he allow any trace of a hope to appear without exposing the illusion on which it is based. It is clear that he regarded the dominance of material interests and the 'feeble and imperfect consciousness of the worth and force of the inner life' as a condition of humanity and not peculiar to Costaguana.

Costaguana is, however, primarily a prototype of a politically inexperienced nation and it is tempting to see an analogy between it and Poland. It is likely that Conrad was able to express some of his feelings about Poland consciously or unconsciously using the disguise of Costaguana. He might well have been thinking of Russiandominated Poland when he referred to the 'political immaturity of the people... the indolence of the upper classes and the mental darkness of the lower', [137] or when Gould complains: 'The words one knows so well have a nightmarish meaning in this country. Liberty, democracy, patriotism, government—all of them have a flavour of folly and murder,' [138] or when 'The cruel futility of things stood unveiled in the levity and sufferings of that incorrigible people; the cruel futility of lives and of deaths thrown away in the vain endeavour to attain an enduring solution of the problem'. [139] So, too, when Decoud says: '"We are a wonderful people, but it has always been our fate to be"—he did not say "robbed", but added, after a pause—"exploited!"' [140] And his analysis of the predicament of Costaguana fits closely to that of Poland:

> There is a curse of futility upon our character: Don Quixote and Sancho Panza, chivalry and materialism, high-sounding sentiments and a supine morality, violent efforts for an idea and a sullen acquiescence in every form of corruption. We convulsed a continent for our independence only to become the passive prey of a democratic parody, the helpless victims of scoundrels and cut-throats.... [141]

There is little doubt that Conrad had strongly ambivalent feelings towards Polish aspirations which were closely bound up with his attitude towards his father. He had seen at first hand one of the tragic consequences of the political agitation which culminated in the 1863 rising; the exile and disillusionment of his father and the premature death of his mother.

In fact the situation between Mr and Mrs Gould is analogous to that between Conrad's parents if political action is substituted for material interests; it is particularly emphasised when Conrad says that Gould is haunted by a fixed idea, and 'a man haunted by a fixed idea is insane. He is dangerous even if that idea is an idea of justice; for may he not bring the heaven down pitilessly upon a loved head?' [142] or when Decoud, speaking of Mrs Gould, points to 'some subtle wrong... that sentimental unfaithfulness which surrenders her happiness, her life, to the seduction of an idea'. [143]

As a result of his experiences, and above all because he had left Poland, Conrad, while retaining a deep attachment to the country, refused to take her political aspirations seriously; for if he admitted that there was a genuine chance that Poland might regain her freedom he would have felt bound to remain and participate in the struggle. In the Author's Note to *Nostromo* he says that Antonia Avellanos is modelled on his 'first love' and adds: 'I was not the only one in love with her; but it was I who had to hear oftenest her scathing criticism of my levities—very much like poor Decoud—or stand the brunt of her austere, unanswerable invective.'[144]

Although this must be treated circumspectly in view of Eastwick's Antonia Ribera it is not too far-fetched to see Conrad's own dilemma reflected in Decoud's attitude. Decoud at first, like Mrs Gould, finds it hard to take the affairs of Costaguana seriously; they smack of *opéra bouffe*. But he cannot withhold his sympathy for long: 'He was moved in spite of himself by that note of passion and sorrow unknown on the more refined stage of European politics?',[145] and: 'To contemplate revolutions from the distance of the Parisian boulevards was quite another matter. Here on the spot it was not possible to dismiss their tragic comedy with the expression, "Quelle Farce!"... "I suppose I am more of a Costaguanero than I would have believed possible," he thought to himself.' [146] In several of his utterances, and even of his actions, he shows signs of a passionate concern for his country's fate akin to that of Don José and Antonia Avellanos.

When Conrad condemns Decoud's attitude to life, or at least his pose of scepticism, he is perhaps recalling his own situation in Marseilles:

He imagined himself Parisian to the tips of his fingers. But far from being that he was in danger of remaining a sort of nondescript dilettante all his life. He had pushed the habit of universal raillery to a point where it blinded him to the genuine impulses of his own nature.

When Decoud says: 'What is a conviction? a particular view of our personal advantage either practical or emotional', [148] he is the witty, cynical boulevardier but when 'it seemed to him that every conviction, as soon as it became effective, turned into that form of dementia the gods send upon those they wish to destroy', [149] he is expressing the view of the mature Conrad. The statement that Decoud 'had no faith in anything except the truth of his own sensations' expresses in negative form what was the cornerstone of Conrad's own outlook, [150] and when Father Corbelàn calls Decoud 'neither the son of his own country nor of any other', [151] he designates Conrad's own predicament.

A FEW weeks after *Nostromo* was finished, in October of 1904, the Conrads went to London to prepare for an operation on Jessie's knee. [1] They took a flat at 99b Addison Road. 'It was typical of Joseph Conrad with his inherent extravagance of everything', wrote Jessie, 'that the night before I left the flat in Addison Road to go into the Nursing Home, we had thirty guests for a kind of impromptu supper. I remember Mr and Mrs E. V. Lucas, A. J. Dawson.... Henry Tonks, Augustus John, among many others.' [2]

While in London Conrad turned out some incidental pieces in order to earn some money: an article on Henry James, [3] two more of his sea 'sketches', [4] and an embryo version of *'Gaspar Ruiz'* for the *Strand Magazine.* [5] He was, as usual, very short of money and the cost of Jessie's operation was going to be an additional burden. But the Conrads had decided that they must have a rest and, despite their lack of money, had arranged to go to Capri as soon as Jessie was well enough. Pinker probably put up some of the money, no doubt fearing that Conrad would have a nervous breakdown if he did not get away, and it may be that other friends helped too.

They set off on 15 January. [6] It was an eventful journey. According to Jessie it started badly, as Conrad could not find his favourite glasses and had to leave without them, whereas Jessie herself forgot part of her false teeth. Then Conrad apparently took a dislike to the nurse who was to look after Jessie. Finally, Jessie, still being almost immobile, had to be carried in a chair. Boarding the ship at Dover one of the carriers 'got his hand stuck firmly between the chair and the rail of the gangway. No doubt it pinched horribly and my fortitude was severely tried while I sat poised aloft, in a frail chair without arms even, on the top of the rail, watching the swirling waters between the ship and the quay, and listening to the howls of dismay from the onlookers, who expected every moment to see me tipped into the water.' [7] In Rome she was left hanging on to the door of the railway carriage when the chair was by mistake taken away from underneath her. In Naples the Conrads were held up for five days because it was too rough to land Jessie. [8] Finally:

My landing was accomplished in a truly marvellous manner. A number of Italian seamen appeared and amid loud, unintelligible chatter, I was hoisted over the side of the vessel and passed by willing hands down the gangway into the small boat lying alongside. I simply shut my eyes and let myself go. Still in the wooden chair, I was landed on the 'Granda Marina', without a pause as it seemed to me. Poor Joseph Conrad was loud in praise of the feat performed by the seamen—after it was all over. 'It took a sailor to do things properly.' The dear man seemed to have forgotten his agitation during the process.

The journey certainly seems to have taken its toll of Conrad's nerves and purse because he wrote to Galsworthy on arrival: The delay of all these days in the hotel has utterly ruined me. In fact to be able to get over to Capri, I had to leave a 150 frcs. unpaid on my bill and am beginning life here in charge of a party of four with 30 frcs. in my pocket....

The nervous irritation of these days in Naples prevented me from doing anything. I got 1000 words of a political article written (and that's all) during the voyage. Here the outlook is very promising; the rooms good, the terrace on the south side. Through the good Canonico we have fallen into the hands of priests. There were three of them waiting on the Marina Grande for our arrival, which took place on a moonlight evening about seven. The whole population surged and yelled round poor Jessie's chair, while we waited on the quay for the large carriage which was ordered but did not turn up in time. I think we will be very comfortable here. But the whole expedition is a mad thing really, for it rests upon what I am not certain of—my power to produce some sixty thousand words in four months. I feel sick with apprehension at times. [21 January 1905, *LL., II*, 9,]

The expedition was not a success as far as writing was concerned. To start with, the nurse got seriously ill and instead of looking after Jessie had to be looked after by her. Conrad complained to Pinker:

I, who now if ever wanted peace to concentrate my thoughts after all the anxieties in London, could not achieve it (as you may guess) in these lodgings. I have worked but badly—there's no use disguising the truth-I've been in a state of exasperation with the eternal something cropping up to distract my mind.... Of course you may say that I ought to disregard all the complications and peg away with my eyes shut to domestic affairs.

I know some men are capable of that sort of thing; and with in organised household one could perhaps abstract oneself for six hours per day. It's another matter with me. You understand that my wife was pretty helpless and required some attention; the child too. For me to have to lay down my pen ten times in the course of the day is fatal. I wish there had been something of a hack-writer in my composition. [5 February 1905, *LL., II,* 11]

Conrad himself then caught influenza and bronchitis and suffered from insomnia and nerves. [10] But even after these troubles were over he found that he could not work well. Near the end of the four months he told Hueffer: 'This climate, what between Tramontana and Sirocco, has half killed me in a not unpleasant languorous, melting way. I am sunk in a vaguely uneasy dream of visions, of innumerable tales that float in an atmosphere of voluptuously aching bones.' [11]

In consequence he only succeeded in writing a long political article which he called *'Autocracy and War'* and a little of a story which he was to lay aside for some years and was eventually to develop into *Chance.* [12] He also did some reading for a projected 'Mediterranean novel' in the library of a Dr Cerio; the subject was to be the struggle for Capri in 1808 between the French and the British. [13]

'Autocracy and War' is Conrad's most important piece of political writing and he evidently set much store by it, hoping that it would cause something of a sensation. [14] It was

prompted immediately by the Russo-Japanese war, but it may well be that *Nostromo* had stimulated Conrad to think particularly about political subjects. He took this opportunity to make a withering indictment of Russia.

He contrasted the two armies. The Japanese 'has for its base a reasoned conviction; it has behind it the profound belief in the right of a logical necessity to be appeased at the cost of so much blood and treasure. And in that belief, whether well or ill founded, that army stands on the high ground of conscious assent, shouldering deliberately the burden of a long-tried faithfulness.' Whereas the Russian army, 'torn out from a miserable quietude resembling death itself, hurled across space, amazed, without starting-point of its own, or knowledge of the aim, can feel nothing but a horror-stricken consciousness of having mysteriously become the plaything of a black and merciless fate'. [15] He saw this war as the first step in the destruction of the Russian myth. But:

Above it all—unaccountably persistent—the decrepit, old, hundred years old, spectre of Russia's might still faces Europe from across the teeming graves of Russian people. This dreaded and strange apparition, bristling with bayonets, armed with chains, hung over with holy images; that something not of this world, partaking of a ravenous ghoul, of a blind Djinn grown up from a cloud, and of the Old Man of the Sea, still faces us with its old stupidity, with its strange mystical arrogance, stamping its shadowy feet upon the gravestone of autocracy, already cracked beyond repair by the torpedoes of Togo and the guns of Oyama, already heaving in the blood-soaked ground with the first stirrings of a resurrection.... [16]

The Russian autocracy is condemned absolutely:

Spectral it lived and spectral it disappears without leaving a memory of a single generous deed, of a single service rendered—even involuntarily-to the polity of nations. Other despotisms there have been, but none whose origin was so grimly fantastic in its baseness, and the beginning of whose end was so gruesomely ignoble.... An attentive survey of Russia's literature, of her Church, of her administration and the crosscurrents of her thought, must end in the verdict that the Russia of to-day has not the right to give her voice on a single question touching the future of humanity, because from the very inception of her being the brutal destruction of dignity, of truth, of rectitude, of all that is faithful in human nature has been made the imperative condition of her existence. [17]

His close knowledge of Russia, and, no doubt too, a temperamental predisposition led him to a grim prediction of her future which was far more accurate than the optimistic hopes of the liberal Garnett and his friends:

As her boasted military force that, corrupt in its origin, has ever struck no other but faltering blows, so her soul, kept benumbed by her temporal and spiritual master with the poison of tyranny and superstition, will find itself on awakening possessed of no language, a monstrous full-grown child having first to learn the ways of living thought and articulate speech. It is safe to say tyranny, assuming a thousand protean shapes, will remain clinging to her struggles for a long time before her blind multitudes succeed at last in trampling her out of existence under their millions of bare feet. [18]

To Conrad, as a Pole, Germany, or rather Prussia, 'which has been the evil counsellor of Russia on all the questions of her Polish problem', [19] was scarcely less hateful than Russia. But whereas Russia was an object of contempt, Germany was a sinister menace. Germany, with 'a people trained to the worship of force', [20] is 'a powerful and voracious organisation, full of unscrupulous self-confidence, whose appetite for aggrandisement will only be limited by the power of helping itself to the severed members of its friends and neighbouts.'[21] The article ends with the prophetic warning: '*"Le Prussianisme-voilà l'ennemi"*.'

As Conrad was accomplishing so little during his stay on Capri he was again getting very short of money and there came a point when Pinker felt that he could advance no more. [23] But then there was a piece of good news. For some time William Rothenstein had been organising support to get Conrad a grant of money from a confidential official fund;

Gosse and others had taken the matter up and in March Rothenstein was able to write to Conrad that the Prime Minister, Balfour, had obtained the King's consent to a grant.

This grant, of £500, was the occasion of a small rumpus. When Conrad heard that Henry Newbolt was to be a sort of trustee he took this as an aspersion on his character, implying that he was an irresponsible bohemian. He wrote an indignant letter to Gosse who was of course much put out by this apparent ingratitude and had in turn to be mollified by Rothenstein.

Galsworthy and Ada came to Capri while the Conrads were there and Conrad also made a number of new friends, the most important of whom were Norman Douglas and a compatriot named Count Szembek. Douglas was just beginning his writing career and Conrad enthusiastically took him up, asking Pinker to try to place a couple of his pieces in magazines.

The Conrads got back to England on 17 May, having apparently met Marguerite Poradowska in Marseilles on the joumey. [27] One Day More was to be performed by the Stage Society in a month's time, which involved a certain amount of work and a lot of worry. At the end of June Conrad gave Galsworthy a 'résumé' of his activities since his return from Capri: 'Gout. Tinkering at the play. Worry. Two *Mirror* papers. Touch of gout. Rehearsals of the play, with going up to London for the purpose (which is a game not worth the candle). Loss of time. Some experience (which may or may not be of use).'

The play was performed on Sunday 25 June and the two following days; the Conrads went to the last performance. Conrad summed up the affair to Galsworthy:

As to the success of my thing, I can't say anything. I've heard that some papers praised it and some ran it down. On Tuesday when we went (like the imbeciles we are) there was some clapping but obviously the very smart audience did *not* catch on. And no wonder! On the other hand the celebrated 'man of the hour', G. B. Shaw, was ecstatic and enthusiastic. 'Dramatist!', says he. With three plays of his own running simultaneously at the height of the season he's entitled to speak. Of course, I don't think I am a dramatist. But I believe I've three or even five acts somewhere in me. At any rate the reception of the play was not such as to encourage me to sacrifice six months to the stage. Besides I haven't the six months to throw away.

In the end: loss of time. A thorough unsettling of the writing mood. Added weariness. [30 June 1905, *LL., II*, 21]

Although the same objections could be made to the play as to the story it is a neat and, within its limitations, effective piece of theatre.

The episode seems to have heightened Conrad's ambivalence towards the theatre. Twelve years later, when he was helping Macdonald Hastings with a dramatisation of Victory, he wrote to Christopher Sandeman:

I have a secret horror of all actors and (not so much) of actresses since they murdered for me a one-act play I wrote once (off my own bat) and had some illusions about it. [(End of April 1917), *LL., II*, 191]

The next few months were uneventful. There were visits from a few close friends, such as the Galsworthys and the Hopes; [29] and Conrad saw a certain amount of Hueffer, who, he told Wells, 'is a sort of lifelong habit—of which I am not ashamed, because he is a much better fellow than the world gives him credit for'. [30] There was also, according to Jessie, a visit from a figure from Conrad's past, Roger Casement. [31] Conrad's health was not good at this time and he told Douglas in October that he had not had 'more than three weeks of decent health in the whole time since I left Capri. [32] Then to complete the usual catalogue of woes Borys went down with scarlet fever while the Conrads were visiting London in November. [33] However, as if to make up for the unproductiveness of the rest of 1905, Conrad managed to end the year with a spurt of work. He finished two more pieces for *The Mirror of the Sea* [34] and seems to have developed *'Gaspar Ruiz'* into its final form. [*] Then he wrote three other short stories, *'The Brute'*, *'An Anarchist'* and *'The Informer'*; [*] and he also continued to work on *Chance*.

'Gaspar Ruiz' is set in Chile during her war of

independence and is a by-product of Conrad's reading for *Nostromo*. He found the 'seed' for the story in Captain Basil Hall's book, *Extracts from a Journal, written on the Coasts of Chili, Peru, and Mexico.* [35] He again captured the atmosphere of a warring South American state, but it is a slight, melodramatic story and, even apart from the enormous physique of Gaspar Ruiz himself, emotions and actions give the impression of having been blown up to more than life-size. Gaspar Ruiz is a simple, humane man of the people who is unjustly sentenced to death as a deserter by the republicans. He escapes and is looked after by an aristocratic royalist girl with an implacable desire for revenge on the republicans. Having saved the life of a republican general in an earthquake he is pardoned and rises to a position of responsibility. Then, enraged by the machinations of the civil governor of the province of which he is 'military guardian', he leads a rising against the republicans. Urged on by the girl, who has become his wife and borne him a child, he successfully holds out against the government. But his wife and child are finally captured through treachery and he is killed trying to rescue them; his back is broken when he has a cannon fired from it in place of the gun-carriage which has been lost over a precipice. Before he dies, the girl, who until now seems only to have been using Gaspar Ruiz as an instrument of revenge, declares her love for him and when he is dead throws herself to her death in an abyss.

The story is told by an old officer of the republican army, but the presentation is as slipshod as the characterisation is crude; whenever Conrad needs to give some information which the narrator could not know he drops him and takes over himself.

'The Brute' is a short story about an unpredictable ship which had the reputation of killing a man every voyage. Conrad says that he first heard about the ship from Captain Blake, under whom he served as Second Officer on the *Tilkburst* in 1884. [36] The 'brute' is eventually run on the rocks because the Officer of the Watch was occupied with a woman passenger; this was the fate of another ship which Conrad

grafted on to the story of the brute. [37] It is a slight story, little more than a pot-boiler.

The two other products of this winter's work are, however, more substantial. *'An Anarchist'* is a savage, almost mad story about a man who becomes a victim of society in rather the same way as does Anatole France's *Crainquebille*. 'The principal truth discoverable in the views of Paul the engineer was that a little thing may bring about the undoing of a man.' [38] He is a decent, hard-working man who gets drunk when celebrating one day and is arrested for causing a disturbance and shouting anarchist slogans. At his trial:

Whatever chance he had was done away with by a young socialist lawyer who volunteered to undertake his defence. In vain he assured him that he was no anarchist; that he was a quiet, respectable mechanic, only too anxious to work ten hours per day at his trade. He was represented at the trial as the victim of society and his drunken shoutings as the expression of infinite suffering. The young lawyer had his way to make, and this case was just what he wanted for a start. The speech for the defence was pronounced magnificent. [39]

He received the maximum sentence for a first offence.

When he comes out his old employer refuses to take him back and he falls into the hands of a group of anarchists who terrorise and exploit him. He is involved in a bank robbery and is sentenced to the penal colony at Cayenne. During a convicts' revolt he and two of the anarchists with whom he has been associated escape in a boat. He has managed to get hold of a pistol and he forces the two men to row to the point of exhaustion. 'It made me smile. Ah! They loved their life these two, in this evil world of theirs, just as I used to love my life, too, before they spoiled it for me with their phrases.' [40]

Eventually he sees a sail on the horizon:

I remembered their lies, their promises, their menaces, and all my days of misery. Why could they not have left me alone after I came out of prison? I looked at them and thought that while they lived I could never be free. Never. Neither I nor others like me with warm hearts and weak heads. For I know I have not a strong head, monsieur. A black rage came upon me—the rage of extreme intoxication—but not against the injustice of society. Oh, no!

'I must be free!' I cried, furiously.

'*Vive la liberté*!' yells that ruffian Mafile. '*Mort aux bourgeois* who send us to Cayenne! They shall soon know that we are free.'

The sky, the sea, the whole horizon, seemed to turn red, blood red all round the boat. My temples were beating so loud that I wondered they did not hear. How is it that they did not? How is it they did not understand?

I heard Simon ask, 'Have we not pulled far enough out now?'

'Yes. Far enough,' I said. I was sorry for him; it was the other I hated. He hauled in his oar with a loud sigh, and as he was raising his hand to wipe his forehead with the air of a man who has done his work, I pulled the trigger of my revolver and shot him like this off the knee, right through the heart.

He tumbled down, with his head hanging over the side of the boat. I did not give him a second glance. The other cried out piercingly. Only one shriek of horror. Then all was still.

He slipped off the thwart on to his knees and raised his clasped hands before his face in an attitude of supplication. 'Mercy,' he whispered, faintly. 'Mercy for me!—comrade.'

'Ah, comrade,' I said, in a low tone. 'Yes, comrade, of course. Well, then, shout *Vive l' anarchie*.'

He flung up his arms, his face up to the sky and his mouth wide open in a great yell of despair. '*Vive l' anarchie! Vive.*

He collapsed all in a heap, with a bullet through his head.

The story is told by a lepidopterist who finds the 'anarchist', after his escape, being exploited by the callous manager of a cattle estate whose steam-launch he is working. Despite the man's bloodcurdling past he is portrayed as a desolate, sympathetic figure. In his isolation from all around him he is a little like Yanko Goorall of 'Amy Foster'. He is enveloped in an aura of mystery; thus although he is French the manager insists that he comes from Barcelona and he is called Anarchisto de Barcelone 'as if it were his christian name and surname'. The lepidopterist's conclusion is that he was much more of an anarchist than he confessed to me or to himself; and that, the special features of his case apart, he was very much like many other anarchists. Warm heart and weak head—that is the word of the riddle; and it is a fact that the bitterest contradictions and the deadliest conflicts of the world are carried on in every individual breast capable of feeling and passion.

'The Informer' is also a savage story concerned with anarchism, but not of the warm-hearted type. The story is told at one remove; the narrator relates what he has been told by Mr X, the anarchist, for whom he shows a strong distaste. It is by revealing the cynicism of Mr X who is also an 'enlightened connoisseur of bronzes and china' [44] and a luxurious liver, that Conrad expresses his own antipathy towards anarchism. The use of Mr X greatly enriches the texture of the story, as when the girl's misguided belief in the 'informer' Sevrin is portrayed through Mr X's own callous contempt for her behaviour. Through him Conrad also condemns those of the bourgeoisie who foster the anarchists:

'Don't you know yet,' he [Mr X] said, 'that an idle and selfish class loves to see mischief being made, even if it is made at its own expense? Its own life being all a matter of pose and gesture, it is unable to realise the power and the danger of a real movement and of words that have no sham meaning. It is all fun and sentiment.... The demagogue carries the amateurs of emotion with him. Amateurism in this, that, and the other thing is a delightfully easy way of killing time, and feeding one's own vanity—the silly vanity of being abreast with the ideas of the day after tomorrow.'

It is significant of Conrad's contempt for anarchism that in both *'The Informer'* and *The Secret Agent* the central character is a police agent, a traitor to his professed cause. In this story Sevrin is an informer 'from conviction':

A vague but ardent humanitarianism had urged him in his first youth into the bitterest extremity of negation and revolt. Afterwards his optimism flinched. He doubted and became lost. You have heard of converted atheists. These turn often into dangerous fanatics, but the soul remains the same....

The fact is, he was not enough of an optimist. You must be a savage, tyrannical, pitiless, thick-and-thin optimist, like Horne, for instance, to make a good social rebel of the extreme type.

But Sevrin is not a convincing character. His loss of faith should have led him to despair, not to fanaticism. To become a fanatic he should have acquired another faith, but Conrad does not provide him with one; to be merely a fanatical informer is too negative. Despite its incidental interest this is not a well worked out or satisfying story.

Conrad had been 'abominably ill' [48] in December and in the new year, 1906, he and Jessie decided to go to Montpellier to escape the rest of the English winter. Conrad's first task in Montpellier was to prepare the 'sea sketches', which he had written during the last two years, for publication in book form as *The Mirror of the Sea.*

From the beginning Conrad had planned to make a book out of these sketches or essays, and he described his aim in a letter to Colonel Harvey of Harper's. They were to compose 'a volume of sea sketches, something in the spirit of Turgeniev *Sportsman's Sketches,* but concerned with ships and the sea with a distinct autobiographical and anecdotal note running through what is mainly meant for a record of remembered feelings'. [49] But when he started to write these sketches he does not seem to have looked on them as of much importance, telling Wells: 'I've discovered that I can dictate that sort of bosh without effort at the rate of 3,000 words in four hours.'

When, however, he wrote the Author's Note to *The Mirror of the Sea* he called the book 'a very intimate revelation' and said: 'I have attempted here to lay bare with the unreserve of a last hour's confession the terms of my relation with the sea'. [51] The correct assessment of the book is perhaps somewhere between these two judgements and it has been admired most by those, such as Wells and Galsworthy, who liked or understood Conrad's work least.

As was perhaps inevitable from the manner of its composition, *The Mirror of the Sea* is an uneven book containing some fine things like *'Initiation'* or, a very different type of sketch, *'The Tremolino'*, and also some bad, inflated writing like much of *'Rulers of East and West'* or *'Overdue and Missing'*. It lacks unity of approach or design—for instance *'The Heroic Age'*, an essay on Nelson, seems only to have been tagged on at the end because it happened to have been written for the centenary of Trafalgar—and the book is certainly far from being the 'very intimate revelation' which Conrad claimed. Some of the pieces are no more than impersonal and general essays, a form of writing in which Conrad was weakest. There would be no point in mentioning these defects if *The Mirror of the Sea* had not been exalted by some into one of Conrad's most important books. The writing, which has been admired, is often muddled, overstrained, and excessively metaphorical. For instance, the two similes blur this description:

> a white mast, slender like a stalk of straw and crossed by a yard like a knitting needle, flying the signals of flag and balloon, watches over a set of heavy dock-gates.

or,

> What had become of the dazzling hoard of royal jewels exhibited at every close of day? Gone, disappeared, extinguished, carried off without leaving a single gold band or the flash of a single sunbeam in the evening sky. [53]

Jewels cannot be extinguished, nor can they leave flashes of sunbeams in the sky.

Then "'Rulers of East and West'" is burdened with the most elaborate and inconsistent anthropomorphism, much of which merely obscures or belittles the effect, as when Conrad speaks of the west wind as a king 'playing his royal game of quoits with hurricanes, tossing them over from the continent of republics to the continent of kingdoms...'.

Conrad was always at his best when he could find a concrete framework for what he had to say, and it is his portraits of the merchant navy seamen whom he knew, of scenes like those in Sydney harbour or frozen Amsterdam, or of a piece of action like the *Tremolino* episode which stand out as the finest parts of the book.

Conrad was soon feeling refreshed by the move to Montpellier and on 13 February he wrote a cheerful letter to Pinker telling him that the air was 'splendid' and describing a carnival with masked revellers and political riots. A week later he sent Pinker the first thirteen pages of *The Secret Agent*, at this stage called 'Verloc' which he envisaged as a short story. [55] He said that he was doing much of his writing under a sunny wall in the gardens of Peyron.

After he had dealt with *The Mirror of the Sea*, Conrad concentrated on *The Secret Agent* for the rest of the time that he was at Montpellier, although he had to break off to write a review of Galsworthy's *Man of Property*. [56] As usual he felt that he was working too slowly and wrote to Galsworthy towards the end of the visit:

As to myself, my dear Jack, I have always that feeling of loafing at my work, as if powerless in an exhaustion of thought and will. Not enough, not enough! And yet perhaps those days without a line, nay, without a word, the hard, atrocious, agonising days are simply part of my *method* of work, a decreed necessity of my production.... I doubt not only my talent (I was never so sure of that) but my character. Is it indolence,-which in my case would be nothing short of baseness,—or what? No man has a right to go on as I am doing without producing manifest masterpieces. [9 April 1906, *LL., II*, 33]

When the Conrads got back to England the Hueffers lent them their house in Winchelsea for a fortnight. This was not a success. Hueffer came down for both week-ends and Jessie's dislike of his bohemianism was brought to a climax by a series of incidents:

The next day I was cooking the lunch when he appeared with a Panama hat he had washed, and to my amazement opened the oven door and placed that hat on a sheet of paper above my joint. It was a real Panama, but his washing had been strictly confined to the outside only, there was too much grease inside the lining for my liking—even had I not had our meat beneath, and I would have liked above everything to have put it on the fire. I removed it to a chair as close to the fire as possible, and resolutely closed the oven, voicing my displeasure in as few words as possible.

My next surprise was a request put forward by my husband that I should, on a Sunday morning, out of the blue, so to speak, provide a new black ribbon and put it on the hat. But even this fantastic request was possible as it happened that I had some few yards of black ribbon I had been giving the maid to tie her collar with. I dutirully sewed it on the hat.

The next morning before F. M. H. started to go to the station, which he did after nearly making me break the rule I had set for a guest under the same roof as myself—although it was somewhat difficult to fix who was host and who was the guest under the circumstances. He had entered the dining-room for his breakfast after Joseph Conrad had left the room. The first thing that caught his eye was a small cut in the tablecloth. 'Look at that, Elsie will be furious.' I paused in the act of pouring out his coffee and said indifferently: 'I don't suppose she will ever see it.' F. M. H. jumped to his feet with surprising energy, and almost forgot to drawl: 'Not see it, what do you mean? It's the first thing she will see. I must say that when I lent the house I expected ordinary care——'. I rose quickly to my feet and hastily turned another corner of the cloth towards him, saying slowly and distinctly: 'I said she most probably would not see it. You see my name is on the corner. I brought my own linen, and I shall take it home with me. Are you satisfied?'

He uttered a short vexed laugh and stalked out of the house, or rather had started to do so when I recalled him with the remark: 'Oh, by the way, be kind enough to look at the date of the laundry book you gave me last night. You will see the last entry is three weeks before I came into the house, and that week's laundry is entered in the name of Hyde. Moreover, I put away the first day I came into the place everything of yours in the shape of linen *without using it* and we have been using our own.'

I could cheerfully have devoured my husband who entered the room at that moment and caught something of the last remark. 'Pay the laundry bill, of course, my dear fellow.' F. M. H. gave me a supercilious glance and a condescending 'Good morning'. But I took care to forget to settle the account which was distinctly not mine....

The host-guest had only left the house an hour or so when

the young maid appeared at the kitchen door with a miscellaneous collection of masculine garments crumpled out of all recognition in her arms, and asked what was she to do with them. Some she had found on the bed occupied by F. M. H. and some beneath. They turned out to be my husband's robes of ceremony. Frock-coat and striped grey trousers. I was puzzled for it was my pride to keep my husband's wardrobe in proper condition for instant wear. I had carefully pressed and ironed the crease myself and had also laid them flat in the drawer when we had taken temporary possession of that house.

I made my difficult way upstairs, and such was my disgust I could not forbear calling Joseph Conrad and drawing his attention to the wanton treatment of his dress suit and other garments. It was quite plain to see what had happened. F. M. H. had not found the curtains thick enough in the room he had occupied to keep out the early morning light, and had hung one of the blankets over the window. Then not finding himself warm enough in bed, had removed the suits from the drawer to pile on the bed. It was an effective eye-opener to the owner. For once he could not blame me for this calm appropriation and misuse of his wardrobe, because there had been too little clothes on a guest's bed. F. M. H. was in his own place and any responsibility for the dearth of covering was his own, not mine. [57]

Jessie's nerves were probably on edge because she was reaching the end of her pregnancy with her second child. The Galsworthys lent the Conrads their London house in Addison Road when the child was due and it was there, on 2 August 1906, that John Conrad was born. [58]

Throughout the summer and autumn Conrad continued to work at *The Secret Agent*, which he finished early in November.

The Secret Agent is held by some to be one of Conrad's greatest achievements. Although it is in many ways a fine piece of work and is superlatively expressed it has some rather serious flaws and lacks the power and range of *Under Western Eyes*, *Nostromo*, *Lord Jim* or *Victory*.

In the Author's Note Conrad says that the story had two separate sources. He recounts how he was discussing anarchism with a friend, apparently Hueffer, [60] when one of them mentioned the attempt to blow up Greenwich Observatory: 'a bloodstained inanity of so fatuous a kind that it was impossible to fathom its origin by any reasonable or even unreasonable process of thought'. The friend 'remarked in his characteristically casual and omniscient manner: "Oh, that fellow was half an idiot.

His sister committed suicide afterwards."' [61] This gave Conrad the kernel round which he was able to build a plausible story. The other source was, he says, a book of recollections by an assistant commissioner of police in which the author—'I believe his name was Anderson' [62] —reproduced a short dialogue between the Home Secretary and himself after some unexpected anarchist outrage. At one point the Home Secretary said: '"All that's very well. But your idea of secrecy over there seems to consist of keeping the Home Secretary in the dark."' [63]

This, Conrad wrote, was 'the tiniest little drop of the right kind, precipitating the process of crystallisation'. [64] From this ' Winnie Verloc's story' [65] grew. But like most of Conrad's accounts of the origins of a story this is misleading. It is clear that he first conceived of *The Secret Agent* as a short story with Verloc at the centre and it is only in the last third of the book that Winnie emerges at all fully, while the centre of interest does not shift to her until after she has killed Verloc.

The only similarity between the actual Greenwich Bomb Outrage which took place on 15 February 1894 [66] and the use which Conrad made of it is that neither Conrad's Stevie nor the actual perpetrator, Martial Bourdin, damaged the Observatory but were themselves blown up, and they resembled each other physically. Stevie is slight and fair [67] while Martial Bourdin was described as a 'remarkably short man, 5 ft. 1 in. by measurement, well-nourished and proportioned, but inadequately developed'; his hair and moustache were 'silky and fair'. [68] The physical resemblance was probably a coincidence, although Conrad may have come upon an account of the outrage in some book, or details from contemporary reports may have lingered in his mind.

As seems to have been invariably the case when he was not relying on personal knowledge, Conrad did some background reading for the novel. An Assistant Commissioner of Police named Robert Anderson, who had been engaged on Secret Service work, had published a book called *Sidelights on the Home Rule Movement* just as Conrad was starting his novel. It contained a certain amount about the use of police agents to foil the Fenian plots; the author also quotes Sir William Harcourt's remark which caught Conrad's fancy: ' Anderson's idea of secrecy is not to tell the Secretary of State.' [69]

Conrad told Cunninghame Graham that 'Mr Vladmir was suggested to me by that scoundrel General Seliwertsow whom Padlewski shot (in Paris) in the nineties', adding: 'Perhaps you will remember, as there were peculiar circumstances in that case.' [70] The outstanding feature of the Seliwertsow, or Seliwerstow, case was its obscurity. The General, who seems to have had a most unsavoury character, had at one time been head of the notorious Third Section of the Russian police, but had been living in Paris for some years, allegedly as a Russian agent. After mortally wounding him in his hotel room Padlewski disappeared; there were the wildest rumours as to his whereabouts and it was suggested that the French police were most unanxious to have him traced. [71] Conrad no doubt had recourse to other background material, but this has not yet come to light.

Several times Conrad described *The Secret Agent* as an attempt to treat a melodramatic theme ironically and certainly there is plenty of melodrama; a particularly gory death, murder and suicide within a framework of anarchist activities, foreign embassy plotting and police investigation. But, as always with Conrad, the interest is in the treatment and not in the facts themselves.

In the Author's Note he says it was his 'earnest belief that ironic treatment alone would enable me to say all I felt I would have to say in scorn as well as in pity', [72] and in *The Secret Agent* more than any of his other novels the effect is gained through the diversity of ironic treatment. First, the predominantly ironic tone is set by the author's assumed emotional detachment from the action, expressed through the dry, at times sardonic, manner of telling the tale. This is particularly evident in the scenes which are potentially the most dramatic. Thus when Winnie Verloc pushes Ossipon, 'the robust anarchist', into the room where her murdered husband is 'reposing quietly on the sofa':

The true sense of the scene he was beholding came to Ossipon through the contemplation of the hat. It seemed an extraordinary thing, in ominous object, a sign. Black, and rim upward, it lay on the floor before the couch as if prepared to receive the contributions of pence from people who would come presently to behold Mr Verloc in the fullness of his domestic ease reposing on a sofa. From the hat the eyes of the robust anarchist wandered to the displaced table, gazed at the broken dish for a time, received a kind of optical shock from observing a white gleam under the imperfectly closed eyelids of the man on the couch. Mr Verloc did not seem so much asleep now as lying down with a bent head and looking insistently at his left breast. And when Comrade Ossipon had made out the handle of the knife he turned away from the glazed door and retched violently. [73]

Such passages go towards justifying Douglas Hewitt's characterisation of the book as 'more nearly a comedy than any other novel of Conrad'. [74] There is underlying comedy in the last scene between the Verlocs and even macabre humour in Conrad's treatment of Stevie's gory death, as when the police constable repeatedly and self-satisfiedly insists that the body 'is all there'—'I don't think I missed a single piece as big as a postage stamp' [75] —or when Chief Inspector Heat peers at Stevie's remains on the table 'with a calm face and the slightly anxious attention of an indigent customer bending over what may be called the by-products of a butcher's shop with a view to an inexpensive Sunday dinner', [76] or in Winnie Verloc's image of 'a park—smashed branches, torn leaves, gravel, bits of brotherly flesh and bone, all spouting up together in the manner of a firework.... Mrs Verloc closed her eyes desperately, throwing upon that vision the night of her eyelids, where after a rainlike fall of mangled limbs the decapitated head of Stevie lingered suspended alone, and fading out slowly like the last star of a pyrotechnic display.'

Conrad also uses the time-shift to achieve an ironical effect as he did in *Nostromo*. After setting the scene of the novel (pp. 3 - 60) he goes straight to the Greenwich Park explosion, which is discussed by Ossipon and the Professor on the basis of the newspaper report. Then after the reader has realised that Stevie was the victim of the explosion * Conrad goes back to events which take place before Verloc and Stevie set out for Greenwich Park. Thus the reader is aware of the poignant irony in Winnie Verloc's comments on the relationship between her husband and Stevie. She congratulates herself on Verloc's growing affection for Stevie and thinks with pride that they 'might be father and son'. [78] To Winnie this bond has seemed the culmination of her seven years' effort to ensure Stevie's security. She has forced the two together and, with assertions such as 'You could do anything with that boy, Adolf.... He would go through fire for you', [79] has inadvertently suggested the answer to Verloc's problem. The reader knows what Stevie has actually done for Verloc.

In the great scene of the book, that between Winnie and Verloc which leads up to the stabbing, the irony is gained through the reader's knowledge of the situation in contrast with Verloc's total unawareness.

The reader knows that Winnie is obsessed with Stevie's welfare to the exclusion of everything else, and that she married Verloc only because he was willing to take over Stevie along 'with the furniture'. [80] He knows Winnie's reaction to the news of Stevie's death: her 'moral nature had been subjected to a shock of which, in the physical order, the most violent earthquake of history could only be a faint and languid rendering'. [81] He thus experiences the full ironical impact of Verloc's fumbling attempts to console Winnie which culminate in the magnificent 'Do be reasonable Winnie. What would it have been if you had lost me?' [82] Verloc's pathetically inadequate advice is to have 'a good cry'. [83]

Not only is Verloc emotionally obtuse but he is unaware of the enormity of his using Stevie for such a task. He even imagines that he is showing restraint and magnanimity in not reproaching Winnie for bringing the police down on them; after all it was she who had put Stevie's address in the coat. His attitude expresses that 'moral nihilism' [84] which Conrad had earlier attributed to him:

'By heavens! You know that I hunted high and low. I ran the risk of giving myself away to find somebody for that accursed job. And I tell you again I couldn't find anyone crazy enough or hungry enough. What do you take me for—a murderer, or what? The boy is gone. Do you think I wanted him to blow himself up?... I don't blame you. But just try to understand that it was a pure accident; as much an accident as if he had been run over by a bus while crossing the street.'

His generosity was not infinite, because he was a human being—and not a monster, as Mrs Verloc believed him to be.

It is a triumph of subtlety that Verloc remains a far from unpleasant human being throughout, so much so that the reader is constantly on the verge of accepting his point of view, and sympathises with him sitting in the parlour of the Cheshire Cheese thinking over the best way to break the news. Of course it is easy enough to make a villain appear pleasant, but Conrad never blurs the moral issue and the impact of Verloc's crime is all the greater because Conrad shows how easily it happened.

The Verlocs remain at cross-purposes to the end:

'Come here,' he said in a peculiar tone, which might have been the tone of brutality, but was intimately known to Mrs Verloc as the note of wooing.

She started forward at once...

But she was coming to kill him, not to answer his call, and Mr Verloc dies 'in the muttered sound of the word "Don't" by way of protest'. [87]

Conrad told Cunninghame Graham: 'I don't think that I've been satirising the revolutionary world. All these people are not revolutionaries,—they are shams'; [88] and some years later he insisted to another correspondent: 'I hope you have seen that the purpose of the book was *not* to attack any doctrine, or even the men holding that doctrine'.

But if it wasn't Conrad's main purpose to satirise anarchism and anarchists he leaves no doubt as to his contempt for them and treats them throughout with scornful irony, untouched by pity. In his Author's Note he speaks of 'the criminal futility of the whole thing, doctrine, action, mentality... the contemptible aspect of the half-crazy pose as of a brazen cheat exploiting the poignant miseries and passionate credulities of a mankind always so tragically eager for self-destruction'. [90] Then in the novel he describes Karl Yundt, the most repellent of the anarchists, as 'an insolent and venomous evoker of sinister impulses which lurk in the blind envy and exasperated vanity of ignorance, in the suffering and misery of poverty, in all the hopeful and noble illusions of righteous anger, pity, and revolt'. [91]

It is true that Karl Yundt, Michaelis and Ossipon are shams, for there is no accord between their words and their actions; Yundt, for instance, 'had never in his life raised personally as much as his little finger against the social edifice'. [92] But Conrad so hated revolutionary views and activity that he found it almost impossible to allow revolu tionaries any sincerity. At the best his sincere revolutionaries are victims of an illusion, like Haldin and Sophia Antonovna in *Under Western Eyes*; at the worst their creed is based, like the Professor's, on 'ambition' and 'vengeful bitterness'.

Indeed, Conrad says that 'the way of even the most justifiable revolutions is prepared by personal impulses disguised into creeds'. [94] But the anarchists in *The Secret Agent* are not very convincing; or rather they are slight, two-dimensional characters, and Conrad gives less care to their presentation than he does to that of Chief Inspector Heat or the Assistant Commissioner. Yundt is a caricature, Michaelis is a harmless absurdity, and Ossipon is a rogue portrayed with a few vigorous strokes which tend to be repeated at each of his appearances. The Professor comes in a slightly different category, in that he is a genuine nihilist and there is some attempt to present his views.

He is the embodiment of all that is anti-social and destructive. His single-minded ruthlessness and his incorruptibility raise him above the others, so that he is Chief Inspector Heat's only formidable opponent; Heat knows that the Professor always carries a bomb on him which he will not hesitate to explode if he is molested by the police. But, although it is a tribute to his pre-eminence among the anarchists that he is given the last paragraph of the book, even he is no more than a stock figure.

As a corollary to the moral repulsiveness of the anarchists Conrad emphasises their physical defects. Karl Yundt is

> old and bald.... An extraordinary expression of underhand malevolence survived in his extinguished eyes. When he rose painfully the thrusting forward of a skinny groping hand deformed by gouty swellings suggested the effort of a moribund murderer summoning all his remaining strength for a last stab. He leaned on a thick stick, which trembled under his other hand.... His worn-out passion, resembling in its impotent fierceness the excitement of a senile sensualist, was badly served by a dried throat and toothless gums which seemed to catch the tip of his tongue. [95]

Michaelis's repulsive corpulence is constantly mentioned. His voice 'wheezed as if deadened and oppressed by the layer of fat on his chest. He had come out of a highly hygienic prison round like a tub, with an enormous stomach and distended cheeks of a pale, semitransparent complexion, as though for fifteen years the servants of an outraged society had made a point of stuffing him with fattening foods in a damp and lightless cellar'.

Ossipon is always ironically referred to as 'the robust anarchist', because, although he has a good physique, he is particularly feeble when action is demanded. But he has 'a flattened nose and prominent mouth cast in the rough mould of the negro type', a mark of degeneracy to Conrad, and there is obvious irony in Ossipon's dubbing Stevie a degenerate on the basis of Lombroso's theories. The 'Professor' is a puny, unhealthy man, an 'unwholesome-looking little moral agent of destruction': 'The lamentable inferiority of the whole physique was made ludicrous by the supremely self-confident bearing of the individual.' [99]

Verloc himself is supremely well presented; he makes a stronger physical impact on the reader than any of Conrad's characters. His appearance and habits are a counterpart to his moral indolence. 'He had an air of having wallowed, fully dressed, all day on an unmade bed.' [100] The Chancelier d'Ambassade tells him, 'You are very corpulent', [101] and Mr Vladimir asks him: 'What do you mean by getting out of condition like this?' [102] 'I'll tell you what I think is the matter,' he goes on. 'You are a lazy fellow.'

In fact the whole book could be regarded as a homily on sloth. 'With the insight of a kindred temperament', Mr Verloc pronounces the anarchists—Yundt, Michaelis and Ossipon—'a lazy lot' and Conrad generalises:

Mr Verloc, temperamentally identical with his associates, drew fine distinctions in his mind on the strength of insignificant differences. He drew them with a certain complacency, because the instinct of conventional respectability was strong within him, being only overcome by his dislike of all kinds of recognised labour—a temperamental defect which he shared with a large proportion of revolutionary reformers of a given social state. For obviously one does not revolt against the advantages and opportunities of that state, but against the price which must be paid for the same in the coin of accepted morality, self-restraint, and toil. The majority of revolutionists are the enemies of discipline and fatigue mostly. [103]

The Verlocs' relationship is conditioned by their indolence: 'Their accord was perfect, but it was not precise. It was a tacit accord, congenial to Mrs Verloc's incuriosity and to Mr Verloc's habits of mind, which were indolent and secret. They refrained from going to the bottom of facts and motives.' [104] Winnie Verloc's conviction that 'things did not stand being looked into' [105] is constantly reiterated. 'Mrs Verloc wasted no portion of this transient life in seeking for fundamental information. This is a sort of economy having all the appearances and some of the advantages of prudence.

Obviously it may be good for one not to know too much. And such a view accords very well with constitutional indolence.' [106] Without this indolence the Verlocs could hardly have remained together, but with it they are able to live insulated from each other, like two wires in an electric flex; the breaking of the insulation brings immediate disaster.

Thus Mrs Verloc deliberately ignores her husband's nefarious activities on which their life is built, while Mr Verloc remains unaware that his wife has married him solely for the sake of Stevie's welfare, complacent in 'the idealistic belief in being loved for himself'. [107] For Mrs Verloc has a ruthless streak which enables her to carry out her thoroughly reprehensible deception of Mr Verloc, but also sets her above most of the rest of the characters, inasmuch as she is able to sacrifice herself totally for another person—a quality which she shares with her mother.

It seems that Conrad did not intend Mrs Verloc to be very strongly condemned for her treatment of Mr Verloc. He speaks of 'this woman, capable of a bargain the mere suspicion of which would have been infinitely shocking to Mr Verloc's idea of love', [108] —and, one should add, to that of most people—but emphasises that she loyally carried out her unspoken bargain and was a model wife. He commends her 'exalted faithfulness of purpose, even unto murder' [109] and describes the Verlocs' life as 'an existence created by Mrs Verloc's genius; an existence foreign to all grace and charm, without beauty and almost without decency, but admirable in the continuity of feeling and tenacity of purpose'.

It seems that Conrad intended her to be a sort of feminine counterpart of MacWhirr, but she does not emerge as a very sympathetic or admirable character, and it is only when she becomes the victim of the despicable Ossipon that she arouses pity or concern. It is this that reduces the impact of the book because, although it contains the seeds of a conflict between the altruism or capacity for selfsacrifice of Winnie and her mother on the one side and of the ruthless self-centredness of Verloc and the anarchists on the other, the two women are essentially minor characters.

Winnie's mother plays only an insignificant part, and Winnie herself is on such a low mental level that one wonders whether there was ever an element of choice, therefore of virtue, in her self-sacrifice or whether it was merely as instinc tive as an animal's defence of its offspring; certainly her terror of death at the end is closer to the reaction of an animal scenting blood in a slaughterhouse than to that of a human being. Thus although there is pathos in the book there is no tragedy because there is no sense of waste, no suggestion that the characters were made for better things: Winnie and Stevie might have had a less gruesome fate, certainly, but not a nobler. The final effect is of negation and squalor.

There are other aspects of the book which have barely been mentioned. There is Mr Vladimir, First Secretary of the foreign Embassy (the Russian, of course), whose instructions to Verloc to carry out the bomb outrage on Greenwich Observatory, in order to frighten the British police into rounding up all the known anarchists, set the events of the story in motion. In Mr Vladimir, with his contempt for Western legality, Conrad expresses something of his dislike of Russians and Russian methods. Mr Vladimir is famous for his witticisms, a favourite of society drawing-rooms and a member of an exclusive club, but his civilised manners are only a veneer on innate savagery:

'Aha! You dare be impudent,' Mr Vladimir began, with an amazingly guttural intonation not only utterly un-English, but absolutely unEuropean, and startling even to Mr Verloc's experience of cosmopolitan slums. [111]

And,

The features of Mr Vladimir, so well known in the best society by their humorous urbanity, beamed with cynical self-satisfaction, which would have astonished the intelligent women his wit entertained so exquisitely. 'Yes,' he continued, with a contemptuous smile, 'the blowing up of the first meridian is bound to raise a howl of execration.' [112]

Contrasted with this method of dealing with anarchism is that of the British police, for whom Vladimir at first has an 'immense contempt',— [113] although, 'descended from generations victimised by the instruments of an arbitrary power, he was racially, nationally, and individually afraid of the police. It was an inherited weakness, altogether independent of his judgement, of his reason, of his experience. He was born to it.' [114]

There is a conflict between the aims and approach of the two police officers dealing with the bomb outrage. On one side there is Chief Inspector Heat, the reliable 'old departmental hand' [115] whose rise to prominence has been due to his successful handling of thieves and who 'could understand the mind of a burglar, because, as a matter of fact, the mind and the instincts of a burglar are of the same kind as the mind and the instincts of a police officer.

Both recognise the same conventions, and have a working knowledge of each other's methods and of the routine of their respective trades.' [116] Confronted with an anarchist, Heat 'gave a thought of regret to the world of thieves—sane, without morbid ideals, working by routine, respectful of constituted authorities, free from all taint of hate and despair'. —'Catching thieves... had that quality of seriousness belonging to every form of open sport where the best man wins under perfectly comprehensible rules.

There were no rules for dealing with anarchists.' Heat had therefore devised his own method, which was to use Verloc as a private source of information about anarchist activities in the hope thereby of forestalling any violent action. When he discovers that Verloc was connected with the Greenwich bomb explosion he withholds his knowledge from his superior, the Assistant Commissioner, because he does not want his source of information to be endangered. Instead he wants to make a scape goat of the ticket-of-leave ex-convict, Michaelis, although he is almost certain that Michaelis is innocent, because he 'did logically believe that incarceration was the proper fate for every declared enemy of the law'. [119] The Assistant Commissioner, on the other hand, is repelled by Heat's hole-in-the-corner methods and is determined to destroy the squalid system of embassy spies and double agents; moreover he has strong reasons for not wanting Michaelis to be touched, because Michaelis has been taken up by an elderly rich woman who was 'one of the most influential and distinguished connections of the Assistant Commissioner's wife', [120] and he knows that he will never be forgiven by the woman or by his wife if any harm comes to Michaelis.

Thus when the Assistant Commissioner has managed to wheedle the culprit's name out of Heat and when he discovers that Verloc is also an embassy spy he is determined to teach the foreign power a lesson, even though it means destroying Heat's source of information. He tells the Home Secretary:

'The existence of secret agents should not be tolerated, as tending to augment the positive dangers of the evil against which they are used. That the spy will fabricate his information is a mere commonplace. But in the sphere of political and revolutionary action, relying partly on violence, the professional spy has every facility to fabricate the very facts themselves, and will spread the double evil of emulation in one direction, and of panic, hasty legislation, unreflecting hate, on the other.' [121]

In fact Heat is intent, unknowingly, on fulfilling Vladimir's hopes, whereas the Assistant Commissioner is determined to thwart them. As he tells the Home Secretary: 'For him [Heat] the plain duty is to fasten the guilt upon as many prominent anarchists as he can... whereas I, he would say, am bent upon vindicating their innocence'. [122] Thus, although Heat and the Assistant Commissioner are both genuinely acting as they think right, their conduct coincides with their personal interests.

The wrangle between Heat and the Assistant Commissioner is extremely well done; the one an 'old police hand' [123] and the other new to his job, just back from a tropical colony whose freedom he loved, chained to an office desk, which he hates. Conrad takes great care to make them both rounded and convincing characters. But if the book is to be looked on as ' Winnie Verloc's story' or as Verloc's, or, more correctly, if the theme is thought of in general terms such as an attempt 'to hold up the worthlessness of certain individuals and the baseness of some others', [124] the scenes between Heat and the Assistant Commissioner and still more between the

Assistant Commissioner and the Home Secretary seem to contribute little to the central interest. * Moreover, it is very hard to decide what the central interest is; for, although the ironical treatment provides a unity of mood, the book lacks, unlike most of Conrad's work, a unifying theme, and when it is carefully examined falls apart into a succession of only superficially related scenes; in fact the 'crystallisation' of which Conrad speaks in the Author's Note never occurs.

After he had finished *The Secret Agent*, Conrad, feeling 'horribly seedy and depressed', [125] again decided to escape the English winter by going to Montpellier. Before leaving he was able to dash off a story, *'Il Conde'*, which he apparently finished on 4 December. [126] It is an excellently told but very short and unimportant story about an elderly and intensely civilised Count living in Naples who is the victim of an outrage by an aristocratic young member of a *Camorra*.

The young man stops him in a public place and, threatening him with a knife, demands his money. The Count has left his pocket-book at his hotel and genuinely believes that he has no money to hand over. When the young man has gone he remembers that he has a twenty-five-franc piece tucked away as a reserve. Very much shaken by the incident he goes into a restaurant, but when he is paying his bill he sees the young man again, who comes up and insults him:

'Ah! So you had some gold on you—you old liar—you old *birba*—you *furfante*! But you are not done with me yet.' [127]

The Count decides that he must leave Southern Italy, although he is convinced that his health cannot stand any other climate.

He was not afraid of what could be done to him. His delicate conception of his dignity was defiled by a degrading experience. He couldn't stand that.

This story was apparently based on an experience which happened to the Count Szembek, of whom Conrad had seen quite a lot when he was in Capri. *

The Conrad family left for Montpellier on 16 December, meeting Marguerite Poradowska in Paris on the way. [129] All went well at the start; the weather was 'cold, calm, dry, brilliant',[130] and Conrad rested except for revising the French translations of some of the *Tales of Unrest*. During January of 1907 he must have worked hard. He wrote a lot of *'The Duel'* and seems again to have tried to grapple with *Chance*. He also began to take Spanish lessons as a 'mental stimulant',[132] and did some reading about Napoleon in search of a subject for the perennial ' Mediterranean novel'.

Then troubles began. At the end of January it was discovered that Borys had adenoids and the following month he caught measles, after which he developed what seemed to be bronchitis. The doctor then suspected tuberculosis, saying that both lungs were threatened. Both parents were intensely worried and Conrad wrote to Galsworthy on 5 March:

> The doctor imparted to me his fears yesterday. The most terrific part of it was that for the last month, even before he sickened for measles, I myself had a notion of something of the kind-a sort of gnawing fear which I kept from Jessie of course.... I had no other ground but the expression of his face, which struck me one evening as he sat opposite me. We were having a game of dominoes and I had the greatest difficulty to finish the hundred. Then I went out and walked about the streets for hours. I managed to quiet myself, but the impression remained. It turns out now that poor Jessie on her side had the same fears—and observed the same discretion.... For the last ten days he has got dreadfully thin. We can't get him to eat more than a few mouthfuls and that only he will do for his mother's sake.... The change in his character is also astonishing. But this won't bear being written about.
>
> An analysis would have been made already but we can't get him to expectorate as yet, tho' he is trying his hardost in order to please me. This is the tenth night I haven't slept. I don't mean to say I have had no sleep for all that time; but I hang about his room all night listening and watching. I simply can't go to bed. Then in the afternoon I throw myself down on the sofa and sleep from sheer weariness. For four days I haven't written anything. Jessie is wholly admirable, sharing herself between the two boys with the utmost serenity. [*LL.*, II, 43-4]

The agony must have been increased by the knowledge that both Conrad's parents had died of tuberculosis, but a week later [134] Conrad was able to tell Pinker that the analysis was favourable, although he had been advised by the doctor to take Borys to Geneva instead of returning to England. Conrad had decided on the hydropathic establishment at Champel, to which he had been in the 1890's, hoping that he too might benefit from taking a cure. He was of course worried about the expense and went into detailed calculations for Pinker.

Meanwhile he continued to work at *Chance* and *'The Duel'*, which last he finished on 11 April. [135] It is a delightful tale of how one of Napoleon's officers, Feraud, a fiery little Gascon, compels another, a cautious and gentle Picardian named d'Hubert, to fight a succession of duels with him because he imagines himself insulted. The quarrel lasts for sixteen years, during Napoleon's domination of Europe and after. No one except the antagonists knows its trivial cause, and when d'Hubert finally reveals it, one of the characters comments: 'If that's the tale the fellow made up for his wife, and during the honeymoon, too, you may depend on it that no one will ever know now the secret of this affair'. [136] It is an excellently told story, gently humorous and ironical, but touches no very deep emotions and Conrad was claiming rather a lot to describe it as an attempt to 'capture... the Spirit of the Epoch'.

He also mentions that he 'had heard in my boyhood a good deal of the great Napoleonic legend. I had a genuine feeling that I would find myself at home in it.' Napoleon had a fascination for Conrad, and doubtless his imagination had first been stirred by the glamour surrounding his Uncle Nicholas, whose tales of the Retreat from Moscow particularly impressed him; there is a fine passage on the episode in *'The Duel'*, and Conrad returned to the subject in a later tale, *'The Warrior's Soul'*. Like those of most Poles, his feelings about Napoleon seem to have been ambivalent. Thus in *'Autocracy and War'* he lashed out at him:

The degradation of the ideas of freedom and justice at the root of the French Revolution is made manifest in the person of its heir; a personality without law or faith, whom it has been the fashion to represent as an eagle, but who was, in truth, more like a sort of vulture preying upon the body of a Europe which did, indeed, for some dozen of years, very much resemble a corpse. The subtle and manifold influence for evil of the Napoleonic episode as a school of violence, as a sower of national hatreds, as the direct provocator of obscurantism and reaction, of political tyranny and injustice, cannot well be exaggerated. [139]

But he was also captivated by the magnificence of the Napoleonic legend, and in *'The Duel'* wrote of 'the triumphant return from Elba, a historical fact as marvellous and incredible as the exploits of some mythological demi-god'. [140] Conrad saturated himself in the history and memoirs of the period with the prime aim of preparing the background for his Napoleonic novel, but his reading went far beyond this limited purpose, and his library contained more books connected with this subject than with any other. [141] It was no doubt during his reading about Napoleon at Montpellier that he had come upon an account in a periodical or a book of the story which he used for *'The Duel'*. J. DeLancey Fetguson [142] has discovered a version of the story, allegedly based on fact, in *Harper's Magazine* for September, 1858, and it is clear, from the similarity between the events and details in this version and *'The Duel'*, that Conrad either consciously followed it or, more likely, an earlier French version on which the *Harper's* story was based. The *Harper's* version has no pretensions to literary merit.

Shortly before leaving for Geneva Conrad wrote despairingly to Galsworthy, telling him that he had gout and adding, 'the state of worry in which I am living,—and writing,—is simply indescribable. It's a constant breaking strain.' [143] But worse was to come; the baby came out with whooping-cough just before they started. Nonetheless they did not postpone the journey. Conrad wrote a heartrending letter to Pinker from the Hotel de la Poste at Geneva:

Here I am stranded again with baby at its last gasp with whoopingcough. It began in Montpellier. We started by medical advice, counting on the change of climate to check the disease, but it has developed on the road in the most alarming manner. The poor little devil has melted down to half his size. Since yesterday morning he has had a coughing fit every quarter of an hour or so and will not eat anything. We'll have to resort to artificial feeding very soon. Of course La Roseraie Hotel won't take us now. We stick here isolated at the end of a corridor. Really I haven't got my share of the commonest sort of luck. I suppose *Chance* will have to pay for all this. But if you think I ought to come home I will do so as soon as baby can travel, and will let my cure go to the devil. Borys of course has whooping-cough too, but very mildly. Still, it isn't good for him. My dear Pinker, I feel that all this is almost too much for me. [18 May 1907, *LL.*, II, 48]

Three weeks later he followed this up with a rather hysterical letter to Galsworthy (Borys had by then developed rheumatism in both his ankles):

... All this is ghastly. I seem to move, talk, write in a sort of quiet nightmare that goes on and on. I wouldn't wish my worst enemy this experience....

From the sound next door (we have three rooms) I know that the pain has roused Borys from his feverish doze. I won't go to him. It's no use. Presently I shall give him his salicylate, take his temperature and shall then go to elaborate a little more the conversation of Mr Verloc with his wife. It is very important that the conversation of Mr Verloc with his wife should be elaborated,—made more effective, don't you know,—more *true* to the situation and character of these people.

By Jove! I've got to hold myself with both hands not to burst into a laugh which would scare wife, baby and the other invalid,—let alone the lady whose room is on the other side of the corridor! [6 June 1907, *LL.*, II, 51-2]

Nonetheless, despite these appalling troubles, Conrad was able to do some very important and extensive revision of *The Secret Agent* for book form, writing in almost 30,00 words. [145] This was no doubt largely due to Jessie's ability to deal with the situation.

Conrad told Rothenstein that 'Jessie has been simply

heroic in the awful Montpellier adventure, never giving a sign of anxiety not only before the boy, but even out of his sight; always calm, serene, equable, going from one to the other and apparently never tired though cruelly crippled by her leg'. [146] As Jessie has been subjected to so much disparagement it is perhaps worth mentioning that there could have been few people temperamentally better equipped than her to cope with such a situation; her efficiency and equability may well have saved Conrad from a nervous breakdown, then and at other times.

Gradually the troubles subsided, and by the middle of August the Conrads were back at the Pent, but looking for another house. [147] They finally found one called Someries, in Bedfordshire, on the Luton Hoo estate, and moved there in September. [148] Conrad seems to have struggled on with *Chance* during most of the rest of the year, but when he found that he could make little progress he started another story which he called *Razumov* and which was to become *Under Western Eyes*.

During the autumn he also wrote, out of friendship for Edward Garnett, an attack on the censorship of plays which was published in slightly emasculated form in the *Daily Mail*. [150] It is a splendid piece of scathing derision. Of the Censor Conrad says: 'He has power. He can kill thought, and incidentally truth, and incidentally beauty, providing they seek to live in a dramatic form. He can do it, without seeing, without understanding, without feeling anything; out of mere stupid suspicion, as an irresponsible Roman Caesar could kill a senator.' [151] And his final paragraph is:

Frankly, is it not time to knock the improper object off its shelf? It has stood too long there. Hatched in Pekin (I should say) by some Board of Respectable Rites, the little caravan monster has come to us by way of Moscow—I suppose. It is outlandish. It is not venerable. It does not belong here. Is it not time to knock it off its dark shelf with some implement appropriate to its worth and status? With an old broom handle for instance.

It is still there.

1908 was Conrad's fiftieth year, and it did not start well.

In a listless letter to Marguerite Poradowska sending her the new year's greetings, he wrote: '*Moi je suis fatigué et attristé. Le travail m'est très difficile et les affaires en general ne marchent pas*'. [1] He had reason to be depressed. Although in the judgement of today he had already achieved enough to set him among the greatest novelists of all nations and his last two novels had shown his powers at their height, the situation appeared very different at the time. Thus whereas his early work had been duly recognised and *The Nigger of the 'Narcissus'*, followed by *Lord Jim,* had carried him to the crest of critical acclaim, his two latest novels had had a mixed reception. The critical reaction to *Nostromo, which he knew to be his most ambitious book and which had cost him so much effort, must have been particularly galling.*

In the reviews he was treated with a respect which acknowledged his position as one of the leading novelists of the day, and there was much praise for the book, the ever-loyal Garnett above all doing his best to point out its quality; [2] *but there was much wistful harking back to the earlier tales, while in places, such as The Times literary Supplement,* [3] *where it was reasonable to expect some measure of understanding and appreciation, Nostromo was handled with fatuous obtuseness.*

The reaction to The Secret Agent had been similar and there were a number of complaints that Conrad's method, particularly his use of the time-shift, put his work above the head of the average reader. This was the most worrying aspect; the sales of both books had been mediocre, and Conrad was increasingly becoming a novelist of the élite without popular appeal. Several years back Henry James had already concluded that Conrad's work was 'of the sort greeted more by the expert and the critic than (as people say), by the man in the street', [4] and the reviewer of The Secret Agent in the Athenaeum stressed the same point:

The subtlety of his mental processes, the keenness of his artistic senses, have placed him further away from the great reading public—if infinitely nearer to the select few who have trained faculties of literary appreciation —than many a writer of far less worth. [5]

Conrad was, understandably, becoming obsessed by his failure to establish himself as a 'selling' author, confessing to Galsworthy:

Ah my dear, you don't know what an inspiration-killing anxiety it is to think: is it saleable? There's nothing more cruel than to be caught between one's impulse, one's act, and that question, which for me simply is a question of life and death. There are moments when the unholy[?] fear sweeps my head clear of every thought. It is agonising—no less. And —you know—that pressure grows from day to day instead of getting less. [6 January 1908, *LL., II,* 65]

In the same letter he looked back on his financial achievement during the twelve years of his writing career. He worked out that he had written eleven novels (volumes, to be precise) and had lived at an average rate of £650 a year. If, he said, each book had brought him in £1,000 he would have had £5,000 in hand, but as it was he owed Pinker £1, 572 and had other debts as well.

A further ground for depression was Someries. Conrad seems to have disliked the house and area from the start. He wrote to Elsie Hueffer: 'You have no idea of the soul corroding bleakness of earth and sky here when the east wind blows'.[6] The climate affected his health and he told Galsworthy: 'I've known not a single moment of bodily ease since we got into this new house'.[7] As a result of all these physical and mental afflictions he went down with an attack of gout.[8]

But after he had recovered from his illness he became more cheerful, and as he did most of the writing of *Under Western Eyes* during 1908 it can be considered a good year so far as work was concerned. The second version of '"The Black Mate'" also made its appearance, in the *London Magazine* for April. The year was otherwise uneventful. In August Conrad was still complaining about Someries, telling Galsworthy that he would like to spend a few weeks in Kent,[9] and at the end of August the family went to stay for a month in the village of Aldington, near the Hueffers.

It was probably then that Conrad first met Arthur Marwood, who was living close by, and was a friend of

Hueffer's.[11] In retrospect Marwood appears a slightly mysterious figure; not because he was in fact mysterious but because all that has been preserved of him are a few rather slight reminiscences by friends and some articles on economic subjects.

The comments of his friends or acquaintances [12] agree in their expression of extreme admiration for his character, his profound intelligence, and his encyclopaedic knowledge. Conrad undoubtedly had a very great respect for Marwood and saw a lot of him in the following years. At one period, at least, the two men met regularly once a week. [13] Marwood had apparently been a sick man for most of his life and he died in 1916 when he was forty-seven. He came from a well-to-do Yorkshire family, and Hueffer regarded him as the ideal English gentleman, using him as the model for Christopher Tietjens in that series of novels. [14]

Hueffer and Conrad had resumed their intimacy, and it was on Hueffer's suggestion that Conrad started, probably when he was at Aldington, to write his reminiscences for the *English Review,* which was to be started in a new form in December under the editorship of Hueffer. When the first number was being prepared for press, to Jessie's dismay, Hueffer arrived at Someries with all the copy and several assistants. According to Jessie:

Lights blazed from every room downstairs—no expense was spared. To have some four or five strangers quartered on one without more notice than an hour or so was not exactly comfortable. Only the baby and the maids slept that night. Orders, directions, or suggestions were shouted from room to room. It was an uproar all night, and the next day the house was in a chaos. My monthly stock of provisions were soon devoured, and the great trouble was that we had to use lamps and candles.... [15]

Conrad, too, recalled that night in a letter to Hueffer, to be printed in the *transatlantic review.*

You arrived one evening with your amiable myrmidons and parcels of copy. I shall never forget the cold of that night, the black grates, the guttering candles, the dimmed lamps—

and the desperate stillness of that house, where women and children were innocently sleeping, when you sought me out at 2 a.m. in my dismal study to make me concentrate suddenly on a two page notice of the *Ile des Pingouins. A marveuously successful instance of editorial tyranny! I suppose you were justified. The Number One of the E.R. could not have come out with two blank pages in it. It would have been too sensational. I have forgiven you long ago.*

Thus the first number of this distinguished review appeared with two contributions from Conrad. Other contributors were Hardy with the poem *'A Sunday Morning Tragedy'*, Henry James with *'The Jolly Corner'*, Wells with an instalment of *Tono-Bungay, Galsworthy, Hudson, Cunninghame Graham, W. H. Davies, and Marwood with the first part of 'A Complete Actuarial Scheme for Insuring John Doe against all the Vicissitudes of Life'.*

It was lavish fare, a hundred-and-ninety-two pages for half-acrown. Hueffer was a remarkable editor with a flare for discovering new talent as well as mustering the old, but he was a most incompetent business man. The Review lost heavily from the start and after a few months financial control was taken out of Hueffer's hands, although he was allowed to stay on as editor.

Conrad's reminiscences had been running for seven months when they became the cause, or the occasion, of a quarrel between Hueffer and himself. An attack of gout had prevented Conrad from writing the instalment for July [18] and, to his great annoyance, Hueffer had printed a dramatic note in the July number saying:

We regret that owing to the serious illness of Mr Joseph Conrad we are compelled to postpone the publication of the next instalment of his Reminiscences.

But, for reasons that remain obscure, Conrad decided not to contribute any further reminiscences. This must have called forth an indignant outburst from Hueffer, whose resentment was probably aggravated by his own insecure position as editor. He no doubt felt that he particularly needed the support of his friends at this moment. But only Conrad's reply has been preserved. He starts with the formal 'Dear Hueffer' instead of his usual 'My dear Hueffer', 'My dear Ford', or some other affectionate term of address, and continues:

If you think I have discredited you and the Review, why then it must be even so. And as far as the Editor of the E.R. is concerned, we will let it go at that, with the proviso that I don't want to hear anything more about it.

But as writing to a man with a fine sense of form and a complete understanding, for years, of the way in which my literary intentions work themselves out, I wish to protest against the words,—Ragged condition.

It is so little ragged to my feeling, and in point of literary fact, that in the book (if the book ever appears) the whole of the contribution to the E.R. as it stands now without the addition of a single word shall form the Part First.

It expresses perfectly my purpose of treating the literary life and the life on parallel lines, with a running reference to my early years. It treats of the inception of my first book and of my first contact (psychologically and de facto) with the sea. It begins practically with the first words of appreciation of my writing I ever heard and ends with the first words ever addressed to me personally in the English tongue. And actually the very phrase ending the seventh instalment is to my mind an excellent terminal, a perfect pause carrying out the spirit of the work....

It is another instalment which would make the thing *ragged*. It would have to begin another period and another phase. On a dispassionate view I see it so clearly that nothing on earth would induce me to spoil the thing as it now stands by an irrelevant single instalment.

I will say no more, except to add that my contributions were for a *person* not for an *editor*. The *E.R.*, I hear, is no longer your property and there is, I believe, another circumstance which for a purely personal reason (exceptionally personal, I mean) makes me unwilling to contribute anything more to the *E.R.* This reason has, of course, nothing to do with you, you understand. It is not a critical reason. A pure matter of feeling. If I have discredited the R., well, I must bear the disgrace. [31

July 1909, *LL., II,* 101-2] Conrad's 'purely personal reason' apparently did have something to do with the change in ownership. He had acquired an intense dislike for Dr David Soskice, Hueffer's brother-in-law, who had been called in to try to save the *Review* financially, and he wrote to Galsworthy: 'I hear Ford is enraged with me for not giving him more of my Reminiscences. He says I made a fool of him. I don't see how that can be. A Russian his got hold of the *E.R.* and I cannot contribute any more.' [20] It must remain in doubt whether this was the real reason or whether, as seems more likely, Conrad was merely seizing a pretext to cut himself off from Hueffer, whose behaviour in the affair had exasperated him.

Conrad let himself go on the subject in a letter to Pinker: 'I am made responsible for the failure of a negotiation with McClure for the sale of the *E.R.*,' he said; and he had heard that Hueffer was going about saying he had 'called Conrad out'. He went on:

His conduct is *impossible*.... He's a megalomaniac who imagines that he is managing the Universe and that everybody treats him with the blackest ingratitude. A fierce and exasperated vanity is hidden under his calm manner which misleads people.... I do not hesitate to say that there are cases, not quite as bad, under medical treatment....

Generally he is behaving like a spoilt kid—and not a nice kid either. (Wednesday (probably July 1909)]

Conrad's quarrel with Hueffer seems to have produced an estrangement which was never fully healed. But before the break the two men collaborated on a worthless trifle entitled *The Nature of a Crime,* * which appeared in the April and May numbers of the *English Review* under the pseudonym of Baron Ignatz von Aschendrof. No trace of Conrad's influence is apparent either in the writing or in the conception, except that the story of Nicholas Bobrowski's stepfather filching his stepson's inheritance which Conrad told in his reminiscences may have suggested the plot. However, about four hundred words of the manuscript in Conrad's handwriting have survived, [21] which proves that he had some connexion with the story.

The design of the reminiscences was essentially discursive and time was deliberately banished, but Conrad handled his material with consummate adroitness and there is no impression of scrappiness. Nonetheless Hueffer was justified in claiming that the seventh instalment provided a weak ending to the series. However, Conrad more than stood by the intention expressed in his letter; he never added anything to his reminiscences and they were printed in book form virtually without alteration, although this was due more to chance than design. It is clear from a letter to E. V. Lucas [22] that he wanted to continue them, and he was possibly dissuaded from doing so by Pinker, who had failed to place them serially in America and seems never to have been particularly enthusiastic about thm. [23]

In the "'Familiar Preface'" to *A Personal Record,* [+] which is a very fine piece of writing, almost equal to the preface to *The Nigger of the 'Narcissus'*, Conrad described the intention of the book:

> They [the reminiscences] have their hope and aim. The hope that from the reading of these pages there may emerge at last the vision of a personality; the man behind the books so fundamentally dissimilar as, for instance, *Almayer's Folly* and *The Secret Agent*, and yet a coherent, justifiable personality both in its origin and in its action. This is the hope. The immediate aim, closely associated with the hope, is to give the record of personal memories by presenting faithfully the feelings and sensations connected with the writing of my first book and with my first contact with the sea. [24]

The decision to leave Poland and the decision—although he would protest at the implication of so conscious a mental processto write were the two most important events in Conrad's life. They were also two events about which he was particularly sensitive because they were bound up with his personal honour.

Although honour and dishonour, in their particular aspects of fidelity and betrayal, were constantly recurring themes throughout Conrad's work, it is clear from *Under Western Eyes* and "'The Secret Sharer'" that he was specially concerned with them at this time. It is thus not surprising to find that much of *A Personal Record* reads like an *apologia pro vita sua.* When he comes to deal with his going to sea, Conrad brings into the open certain charges which had been made or which he sensed:

Alas! I have the conviction that there are men of unstained rectitude who are ready to murmur scornfully the word desertion. Thus the taste of innocent adventure may be made bitter to the palate. The part of the inexplicable should be allowed for in appraising the conduct of men in a world where no explanation is final. No charge of faithlessness ought to be lightly uttered. [25]

In the next paragraph he adds that 'it would take too long to explain the intimate affiance of contradictions in human nature which makes love itself wear at times the desperate shape of betrayal'. [26] Then he returns to the subject much later when he says: 'I have been charged with the want of patriotism, the want of sense, and the want of heart too [for going to sea]", [27] and confesses: 'I catch myself in hours of solitude and retrospect meeting arguments and charges made thirtyfive years ago by voices now for ever still'. [28]

If it seems far-fetched to link Conrad's start of a career as an author with the idea of desertion or betrayal, it is only necessary to refer to a discussion on the "'Emigration of the Talents'", which took place in Poland in 1899, to realise that many Poles considered the decision to become a writer in English, for the English, was more important and final than the decision to go to sea; sailors usually come home in the end, writers seldom. The subject of the discussion was whether people of ability, opposed to mere manual workers, had the moral right to emigrate from Poland. Eliza Orzeszkowa, a popular novelist, maintained that such people should stay in Poland, participating in the nation's sufferings and sustaining it through the application of their talents. They should not adopt the materialistic attitude that it pays better to work in other countries.

She goes on to single out Conrad and accuse him, ironically in view of his actual material position, of writing in

English merely because he is so well paid for this. She apparently either sent him the article or wrote to him about it. An interesting sidelight is thrown on the matter in a report by a Pole, W. Chwalewik, based on a conversation with Conrad's early Polish friends living in England. Spiridion Kliszewski expressed the hope that Conrad would devote his talent as a writer to extolling the fame of Poland. Conrad was shocked; raising both arms, he exclaimed: 'Ah, *mon ami, que voulez-vous*? I should lose my public...' Apparently the Kliszewskis were rather disgusted by this attitude and their relations with Conrad cooled off. [29]

It seems that Conrad was not able to rid himself of a sense of guilt, at least until, by becoming a famous writer, he could qualify for the position of a national hero. Aniela Zagórska has related how on his visit to Poland in 1914 he still had a sense of guilt and a fear of being slighted by other Poles. [30] She also showed how deeply Conrad had been affected by Eliza Orzeszkowa's attack; it still rankled. When Aniela Zagórska innocently suggested that Conrad should read Mrs Orzeszkowa novel *Nad Niemnem, she was greeted with the outburst: 'Don't bring me anything by that shrew— — You don't know about it, but she once wrote me a letter— —'* [31]

Elsewhere Karola Zagórska has repeated a conversation between Conrad and herself in which he asked whether she would forgive him because his sons could not speak Polish; on her reassuring him he said: 'Thank you for not having a grudge against me for this'. [32]

Against this background it is easier to understand why Conrad should have played down any element of deliberate intention in his decision to begin writing Almayer's Folly. It also explains why he should have been so anxious to emphasise that it was Garnett who persuaded him to undertake An Outcast of the Islands, because his starting of a second novel was the most decisive step along the path towards becoming a professional author.

It is equally natural that he should have exaggerated the element of choice in his career as a sailor and emphasised the positive aspect of his decision in order to answer the charge that his real reason was to escape from Poland. When he started to write the reminiscences, Conrad told Pinker that it was his 'ambition' to 'make Polish life enter English literature', and this may partly explain why the most vivid and detailed portrait that emerges is of his uncle Nicholas Bobrowski rather than of Conrad himself.

But although the reminiscences are woven round the two most important events in his life, it was never the intention of a man so reticent about himself in public as Conrad to reveal much of himself; Henry James's autobiographical volumes are examples of blatant self-exposure compared with *A Personal Record*. In his objective re-creation of scenes from his past it is as if Conrad were carrying on a long reminiscent monologue in front of a smouldering camp-fire which from time to time flares up to illuminate a part of the speaker. And it is Conrad's public face that is displayed; there is no analysis, no probing below the surface.

By the end of 1908 the Conrads had had enough of Someries and decided definitely to move back to Kent. They had found a cottage in Aldington, of which they were to have half, and seem to have 'made the move early in March. [33] But the change did not improve Conrad's health, and he was in and out of bed for the first seven months of the year. [34] Thus he seems to have seen scarcely any of his friends, and went to London only once, in order to see Galsworthy's play, Strife, in March. [35] But Conrad had one visit that had important repercussions on his work; it was from a Captain Marris who lived in Penang and was married to a Malayan girl. He described the to Pinker:

It was like the raising of a lot of dead—dead to me, because most of them live out there and even read my books and wonder who [the] devil has been around taking notes. My visitor told me that Joshua Lingard made the guess: 'It must have been the fellow who was mate in the *Vidar* with Craig'. That's me right enough. And the best of it is that all these men of 22 years ago feel kindly to the Chronicler of their lives and adventures. They shall have some more of the stories they like. [Monday (October 1909), *LL., II*, 103]

Conrad kept his word. This visit no doubt stirred his memory and prompted him to write the three stories set, broadly speaking, in the Indian Ocean: *'The Secret Sharer'*, *'A Smile of Fortune'*, and *'Freya of the Seven Isles'*. They were published together as ' *Twixt Land and Sea; Tales* and dedicated to Captain Marris.

Conrad wrote *'The Secret Sharer'* some time during the end of November and early December [36] —exceptionally quick for him. It is undoubtedly one of his best short stories, but certain critics, notably Albert Guerard and Douglas Hewitt, have claimed for it a position as a key story in Conrad's work and attributed to it a significance which I do not believe that it can hold. It is intensely dramatic but, on the psychological and moral level, rather slight.

The story is based on an incident which happened on board the *Cutty Sark* in 1880. [37] The *Cutty Sark* had put in to Singapore on 18 September, three days after the chief officer of the *Jeddah* (the *Patna* in *Lord Jim*) had arrived there. * In Conrad's adaptation of the *Cutty Sark* incident, Leggatt, the mate of the *Sephora,* kills a disobedient member of the crew during a storm and is put under arrest by his captain. But he escapes and swims to another ship of which the narrator of the story is captain.

The captain is a young, comparatively inexperienced man who his just been given his first command—here Conrad seems to draw on his own experiences on the *Otago*—'a stranger to the ship' and 'somewhat of a stranger to myself'. [38] He had taken the anchor watch himself and thus spots Leggatt in the water, clinging to a rope ladder; without calling anyone, for 'a mysterious communication was established already between us two', [39] he lets Leggatt come on board and fetches some clothes for him.

> In a moment he had concealed his damp body in a sleeping-suit of the same grey-stripe pattern as the one I was wearing and followed me like my double on the poop. [40]

When the captain has heard Leggatt's story he decides that he must hide him in his cabin. He does this at great risk and strain to himself and at the cost of becoming somewhat estranged from the rest of the crew because of the precautionary antics he has to go through to prevent Leggatt being discovered.

After some eventful days which include a visit from the captain of the *Sephora* he is able to come in close to shore and allow Leggatt to escape. Constantly throughout the story it is emphasised that the young captain regards Leggatt as his double, and in a letter to Pinker Conrad suggested for titles of the story *'The Second Self', 'The Secret Self', 'The Other Self'* [41] (these three phrases, without the definite article of course, occur in the text); he also suggested *'The Secret Sharer'*, but wondered whether it might not be too enigmatic.

The point of this, apart from heightening the dramatic effect, and the point of the story, is to suggest that the fates of these two men were interchangeable, that it was quite possible for an ordinary, decent, conscientious person to kill someone or to commit some action which would make him 'a fugitive and vagabond on the earth'. [42] Thus Leggatt takes his place alongside Jim and Razumov. There is no suggestion of a transcendental relationship between Leggatt and the captain or of the 'double' being a psychological manifestation of an aspect of the original as there is in Poe's vulgar, trashy ' Richard Wilson' or Dostoevsky's obscure nightmare, *'The Double'*.

But that is the way in which Guerard interprets the story. For him the 'hero' is the young captain: 'The real moral dilemma is *his*, not Leggatt's'. [43] He, and Marlow in *'Heart of Darkness'*, 'must recognise their own potential criminality and test their own resources, must travel through Kurtz and Leggatt, before they will be capable of manhood... and moral survival'. [44] The story will bear this interpretation, as long as it is realised that such was no part of the author's conscious intention. However, Guerard goes on to assert that Leggatt is not merely an 'other self', he is a 'lower self', 'the embodiment of a more instinctive, more primitive, less rational self'. * I believe that this misses the whole point.

Leggatt is not a symbol of the unconscious but a man on precisely the same level as the young captain; their selves are interchangeable (the epithet 'secret' might imply the opposite but its context and the whole tone of the story show that the word was intended in its literal sense: Leggatt was 'secret' because he had to be kept secret or hidden). Guerard's interpretation makes nonsense of the last sentence of the story, in which Leggatt departs, 'a free man, a proud swimmer striking out for a new destiny'. This is no way for a symbol of the unconscious to behave; Guerard's answer is that Leggatt is both a symbol and a 'man of flesh and blood'.

He continues: 'By seeing his own dilem mas and difficulties in Leggatt, the captain has turned this man into symbol and spirit.... But at the end, emerging from his selfexamination, the captain can see Leggatt as a separate and real human being.' [46] But there is no indication in the story, explicit or implicit, that the captain sees any of his dilemma or difficulties in L'eggatt or that he performs any self-examination. Nor is there any 'moral dilemma'.

Guerard's interpretation is based partly on what I believe is a mistaken assessment of the narrator's, or Conrad's, attitude to Leggatt's action. He claims that, for Conrad, 'a crime on shipboard... was simply and irrevocably a crime'. [47] But there is no suggestion that Conrad or the captain-narrator condemns Leggatt's action; quite the contrary. At the start the captain says that he knew Leggatt was 'no homicidal ruffian'; [48] and when the foolish mate comments on the event as 'A very horrible affair.... Beats all these tales about murders in Yankee ships', the captain snaps back: 'I don't think it beats them. I don't think it resembles them in the least.' [49] His own opinion is summed up: 'It was all very simple. The same strung-up force which had given twenty-four men a chance, at least, for their lives, had, in a sort of recoil, crushed an unworthy mutinous existence.' [50]

In this connexion it is interesting to see that Conrad softened the crime, if it can be called a crime, which took place on the *Cutty Sark* and also softened the character of the mate. The mate of the *Cutty Sark* was apparently a despotic character with a sinister reputation. [51] An order which he gave to an incompetent negro named John Francis was twice disobeyed, and when he went forward to deal with Francis the insubordinate seaman attacked him with a capstan bar; after a struggle the mate got hold of the bar and brought it down on Francis's head so heavily that he never regained consciousness and died three days later.

Nonetheless the captain of the *Cutty Sark*, who was by no means a hard man, is supposed to have said that it served Francis right, and he helped the mate to escape from the law. When the mate was eventually captured and tried, he was acquitted of murder and the judge, 'with great pain', sentenced him to seven years for manslaughter. [52]

Leggatt was, however, clearly in exemplary sailor, and his provocation was greater; it was in the middle of a storm when the fate of the ship was at stake and the captain had lost his nerve. Leggatt was in the process of performing an action, which probably saved the ship, when one of the sailors was insubordinate; Leggatt 'felled him like an ox. He up and at me. We closed just as an awful sea made for the ship. All hands saw it coming and took to the rigging, but I had him by the throat, and went on shaking him like a rat, the men above us yelling, "Look out! look out!" Then a crash as if the sky had fallen on my head.' [53] Although Leggatt says, 'It's dear that I meant business, because I was holding him by the throat still when they picked us up,' [54] his action was far less deliberate than that of the mate of the *Cutty Sark*.

The object of this digression is to show that Conrad had no wish to condemn Leggatt but considered him an honourable man who had done something that other honourable men might equally well have done under similar circumstances. He was in fact 'simply knocked over' when a reviewer described Leggatt as 'a murderous ruffian', [55] and certainly had no intention that he should be a symbol of the dark impulses of human nature.

Although his interpretation is not so extreme, Hewitt also regards Leggatt as a symbol, 'an embodiment of his [the captain's] original feeling of being a "stranger" to himself, of that fear that there are parts of himself which he has not yet brought into the light of day', and this 'strangeness' is finally exorcised with the departure of Leggatt. [56] But this is again reading a meaning into the story which the text neither explicitly nor implicitly warrants; and despite the young captain's initial feeling of 'strangeness', the passage at the end where he says 'Nothing! no one in the world should stand now between us, throwing a shadow on the way of silent knowledge and mute affection, the perfect communion of a seaman with his first command' [57] can be countered by a similar passage, before Leggatt turns up, where the captain is alone in 'quiet communion' with the ship, his 'hand resting lightly on my ship's rail as if on the shoulder of a trusted friend'. [58]

Although I do not believe that Conrad intended *'The Secret Sharer'* to be interpreted symbolically, it is easy to discover an unconscious symbolism which has no direct literary relevance but is important psychologically and autobiographically. Conrad had just left off writing his reminiscences for the *English Review*, in which he had been particularly concerned to justify his action in leaving Poland and to answer charges of desertion. It is tempting to identify Conrad with Leggatt and to see the implicit justification of Leggatt's action as a justification of Conrad's own, which metaphorically had made him too 'a fugitive and a vagabond on the earth, with no brand of the curse on his sane forehead to stay a slaying hand—too proud to explain'.

It seems that in the twelve months which saw the completion of the reminiscences, the writing of *'The Secret Sharer'* and the finishing of *Under Western Eyes*, Conrad finally succeeded in coming to terms with his sense of guilt with regard to Poland. It is thus that the last sentence of *'The Secret Sharer'* acquires an added significance as an expression of Conrad's desire to be:

> a free man, a proud swimmer striking out for a new destiny.

Chiefly because of his bad health, *'The Secret Sharer'*, the reminiscences, *' The Black Mate'* and a short article for the *Daily Mail* [61] were all that Conrad had been able to complete during the last two years. *Under Western Eyes* was still not finished, and thus although by November Conrad was working well—'The tone of my mind is better than it has been for years—and the old power may come back yet' [62] —he was not able to stave off a financial crisis.

The burden of supporting Conrad had fallen primarily upon Pinker, who had made various arrangements, such as standing security for a loan, to help him. But Pinker was now becoming restless. Conrad told his friend, Perceval Gibbon, that Pinker had written saying 'he hopes to have MS sent regularly, that I've given him nothing to sell for two years and threatening to stop short if he don't get end of *Razumov* in a fortnight.... You imagine how charming it is to be following the psychology of Mr Razumov under these conditions. It's like working in Hell.' [63] Conrad had asked Pinker for some money on account of *'The Secret Sharer'*, but Pinker had dug in his heels and demanded more copy of *Razumov*. Conrad then made a desperate plea to Pinker and asked him whether he meant to 'slam the door'. He poured himself out to Galsworthy:

I have been nearly out of my mind ever since. If he says yes—that was what he meant I wonder if I can restrain myself from throwing the MS in the fire. It is outrageous. Does he think I am the sort of man who wouldn't finish the story in a week if he could? Do you? Why? For what reason? Is it my habit to lie about drunk for days instead of working? I reckon he knows well enough I don't. It's a contemptuous playing with my worry. If he had said—No. I will stick to the lot—I would have been hurt. But this gratuitous ignoring of my sincerity in spirit and also in fact is almost more than I can bear. I who can hardly bear to look at the kids, who without you could not have held[?] the boy at school even—I wouldn't finish the book in a week if I could—unless a bribe of six pounds is dangled before me!—I sit twelve hours at the table, sleep six, and worry the rest of the time, feeling the age creeping on and looking at those I love.

For two years I haven't seen a picture heard a note of music, hadn't a moment of ease in human intercourse—not really.—And he talks of *regular supplies of manuscript* to a man who in these conditions (taking all the time together, ill and well) sends him MS at the rate of 7,600 words a month; and he actually writes as if I were a swindler from whom nothing can be got unless he's pinched. Is it a swindle to write a long novel? He had better get some of his clerks to write stuff he can sell. But sixteen months for a long novel nearly done and some 57,000 words of other work is not so bad—even for a man with his mind at ease, with his spirits kept up by prosperity, with his inspiration buoyed by hope.

There is nothing of that for me! I don't complain, dear Jack. I only state it as an argumentfor when people appraise me later on with severity I wish you to be able to say:—I knew him—he was not so bad. By Jove all the moral tortures are not in prison-life. I assure you I feel sometimes as if I could drop everything and beat at the door—you understand. The thing is that, so far, I don't. But I feel now that if he stops the miserable pound a day I *must* throw the MS in the fire.—And indeed why not. It's nothing—it's a mere swindle—it's no good to me.... I am at the present moment unable to write a line. One must secure a certain detachment which is beyond me. I can hardly sit still. If it wasn't for dear Jess—well I don't know. [22 December 1909]

However he managed to finish the book by the end of the year.

In *Under Western Eyes* Conrad returned to the theme which he had handled in *Lord Jim,* that of guilt and atonement, worked out in the fate of Razumov, which is of course the same theme as that of the mis-titled *Crime and Punishment*. He had a strong antipathy to Dostoevsky. When Edward Garnett sent him his wife's translation of *The Brothers Karamazov,* Conrad wrote back praising the translation but saying of the book:

It's terrifically bad and impressive and exasperating. Moreover, I don't know what Dostoevsky stands for or reveals, but I do know that he is too Russian for me. It sounds to me like some fierce mouthings from prehistoric ages. [65]

And on another occasion he referred to Dostoevsky as 'the grimacing, haunted creature'. [66] It seems almost as if *Under Western Eyes* were a challenge to Dostoevsky on his own ground. The book is 'an attempt to render... the psychology of Russia', [67] but set in a Western European perspective. To achieve this Conrad uses a similar method to that of *Lord Jim*; the events are registered through the 'western eyes' of the elderly teacher of languages, and it is his comments, like those of Marlow, that draw out the moral significance.

As well as being the story of the fate of an individual, *Under Western Eyes* is a terrible indictment of Russia; the Russian autocracy dominates the book and controls the destiny of every character in it. In the Author's Note Conrad wrote:

The ferocity and imbecility of an autocratic rule rejecting all legality and in fact basing itself upon complete moral anarchism provokes the no less imbecile and atrocious answer of a purely Utopian revolutionism encompassing destruction by the first means to hand, in the strange conviction that a fundamental change of hearts must follow the downfall of any given human institutions. These people are unable to see that all they can effect is merely a change of names. The oppressors and the oppressed are all Russians together; and the world is brought once more face to face with the saying that the tiger cannot change his stripes nor the leopard his spots. [68]

This contention underlies the whole book and is constantly reflected in the comments of the teacher of languages. Above all, he stresses his incomprehension of the Russian character and the difference between Russia and the rest of Europe—at one point he calls the book 'a Russian story for Western ears, which, as I have observed already, are not attuned to certain tones of cynicism and cruelty, of moral negation, and even of moral distress already silenced at our end of Europe'. [69] Again, when Haldin has arrived in Razumov's rooms after killing Mr de P— the teacher of languages comments:

It is unthinkable that any young Englishman should find himself in Razumov's situation. This being so it would be a vain enterprise to imagine what he would think. The only safe surmise to make is that he would not think as Mr Razumov thought at this crisis of his fate. He would not have an hereditary and personal knowledge of the means by which a historical autocracy represses ideas, guards its power, and defends its existence. Of course this is only a rhetorical device to emphasise the chasm between East and West. There is a very successful attempt to present what Razumov thought, then and at other times; indeed, the characters in *Under Western Eyes* are more subtly and convincingly developed than those in any other of Conrad's novels. Razumov himself is the most considerable character that Conrad created; his thoughts, words, and actions reveal depths of personality which show that Conrad succeeded in identifying himself imaginatively with him. The only exception is his lamentably uncharacteristic, Dostoevskeyan apologia [71] in which he raves about 'evil', gloats over his abasement of 'madcap' Kostia, and talks of stealing Natalia Haldin's soul from her (there has been no suggestion in what has gone before that this was his design).

Of the other characters, Natalia Haldin is Conrad's most effective portrait of a woman. She is a noble, intensely idealistic girl, an identical type to Antonia Avellanos, but Conrad develops her character more fully and gives her greater warmth. She has a mystical belief in the superior destiny of Russia: 'We Russians shall find some better form of national freedom than an artificial conflict of parties'. [72] And: 'There are nations that have made their bargain with fate.... We need not envy them.' [73]

Then, the anarchists in *The Secret Agent* are mere puppets compared with the revolutionary Peter Ivanovitch and Sophia Antonovna.

Peter Ivanovitch has been physically a victim of autocracy, having been 'imprisoned in fortresses, beaten within an inch of his life, and condemned to work in mines, with common criminals'. [74] It is one of the most significant aspects of the book that despite Peter Ivanovitch's undeniably heroic behaviour Conrad does not present him as a hero, but recounts his experiences in Siberia ironically and gives him a most unsavoury character. In Geneva, Peter Ivanovitch is living off an elderly woman who is 'avaricious, greedy, and unscrupulous', and believes that she has been robbed by her late husband's family. The ménage exists in an atmosphere of squalid farce, and there is a very funny scene where Mme de

S— works herself into a state of hysteria over her supposed wrongs:

'Voleurs! Voleurs! Vol—' 'No power on earth can rob you of your genius,' shouted Peter Ivanovitch in an overpowering bass, but without stirring, without a gesture of any kind. A profound silence fell. [76]

In public Peter Ivanovitch proclaims grandiloquent ideals, but in private life he is a petty tyrant, mercilessly bullying the inoffensive, self-sacrificing secretary and *dame de compagnie,* Tekla.

In contrast to Peter Ivanovitch, two other revolutionaries, Sophia Antonovna and Viktor Haldin, are genuine idealists with noble characters, but their tragedy is that they are Russians, because all Russians are 'under a curse', [77] victims of autocracy 'in their submission or in their revolt'. [78] Their optimism is based on an illusion, and in incidentals they are gullible. Thus, although Ziemianitch is a notoriously worthless person whose drunkenness leads to Haldin's arrest, Haldin looks on him as a 'bright Russian soul' [79] and asserts: 'It's extraordinary what a sense of the necessity of freedom there is in that man'. [80] Sophia Antonovna who proclaims, 'I don't think, young man. I just simply believe,' [81] is taken in by the repellent Nikita and the hypocritical Peter Ivanovitch; the last, superbly ironical, sentence of the book is her ' Peter Ivanovitch is an inspired man'. [82]

But to Conrad their illusion is fundamental. The teacher of languages, speaking with Conrad's voice, proclaims to Natalia Haldin:

In a real revolution—not a simple dynastic change or a mere reform of institutions—in a real revolution the best characters do not come to the front. A violent revolution falls into the hands of narrow-minded fanatics and of tyrannical hypocrites at first. Afterwards comes the turn of all the pretentious intellectual failures of the time. Such are the chiefs and the leaders. You will notice that I have left out the mere rogues. The scrupulous and the just, the noble, humane and devoted natures; the unselfish and the intelligent may begin a movement—but it passes away from them. They are not the leaders of a revolution. They are its victims: the victims of disgust, of disenchantment—often of remorse. Hopes grotesquely betrayed, ideals caricatured—that is the definition of revolutionary success. There have been in every revolution hearts broken by such successes. [83]

Conrad's insistence that revolutionaries are also victims and that revolt is as hopeless as submission again reveals his extreme pessimism and, as in Nostromo, his conviction of the ultimate futility of all political action. Thus Haldin's murder of Mr de P—, which precipitates the events of the novel, typifies both the inverted morality to which a noble character can be driven by autocracy and the utter uselessness of such an act of protest. No good can come of it because the supply of de P—s is inexhaustible; it is 'characteristic of the moral corruption of an oppressed society where the noblest aspirations of humanity, the desire of freedom, an ardent patriotism, the love of justice, the sense of pity, and even the fidelity of simple minds are prostituted to the lusts of hate and fear, the inseparable companions of an uneasy despotism'. [84]

In submission to autocracy it is perhaps possible for coarse fanatics like General T— to get by, but a humane, intelligent, relatively enlightened man like Councillor Mikulin, although he is a loyal servant of autocracy, is always in danger. For autocracy is so crass that it will not allow intelligent submission, but 'devours its friends and servants as well' [85] as its enemies.

This was Razumov's tragedy. He was a decent, hard-working, even admirable, student whose 'main concern was with his work, his studies, and with his own future'. [86] All he wanted was to be left unmolested so that he could concentrate on creating the foundations of an honourable life. But all his hopes for the future were destroyed when Haldin arrived to take refuge in Razumov's rooms after killing Mr de P——. Ironically, had Razumov approved of Haldin's action he could almost certainly have saved his own future and Haldin's life. As he disapproved he gave Haldin up to the authorities, and thereby found himself irretrievably embroiled with the workings of autocracy.

Razumov's condemnation of Haldin is perfectly sincere and valid. Haldin's action was opposed to all that Razumov believed in. Razumov's philosophy, which he jots down under contrasting heads, would have Conrad's own approval:

History not Theory
Patriotism not Internationalism
Evolution not Revolution
Direction not Destruction
Unity not Disruptions

He, as well as the teacher of languages, is often Conrad's mouthpiece and uses arguments which Conrad himself might have used:

Haldin means disruption.... What is he with his indignation, with his talk of bondage—with his talk of God's justice? All that means disruption. Better that thousands should suffer than that a people should become a disintegrated mass, helpless like dust in the wind. Obscurantism is better than the light of incendiary torches. The seed germinates in the night. Out of the dark soil springs the perfect plant. But a volcanic eruption is sterile, the ruin of the fertile ground.

Or,

Visionaries work everlasting evil on earth. Their Utopias inspire in the mass of mediocre minds a disgust of reality and a contempt for the secular logic of human development. [89]

His bitterness against Haldin, 'this man who had robbed me of my hard-working, purposeful existence', [90] is justified:

I, too, had my guiding idea; and remember that, amongst us, it is more difficult to lead a life of toil and self-denial than to go out in the street and kill from conviction. [91]

So is his claim that to give up Haldin is no betrayal:

I shall give him up.... Betray. A great word. What is betrayal? They talk of a man betraying his country, his friends, his sweetheart. There must be a moral bond first. All a man can betray is his conscience. And how is my conscience engaged here; by what bond of common faith, of common conviction, am I obliged to let that fanatical idiot drag me down with him? [92]

This is incontrovertible. And yet why does Razumov's

mind jump from the words 'give up' to "betray'? He could convince himself intellectually, but not emotionally. If an ordinary murderer throws himself on a person's mercy he may hope for a sympathetic response prompted by humaneness or sentimentality, but he cannot expect approval of his action. Haldin, however, was a high-minded idealist who had murdered a ruthless tyrant and could reasonably expect approval, yet Razumov was handing him over to a brutal autocracy. It is not surprising that Razumov was in mental torment.

For although he certainly could not be blamed for his disapproval and had no obligation to help Haldin, he need not have given him up. His self-justification is a little specious, and there is the suspicion that cowardice, fear for his future, was at the bottom of his action; the honourable course would have been to tell Haldin to go away immediately even if at some risk to himself, although, as this alternative never crops up, we must assume either that it did not occur to Conrad or that he wished deliberately to exclude it from consideration.

There is a similarity between Razumov's action and Jim's jump from the pilgrim ship. They were both acts of cowardice committed in exceptional circumstances by unexceptional people with average moral sensibility. Other ordinary people might also have behaved in the same way. This is what separates them from Raskolnikov. Dostoevsky's writing is often tinged with abnormality, showing marks of the author's own abnormality, and Raskolnikov's planning and carrying out of the murder of the old pawnbrokeress is definitely abnormal. Many people may have fantasies such as Raskolnikov's, but it is Dostoevsky's genius alone that is able to make Raskolnikov translate his fantasies into action without seeming a monster.

Razumov's action in giving up Haldin committed him inevitably to further actions because he 'had his being in the willed, in the determined future—in that future menaced by the lawlessness of autocracy—for autocracy knows no law—and the lawlessness of revolution'. [93] This fact is brought home to him in his interview with Councillor Mikulin after Haldin has been executed. For insight and dramatic effect it is one of Conrad's finest scenes; Razumov reaches such a pitch of nervous exasperation that he scarcely knows what he is saying:

'... I protest against this comedy of persecution. The whole affair is becoming too comical altogether for my taste. A comedy of errors, phantoms, and suspicions. It's positively indecent—' Councillor Mikulin turned an attentive ear. 'Did you say phantoms?' he murmured. 'I could walk over dozens of them.' Razumov, with an impatient wave of his hand, went on headlong, 'But, really, I must claim the right to be done once for all with that man. And in order to accomplish this I shall take the liberty——'

Razumov on his side of the table bowed slightly to the seated bureaucrat.

'—To retire—simply to retire,' he finished with great resolution.... An unhurried voice said-'Kirylo Sidorovitch.' Razumov at the door turned his head. 'To retire,' he repeated. 'Where to?' asked Councillor Mikulin softly. [94]

This scene ends Part I. The rest of the novel, except for a short retrospect, is set in Geneva, that 'serious-minded town of dreary hotels, tendering the same indifferent hospitality to tourists of all nations and to international conspirators of every shade'; [95] 'the very perfection of mediocrity attained at last after centuries of toil and culture'. [96] Razumov has come to the city as an agent of the Russian Government to report on the plottings of the revolutionaries, and they have accepted him enthusiastically in the belief that he was Haldin's partner in the killing of Mr de P——.

He had tried to resume his student's life as if nothing had happened, but it was impossible:

Everything abandoned him—hope, courage, belief in himself, trust in men. His heart had, as it were, suddenly emptied itself. It was no use struggling on. Rest, work, solitude, and the frankness of intercourse with his kind were alike forbidden to him. Everything was gone. [97]

Therefore he succumbed to Mikulin's blandishments.

In Part I the teacher of languages has told the story as set down in Razumov's diary. Henceforth, although he still has occasional recourse to the diary, the teacher of languages takes part in the action and relates the events as he himself has experienced them or as they are reported to him by other characters. The tempo of the rest of the novel is also different from that of Part I, where the tension is sustained with the help of dramatic external events. Henceforth the interest is concentrated on Razumov's tormented mind, on the mental torture which he is forced to undergo in the process of working out his fate and achieving final atonement. (It is worth noting the similarity in structure, as well as in theme, between *Under Western Eyes* and *Lord Jim*: the first part centres on the vital 'act', and the rest, set in a different place with a variety of new characters, is devoted to the consequences of this act.)

Razumov's straightforward, honest character is singularly illadapted to the role of informer. He cannot disguise his embitterment and enforced cynicism, which express themselves in apparently boorish behaviour. However, the Russian colony is, with the notable exception of Nikita, predisposed in his favour and consistently misinterprets his behaviour. Razumov finds his false position unpleasant enough in his relations with the revolutionaries, but the presence of Haldin's mother and sister in Geneva makes the situation wholly odious. Both look to Razumov for information about the fate of Haldin and for some solace in their grief: but that is what he cannot give. Natalia Haldin has worshipped her brother, and the only person that he mentioned in his letters was Razumov, speaking of his 'unstained, lofty, and solitary existence'. [98] Razumov at first avoids the Haldins, but eventually meets Natalia. She describes their meeting to the teacher of languages; when she had mentioned the name of Victor Haldin 'You should have seen his face. He positively reeled. He leaned against the wall of the terrace. Their friendship must have been the very brotherhood of souls!' [99]

After this Razumov again avoids Natalia for a time, but then they start seeing each other regularly and Razumov finds that he is falling in love with her. Finally the situation becomes intolerable to him, and at the moment when his position among the revolutionaries is most secure he confesses to

Natalia the part which he his played in the death of Haldin. *
At the same time he exposes the extent of his loneliness:

'Do you know why I came to you? It is simply because there is no one anywhere in the whole great world I could go to. Do you understand what I say? Not one to go to. Do you conceive the desolation of the thought—no one—to—go—to?'[100]

This constantly recurring theme in Conrad's work has been touched on at the start of the novel. Razumov is a bastard and is not overtly acknowledged by his father, whom he knows as a remote, almost inaccessible aristocrat. 'He was as lonely in the world as a man swimming in the deep sea. The word Razumov was the mere label of a solitary individuality. There were no Razumovs belonging to him anywhere.'[101]

At the crucial point, when he is deciding what to do about Haldin:

Razumov longed desperately for a word of advice, for moral support. Who knows what true loneliness is—not the conventional word, but the naked terror? To the lonely themselves it wears a mask. The most miserable outcast hugs some memory or some illusion. Now and then a fatal conjunction of events may lift the veil for an instant. For an instant only. No human being could bear a steady view of moral solitude without going mad. [102]

And again, when Mikulin is trying to persuade him to go to Geneva as an agent:

The obscure, unrelated young student Razumov, in the moment of great moral loneliness, was allowed to feel that he was an object of interest to a small group of people of high position.

Before he confesses Razumov asks Natalia whether she believes in the 'efficacy of remorse', and she replies with a firm 'Yes'. [104] Through his confession Razumov feels that he has atoned for his action of giving up Haldin and expresses his conviction through a magnificent piece of verbal ambiguity; on the way back to his lodgings he is drenched by a shower and the owner of the house remarks:

'You've got very wet.' 'Yes, I am washed clean,' muttered

Razumov. But he has still not completed his task. After writing his *apologia,* designed for Natalia Haldin, 'he sat down with the watch before him. He could have gone out at once, but the hour had not struck yet. The hour would be midnight. There was no reason for that choice except that the facts and the words of a certain evening in his past were timing his conduct in the present.' [106] He had decided that he must also confess his role to the revolutionaries. Again there is a close parallel with Jim going to meet his doom at the hands of Doramin.

He finds them in conclave. Their reaction is one of horror, and with some demur they allow the loathsome brute Nikita, terrorist killer, and undisclosed police agent, to deafen him by breaking his eardrums. Then, wandering about the streets afterwards, he is run into by a tram which he does not hear coming, and badly injured. He will be an invalid for the rest of his life; he returns to Russia and is looked after by Tekla, who has dedicated herself to him, just as Sonia dedicated herself to Raskolnikov and followed him to Siberia.

Thus there is a parallel between the course of events in *Under Western Eyes* and in *Crime and Punishment*. Razumov and Raskolnikov commit an act, cowardly or criminal, which causes them mental agony and isolates them by destroying the possibility of normal relations with other human beings, and their torment finally drives them to confess. But their confessions emphasise above all the difference between the two authors. Raskolnikov's confession is the beginning of a process which leads to full repentance and to spiritual regeneration, whereas Razumov's confession is a culmination and is conclusive; Raskolnikov finds his god, but for Razumov, as for Conrad, there is no god. Thus while Sonia is midwife to Raskolnikov's rebirth there is no suggestion that Tekla in any way influenced Razumov spiritually. After Razumov's confession Conrad virtually withdraws his interest from him.

The aim, tone, and form of the two books are absolutely opposed. *Under Western Eyes* is an indictment; its mood is fatalistic, and Conrad's compassion is controlled by a predominantly ironical approach. *Crime and Punishment* is an assertion of ultimate human goodness and the mercy of God, ending on a note of hope and faith, while Dostoevsky's compassion and other emotions constantly spill over in their abundance. On one hand there is carefully organised structure and on the other disordered exuberance; and ultimately it is a matter of temperament and belief which of the two books is judged the greater.

In *Under Western Eyes* there are verbal echoes of *Crime and Punishment*. It may perhaps be fanciful to suggest that they are deliberate, but the fact remains that some of the most dramatic phrases of *Under Western Eyes* have their less dramatic counterpart in Dostoevsky's novel. Thus Razumov's 'Do you conceive the desolation of the thought—no one—to—go—to?' [107] recalls Marmeladov's 'Do you understand, sir, do you understand what it means when you have absolutely nowhere to turn?" [108] Razumov calls Natalia Haldin a 'predestined victim' [109] just as Raskolnikov calls Sonia Marmeladov an 'eternal victim'. [110] Natalia Haldin says: 'It is impossible to be more unhappy', [111] and Sonia says to Raskolnikov: 'There is no one—no one in the whole world now so unhappy as you'. [112] Then Razumov's 'It was myself, after all, whom I have betrayed' [113] recalls Raskolnikov's 'I murdered myself, not her'! [114]

As usual, Conrad dropped a few not very revealing hints about the background of *Under Western Eyes*. He said that he had been 'induced to write this novel by something told me by a man whom I met in Geneva many years ago (Razumov's fate) and by the rubbishy character of stories about Russian revolutionists published in magazines'. [115] In the Author's Note, on the other hand, he wrote that the course of the action and 'the various figures playing their part in the story... owe their existence to no special experience but to the general knowledge of the condition of Russia... '. [116]

Conrad had had plenty of opportunity to gather information about the Russian revolutionary movement from the Garnett family, who were friendly with several distinguished refugees, including Prince Peter Kropotkin and Felix Volkovsky. The Garnetts had also known well S. M. Kravchinsky, called Stepniak, who had fled from Russia after killing the chief of police, General Mesentzev; Stepniak had eventually settled in England, but in 1895 was knocked down and killed when crossing a railway track; according to David Garnett he had not heard the engine approaching because he had the capacity to make himself deaf at will, and this may have given Conrad the idea for Razumov's accident. [117]

Conrad must also have followed the frequent newspaper reports of the appalling conditions in Russia which led to periodical assassinations or attempted assassinations. It is easy enough to identify Father Zosim with Father Gapon, General T— with the notorious General Trepov, or Mr de P— with the even more infamous Minister of the Interior, de Plehve; and in fact Conrad told Galsworthy [118] that Haldin's crime was supposed to be based on the murder of de Plehve, who was blown to bits in his carriage in 1904 by a man named Sasonov—like Haldin, a student of Moscow University. [119] Sasonov was arrested on the spot, and so there is no parallel between his fate and that of Haldin.

Another matter connected with Russia which was fully reported in the press was the discovery that a certain Evno Asev was a double agent: he had for many years been an important agent of the Russian police who had managed to insinuate himself into the inner councils of the revolutionaries, but had at the same time double-crossed his employers and had failed to warn them about terroristic activities in which he was involved.

Lopuhin, the comparatively liberal head of the Police Department, had been shocked by the Government's apparent adoption of the role of *agent provocateur* of political unrest and in a conversation on a train journey had disclosed that Azev was a police agent to a journalist named Burtsev, who was closely connected with the revolutionaries. The Russian Government was appalled that its dirty linen should be washed so publicly but could not prevent the matter being debated in the Duma; however, it had its revenge on Lopuhin who was sentenced to Siberia. [120]

Councillor Mikulin is based at least in part on Lopuhin and is given the same fate; moreover, as Conrad does not seem at first to have intended to make Razumov a police agent, [121] the revelations connected with Azev may have prompted him to develop the plot along these lines, although he had already shown in *The Secret Agent* how much he knew about such police practices. The famous conversation on the train between Lopuhin and Burtsev crops up when Conrad makes Mikulin meet Peter Ivanovitch in a railway carriage and hint to him that Nikita is a police agent.

It is not known what else in the way of press reports, magazine stories and books * Conrad drew on, or whether other events or characters have a source. Peter Ivanovitch gives the impression of having been, in part at least, modelled on an actual person, and it may be that Conrad was to some extent having a dig at Tolstoy: there is the same contrast between proclaimed ideals and a squalid home life; and an allusion in a cancelled passage [122] to Peter Ivanovitch as author of *The Resurrection of Yegor'* and the 'thrice famous Pfennig Cantata' suggests that Conrad at least had Tolstoy in mind. Then some facets of Peter Ivanovitch, such as his sentimental feminism, may be a guying of Kropotkin. But whether or not there are specific prototypes, Conrad's characters had their parallels among contemporary revolutionaries and those of a past generation.

Conrad apparently took the last batch of manuscript of *Under Western Eyes* up to Pinker in London to be typed and had a blazing row with him. He returned to the country with the symptoms of an acute attack of gout, but it was soon plain that he was suffering from a complete breakdown in health, no doubt the culmination of a long period of emotional stmin. [123] Jessie wrote to Meldrum:

Poor Conrad is very ill and Dr Hackney says it will be a long time before he is fit for anything requiring mental exertion.... There is the MS complete but uncorrected and his fierce refusal to let even I touch it. It lays on a table at the foot of his bed and he lives mixed up in the scenes and holds converse with the characters.

I have been up with him night and day since Sunday week and he, who is usually so depressed by illness, maintains he is not ill, and accuses the Doctor and I of trying to put him into in asylum. [6 February 1910]

Conrad was laid up for three months. [124] After his illness he told Clifford: 'It seems I have been very ill. At the time I did not believe it, but now I begin to think that I must have been. And what's more, I begin to see the horrible nervous tension of the last two years (of which even my wife knows nothing) had to end in something of this Sort.' [125] And he wrote to Norman Douglas more than a month later:

'I am all of a shake yet; I feel like a man returned from hell and look upon the very world of the living with dread'. [126]

It had particularly rankled with Conrad that Pinker had told him during their row on the eve of his illness to speak English if he could. [127] Thus, when Conrad was recovering, one of the first things he did was to write Pinker a formal letter beginning 'Dear Sir' instead of the usual 'My dear Pinker', and ending 'Yours faithfully':

As it can't have escaped your recollection that the last time we met you told me that I 'did not speak English to you' I have asked Robert Garnett [Edward's brother and a solicitor] to be my mouthpiece—at any rate till my speech improves sufficiently to be acceptable. [23 May 1910]

The estrangement lasted for nearly two years, and although Conrad's letters to Pinker gradually became warmer he was still addressing him as 'Dear Sir' in March 1912.

Chapter 12

Chronology

1857:	Jozef Teodor Konrad Korzeniowski born December 3 in Berdichev (or vicinity) to Apollo Nalecz Korzeniowski and Evelina (Ewa) Bobrowska.
1862:	May 8, Apollo Korzeniowski exiled to Vologda, Russia, accompanied by his wife and son.
1865:	June 6, Conrad's mother dies. Conrad in care of maternal uncle, Tadeusz Bobrowski.
1869:	Apollo Korzeniowski and son return to Cracow in February. Apollo dies on May 23. Conrad attends (sporadically) school in Cracow.
1873:	In May leaves for a three-month-long stay in Switzerland and northern Italy. First view of the sea.
1874:	On October 14 leaves Cracow for Marseilles.
1875:	Apprentice on the *Mont-Blanc*, bound for Martinique.
1876-1877:	From January to July in Marseilles; from July to February 1877 on schooner *Saint-Antoine* to West Indies.
1877:	Acquires (with three other men) the *tartane*, the *Tremolino* which carries arms illegally to the supporters of Don Carlos, the Spanish pretender.
1878-1879:	In February attempts suicide by shooting himself through the chest. On April 24 leaves

Marseilles on British steamer *Mavis*. On June 18 sets foot in England at Lowestoft. Serves as ordinary seaman on coaster *The Skimmer of the Sea*.

1883: Passes mate's examination on July 4. Meets uncle Bobrowski at Marienbad. Mate on the sailing ship *Riversdale*.

1884: Second mate on the *Narcissus*, bound from Bombay to Dunkirk.

1885-1886: Second mate on the *Tilkhurst*; August 19, receives British certificate of naturalization. November 11, passes examination, receives his "Certificate of Competency as Master"; first story, "The Black Mate," submitted to Tit-Bits.

1887: First mate on *Highland Forest*. Hurt by a falling spar, hospitalized in Singapore (experience recalled in Lord Jim). Second mate on steamship *Vidar* (Singapore-Borneo).

1888: On *Melita* (bound for Bangkok), then his first command on the baroque the *Otago* (Bangkok-Sydney-Mauritius-Port Adelaide). Experiences desçribed in The Shadow-Line, Victory, "The Secret Sharer," "A Smile of Fortune," and other works.

1889: Summer in London; begins writing Almayer's Folly.

1890: First trip to Poland since he left in 1874. In May he leaves for the Congo. Second in command, then in command of S. S. *Roi de Belges*.

1891-1893: First mate on *Torrens*. English passenger (Jacques) reads the first nine chapters of Almayer's Folly, offers encouragement; meets John Galsworthy aboard the ship. Visits uncle Bobrowski in Poland.

1893-1894: Second mate on *Adowa* (London-Rouen-London). Ends his career as seaman on January 14, 1894. Uncle Bobrowski dies on

January 29, 1894. In April Conrad sends Almayer's Folly to T. Fisher Unwin.

1894-1895: Writes An Outcast of the Islands.

1896: Match 24, marries Jessie George.

1897: Completes The Nigger of the "Narcissus"; friendship with R. B. Cunninghame Graham.

1898: Son Alfred Borys born January 14. In October moves to Petit Farm, Kent.

1899: In February completes Heart of Darkness.

1900: Finishes Lord Jim.

1904: Nostromo. Writes The Mirror of the Sea. Wife ill, practically an invalid.

1905: Spends four months in Europe.

1906: Spends two months in France. Second son John Alexander born August 2.

1907: Children ill in France. Returns to Pent Farm in August. The Secret Agent.

1908: A Set of Six.

1910: In June moves to Capel House, Kent. Seriously ill.

1911: Under Western Eyes.

1912: 'Twixt Land and Sea, Tales.

1913-1914: Chance. Writes Victory. Leaves for Poland in July 1914; meets Stefan Zeromski in Zakopane; caught by the war in August; escapes and returns to Capel House November 3.

1915: Victory. Within the Tides.

1916: Borys fights on the French front.

1917: The Shadow-Line. Writes prefaces for a new collected edition of his works.

1918: Borys, gassed and wounded, is hospitalized in Le Havre.

1919: The Arrow of Gold. Moves to Oswalds, Bishopbourne, near Canterbury, where he spends the last years of his life.

1920: The Rescue.

1921: Visits Corsica. Notes on Life and Utters.

1923: Visits New York (April-June). Reading from

	his Victory at home of Mrs. Arthur Curtiss James, May 10. The Secret Agent, Drama in Four Acts (adaptation of the novel). The Rover. Laughing Anne, a play (adaptation of "Because of the Dollars").
1924:	Jacob Epstein does Conrad's bust. In May Conrad declines knighthood. Health deteriorates and he is bedridden. His wife is also ill. Both sons and Richard Curle are with them. Dies of heart attack August 3. Buried in Canterbury.
1925	Suspense (incomplete). Tales of Hearsay.
1926:	Last Essays.
1928:	The Sisters (written in 1896; incomplete.)
1936:	Jessie Conrad dies December 6. Buried near her husband at Canterbury.
1978:	Alfred Borys Conrad, the eider son of Conrad, dies on November 13.

Bibliography

Allen J. The Thunder and the Sunshine; a Biography of Joseph Conrad,New York, 1958.

Aubry G. J. Joseph Conrad; Life and Letters, 2 vols., 1927.The Sea Dreamer; a Definitive Biography of Joseph Conrad,translated by Helen Sebba, 1957. (This is a transla-tion of the author's Vie de Conrad, 1947.)Joseph Conrad; Lettres Française ave une Introduction etdes Noted, [1930].

Bennett A. The Journals of Arnold Bennett, 3 vols., 1932.

Berryman J. Stephen Crane, 1950.

Blackburn W. Joseph Conrad; Letters to William Blackwood and David S.Meldrum, edited with an Introduction, Duke University Press, 1958; and Cambridge University Press,1959.

Bobrowski T. Pamiêtniki, 2 vols., Lwòw, 1900.

Buszcyñski S. Mato znany poeta, Cracow, 1870.

Clifford H. A Talk on Joseph Conrad and his Work, Colombo, 1927.

Conrad Jessie Joseph Conrad and His Circle, 1935.Joseph Conrad as I Knew Him, 1926.

Crankshaw E. Joseph Conrad; some Aspects of the Art of the Novel, 1936.

Curle R. Conrad to a Friend; 150 Selected Letters from Joseph Conrad to Richard Curle, edited with an Introductionand Notes, 1928.The Last Twelve Years of Joseph Conrad, 1928.Caravansary and Conversation, 1937.

Estreicher K. Bibliografia Polska, XIX. Stólecia, Vols. II and V, Cracow,1874 and 1880.

Ford F. M., see Hueffer.

Galsworthy J. Castles in Spain and Other Screeds, 1927.

Garnett D.The Golden Echo, 1953.

Garnett E. Letters from Conrad, 1895 to 1924, edited with Intro-duction and Notes, 1928.

Gee J. A. andP. J. Sturm Letters of Joseph Conrad to Marguerite Poradowska, 1890-1920, translated from the French and edited withan Introduction, Notes and Appendices, Yale University Press, 1940.

Goldring D. The Last Pre-Raphaelite; a Record of the Life and Writingsof Ford Madox Ford, 1948.

Gordan J. D. Joseph Conrad; the Making of a Novelist, Harvard University Press, 1940.

Hart-Davis R. Hugh Walpole; a Biography, 1952.

Hewitt D. Conrad; a Reassessment Cambridge, 1952.

Hueffer F. M. Joseph Conrad; a Personal Remembrance, 1924.Return to Yesterday, 1931.

Keating G. T. A Conrad Memorial Library; the Collection of George T.Keating, Garden City, N. Y., 1929.

Leavis F. R. The Great Tradition; George Eliot Henry James, JosephConrad, 1948.

Marrot H. V. The Life and Letters of John Galsworthy, 1935.

Mégroz R. L. A Talk with Joseph Conrad; and a Criticism of his Mindand Method, 1926.

Morf G. The Polish Heritage of Joseph Conrad [1930].

Quinn J. The Library of John Quinn, 5 Parts, Anderson Galleries,New York, 1923-4.

Rothenstein W. Men and Memories, 2 Vols., 1931-2.

Symons A. Notes on Joseph Conrad; with some Unpublished Letters, 1925.

Taborski R. Apollo Korzeniowski; ostatni dramatopisarz romantyczny,Wroclaw, 1957.

Tschiffely A. F. Don Roberto; being the Account of the Life and Works ofR. B. Cunninghame Graham, 1852-1936, 1937.

Ujejski J. Joseph Conrad, traduit par Pierre Duméril, 1939.(French translation of O Konradzie Korzeniowskim, Warsaw, 1936.)